The American History Series

SERIES EDITORS

John Hope Franklin, *Duke University*

A. S. Eisenstadt, *Brooklyn College*

DATE DUE

James Kirby Martin
UNIVERSITY OF HOUSTON

Mark Edward Lender
KEAN UNIVERSITY OF NEW JERSEY

A Respectable Army

The Military Origins of the Republic

1763–1789

SECOND EDITION

HARLAN DAVIDSON, INC.
WHEELING, ILLINOIS 60090-6000

Library of Congress Cataloging-in-Publication Data

Martin, James Kirby, 1943–

A respectable army : the military origins of the Republic, 1763–1789 / James Kirby Martin, Mark Edward Lender.— 2nd ed.

p. cm. — (The American history series)

Includes bibliographical references and index.

ISBN-13: 978-0-88295-239-0 (alk. paper)

ISBN-10: 0-88295-239-0 (alk. paper)

1. United States—History—Revolution, 1775–1783—Campaigns. 2. United States. Continental Army—History. I. Lender, Mark Edward, 1947– II. Title. III. Series: American history series (Wheeling, Ill.)

E230.M34 2006

973.3'3—dc22

2005006563

Cover photograph: "A Band of Continental Soldiers"
Photograph by Anthony Vertucci

Manufactured in the United States of America
13 12 11 10 09 2 3 4 5 6 VP

For
Frederick William Martin

FOREWORD

Every generation writes its own history for the reason that it sees the past in the foreshortened perspective of its own experience. This has surely been true of the writing of American history. The practical aim of our historiography is to give us a more informed sense of where we are going by helping us understand the road we took in getting where we are. As the nature and dimensions of American life are changing, so too are the themes of our historical writing. Today's scholars are hard at work reconsidering every major aspect of the nation's past: its politics, diplomacy, economy, society, recreation, mores and values, as well as status, ethnic, race, sexual, and family relations. The lists of series titles that appear on the inside covers of this book will show at once that our historians are ever broadening the range of their studies.

The aim of this series is to offer our readers a survey of what today's historians are saying about the central themes and aspects of the American past. To do this, we have invited to write for the series only scholars who have made notable contributions to the respective fields in which they are working. Drawing on primary and secondary materials, each volume presents a factual and narrative account of its particular subject, one that affords readers a basis for perceiving its larger dimensions and importance. Conscious that readers respond to the closeness and immediacy of a subject, each of our authors seeks to restore the past as an actual present, to revive it as a living reality. The individuals and groups who figure in the pages of our books appear as real people who once were looking for survival and fulfill-ment. Aware that historical subjects are often matters of controversy, our authors present their own findings and conclusions. Each volume closes with an extensive critical essay on the writings of the major authorities on its particular subject.

The books in this series are designed for use in both basic and advanced courses in American history, on the undergraduate and gradu-ate levels. Such a series has a particular value these days, when the format of American history courses is being altered to accommodate a greater diversity of reading materials. The series offers a number of distinct advantages. It extends the dimensions of regular course work. Going well beyond the confines of the textbook, it makes clear that the study of our past is, more than the student might otherwise under-stand, at once complex, profound, and absorbing. It presents that past as a subject of continuing interest and fresh investigation. The work of experts in their respective fields, the series, moreover, puts at the disposal of the reader the rich findings of historical inquiry. It invites the reader to join, in major fields of research, those who are ponder-ing anew the central themes and aspects of our past. And it reminds the reader that in each successive generation of the ever-changing American adventure, men and women and children were attempting, as we are now, to live their lives and to make their way.

John Hope Franklin
A. S. Eisenstadt

CONTENTS

PREFACE

When we initially put pen to paper in preparing the first edition of *A Respectable Army,* published in 1982, the proponents of the "new" military history were just gaining full momentum. Their objective was to reach beyond the traditional focus of military studies—the flow of guns, combat, and tactics that influenced the immediate outcome of battles and martial conflicts, often with little reference to broader historical contexts. The new military historians wanted to relate these time-honored considerations to the larger sweep of historical development and change. Virtually every subject, among them soldiers and societies, ideological constructions about standing forces, civil-military relations, and warfare and societal memories, started to come under careful scrutiny in the search for connections between martial issues and the critical matter of explaining the ever-changing contours of human history.

The late Walter Millis was an early proponent of the new military history. In his highly influential overview volume, *Arms and Men: A Study in American Military History,* he discussed how the experience and impact of war had lasting reverberations in molding the core ideals and values of the United States. Along the way, he offered an insightful statement regarding the War for Independence as a key component of the American Revolution. Wrote Millis: "The United States was born in an act of violence. . . . In light of that beginning, it is strange how little attention later generations were to give to the military factor in the origins and development of our institutions."

We number ourselves among those historians who believe the Revolution cannot be fully appreciated without reckoning with the War for Independence and its effects in helping to shape the new American republic. With this thought in mind, we had to hurdle two major obstacles. First, we had to move beyond the deeply ingrained national mythology about the essence of the war effort, so neatly personified by the imagery of the embattled freehold farmer as the quintessential warrior of the Revolution. Second, we had to integrate, not persist in keeping separate, the fascinating history of the real Continental army into the mainstream of writing about the nation-making experience of the United States.

Our conclusion is that the hard-core regulars of Washington's bedraggled and poorly supported army truly acted out the essence of republicanism and gave that concept concrete meaning in their era. What is so striking is that the Continentals were able to contain their mounting bitterness toward the society that spawned and spurned them, permitting the soldiery to measure up to the highest of Revolutionary ideals—virtuous citizenship in serving the greater good of the new American nation. The army did so in the face of a population, ostensibly committed to Revolutionary idealism, that proved more adept at words than deeds, at talking more than doing. Washington's standing army, so serious a potential threat to liberty according to the ideological strains of the times, was ironically the lifeblood of freedom and republican virtue during the Revolution. Such irony helps explain why the origins of the United States cannot be treated separately from military considerations.

In the process of putting together this newly revised study, we questioned every word, argument, and conclusion that appeared in the first edition. Besides drawing on our own research of the past two decades, we have utilized the invaluable outpouring of recent scholarship, which we believe has generally confirmed our earlier findings. Wherever necessary, we have made modifications, such as in our discussion of the militia's role in successfully resisting and ultimately defeating British forces in America. Nor have we ignored important military engagements (the flow of guns and battles) in seeking to broaden the scenario and significance of the Revolutionary War and provide a more inclusive portrayal of America's national origins. Our hope is that this revised edition, with its modifications, may obtain the same kind of positive reception—and widespread acceptance—that its predecessor version has so long enjoyed.

In our efforts to present a succinct, engaging commentary, we have received an abundance of generous assistance (accepting that we remain responsible for any errors in fact or judgment). Historians Richard H. Kohn, Theodore Crackel, Ira D. Gruber, Charles Royster, the late Hugh F. Rankin, and the late Howard H. Peckham offered critical commentary relating to the first edition. We also remain appreciative to former graduate students Robert J. Babbitz, David J. Fowler, and Robert T. Miller, as well as to Maureen Hewitt and Karen W. Martin for editorial and stylistic advice, and to Gail Heseltine and Wendy Yin for help in preparing the original manuscript for publication. Historians Charles Patrick Neimeyer, Irving Levinson, and Donald B. Connelly provided incisive commentary in support of this new edition. Lucy Herz has graciously steered us through the current editorial process, and we would be remiss not to mention our good friend Andrew Davidson, publisher extraordinaire who has enthusiastically supported us over the years. Certainly too, we are grateful to the series editors, John Hope Franklin and Abraham Eisenstadt, and also to the late Arthur S. Link, all of whom greatly aided us in the development of this study. We each thank our families for their interest, patience, and concern, and we continue to dedicate this volume to Frederick William Martin, a loving brother and humane gentleman and friend.

James Kirby Martin
Mark Edward Lender

Remember officers and Soldiers, that you are Freemen, fighting for the blessings of Liberty—that slavery will be your portion, and that of your posterity, if you do not acquit yourselves like men.

George Washington, General Orders, New York, August 23, 1776

In a Word, the next will be a trying Campaign and as All that is dear and valuable may depend upon the issue of it, I would advise that nothing should be omitted that shall seem necessary to our success. Let us have a respectable Army, and such as will be competent to every Exigency.

George Washington, to the President of the Continental Congress,
Headquarters at Keiths, Pennsylvania, December 16, 1776

We therefore still kept upon the parade in groups, venting our spleen at our country and government, then at our officers, and then at ourselves for our imbecility in staying there and starving in detail for an ungrateful people who did not care what became of us, so they could enjoy themselves while we were keeping a cruel enemy from them.

Private Joseph Plumb Martin of the Continental Army,
reflecting back on 1780

CHAPTER ONE

Of Lexington and Concord, and the Myths of the War, 1763–1775

Lexington and Concord

At dawn on April 19, 1775, a select force of 700 British regulars under the command of Lieutenant Colonel Francis Smith approached the outer edges of Lexington, Massachusetts. The column had set out from Boston the night before under instructions from Thomas Gage, who was commander in chief of British military forces in North America as well as the new royal governor of the Bay Colony. Gage had ordered the column to capture and destroy patriot military stores at Concord, another six miles beyond Lexington. The redcoat operation was to have been secret, but many officers in Boston talked unguardedly about the details. Patriot alarm riders had alerted the countryside. As Smith's advance units under Major John Pitcairn marched into Lexington, they saw some 70 Minutemen assembling on the Green. Captain John Parker, the Minuteman leader, was no fool. Completely outnumbered, his intention that fateful morning was not to provoke a fight with the British regulars but to demonstrate whig resolve—to state through the presence of his small militia force that troops of the King's standing army had no legal right in time of peace to trample on the property of freeborn English subjects.

Acting thus as an army of observation, Parker and his troops intended to leave the field once they had made their symbolic martial protest. Witnesses agreed that a British officer rode forward and ordered the Minutemen to disperse. Then, inexplicably, as the defiant patriots began to move aside, a shot rang out. No one knows who fired first, but before the smoke cleared and Major Pitcairn had restored order, eight colonists lay dead or dying with another 10 wounded. Some had been shot or bayoneted to death in their backs. That the redcoats had lost control of themselves chagrined Pitcairn, but he could not turn back the clock. Perhaps he comprehended the grave reality that a civil war that would have profound short- and long-term consequences throughout the western world had just begun.

Within minutes, the redcoats moved on toward Concord, their intended target. There they started to burn or toss into the village pond whatever military stores the patriots had failed to remove. Meanwhile, news of the bloodshed at Lexington swept far and fast. Militiamen began moving toward Concord. Half a mile from town, across the North Bridge, one group of armed freeholders, seeing the rising smoke and fearing that Concord was being put to the torch, pressed forward. The time was 8:30 A.M. Fighting flared with a British light infantry company guarding the bridge. The outnumbered regulars soon retreated, leaving behind three dead comrades; another eight in their unit had received wounds. Blood now had been spilled on both sides.

Lieutenant Colonel Smith, a portly gentleman not known for quick decisions, slowly began to realize that his units were in a precarious position. Partisan colonial forces were gathering on all sides. After some vacillation, Smith ordered his troops to pull out. Citizen-soldiers raked the retreating royal column from behind trees, stone fences, and any other available cover. "We were fired on from all sides," explained a dispirited British lieutenant after the action. He and his comrades could not counter the sniping provincials because the patriots "were so concealed there was hardly any seeing them." Such action went on all the way back to Lexington, with American "numbers increasing from all parts, while ours was reducing by deaths, wounds, and fatigue; and we were totally surrounded with such an incessant fire as it's impossible to conceive."

At Lexington, Smith's beleaguered redcoats linked up with a relief column. General Gage, having suspected the worst, had sent out Hugh, Lord Percy, with another 1,100 regulars. Even with these reinforcements and flanking parties directly challenging the Minutemen, the British continued to suffer heavy casualties as they retreated from Lexington to Charlestown and Bunker Hill, which they reached at sundown. Of the 1,800 British regulars engaged in combat that day, 273 had been killed or wounded or were missing. Counting the Lexington slain, the provincials had lost 95. What had begun as a sortie to destroy supplies had become a full-scale military confrontation, and the British regulars had fared poorly in comparison to the armed American amateurs who stood up in defense of family and property.

The battles of Lexington and Concord set in motion a civil war that would last for eight years, until 1783. Along with other events that soon followed, the martial clash on April 19, 1775, also has served to give credence to an enduring historical mythology about the Revolutionary era. Down to our own time, this mythology has dominated the conceptions that Americans hold about their national origins and their nation as an agency of peace in a sordid, warlike world.

Drawing lifeblood from the battles of Lexington and Concord, the dominant strands in the mythology about the War for Independence may be stated as follows: 1) that provincial Americans were reluctantly forced into war by their overbearing, if not tyrannical parent nation, Great Britain; 2) that the determined colonists willingly displayed public virtue and stouthearted commitment, rushing into combat as citizen-soldiers and steadfastly bearing arms through eight long years of military conflict; and 3) that, united as one family in the cause, they overcame the enemy after hundreds of battles, large and small, thereby assuring through their virtuous behavior that a republican political order would flourish and endure in post–Revolutionary America.

As with any national mythology, some truth (perhaps better stated as accurate observation) may be found in each of these strands. Otherwise, the mythology would have long since been dismissed as literary or patriotic conceit, worthy of study because of metaphorical form and symbolic effect but not because of factual substance. Just enough plausibility exists in these strands to make them believable—up to a limited point. Then they begin to fray and unravel.

One purpose of this volume is to separate popular mythology, aspects of which professional historians have too often enshrined in their writings, from the new historical reality that keeps coming to light about the era of the American Revolution, of which the War for Independence was an integral part. Another purpose is to present a synthesis of the fragments of this new reality. As such, this study investigates how the experience of the war affected the establishment of republican values and institutions in Revolutionary America. Many historians have approached the war as an exclusive "guns-and-battles" phenomenon, not linking the conflict in any way to the larger currents of nation making. The actual experience of the war, however, with all its hope, idealism, conflict, and dissension, was central to the process of constructing a specific form of well-ordered republicanism, as ultimately expressed in the Constitution of 1787. This examination of the historical evidence proposes that the military origins of American republic in the years 1763–89 should not only be evaluated but also given their rightful place in more completely constructing the history of the American Revolution.

At the outset, the story must begin with Lexington and Concord, simply because the salient features of the opening clash lent persuasive form to the mythology that has become so deeply entrenched. These qualities may be summarized by pointing out that the British army ostensibly invaded a peaceful countryside, thereby provoking the initial provincial martial response. The British force consisted of well-trained and disciplined *regulars*, representing a textbook *standing army* acting without apparent provocation in time of peace. In turn, swarms of freedom-loving citizens beat back the British regulars by using irregular tactics. *Citizen-soldiers* organized as militia found themselves in the position of fighting defensively to protect their liberties and property. As such, the beginning of the war fit neatly into the radical whig ideological mood of the era. For the American colonists, the presence of Britain's standing army symbolized the abuse of power. The citizen-soldiers of Massachusetts personified virtuous protectors of liberty.

What commentators, among them some historians, have not appreciated is that the Lexington and Concord paradigm came apart quite early in the conflict. Fitting this model into the whole of the Revolutionary War, they have skewed their interpretations about the nature of the martial contest that followed, including such central issues as the depth and tenacity of patriot commitment, the actual nature of the American military effort, the matter of who actually accepted the burden of combat for rebel society, and the effect of the military confrontation in establishing a sense of national legitimacy, nationhood, and republicanism. To move forward from mythology, this study must begin with the ideological roots of the American rebellion that did reflect the experience of Lexington and Concord.

Of Standing Armies (Power) and Militia (Liberty)

Understanding the ideological framework that helped structure the world view of eighteenth-century American colonists is of prime importance in reckoning with historical reality. A key underlying assumption was that of an ongoing struggle between power and liberty, based on the view that human beings naturally lusted after power and would resort to any form of corruption to satisfy their petty, self-serving objectives. Historian Bernard Bailyn, in *The Ideological Origins of the American Revolution,* has pointed out that Americans, as inheritors of England's radical whig opposition tradition, believed that power "meant the dominion of some men over others, the human control of human life: ultimately force, compulsion." Power, indeed, was constantly juxtaposed with liberty, which was "its natural prey, its necessary victim." While power "was brutal, ceaselessly active, and heedless," liberty "was delicate, passive, and sensitive," in the history of human civilizations more often the victim of power rather than the victor.[1]

According to whig ideology, property-holding citizens organized as militia would naturally stand up to those who would resort to military force as a means of wiping out liberties. An exceedingly significant personage in the struggle between power and liberty, then, was the citizen-soldier, the type of individual who came forth as a Minuteman at Lexington and Concord. From the mid-seventeenth century on, whig opposition writers in England had extolled the citizen-soldier. In particular, they were reacting to the Puritan Oliver Cromwell's "New Model" army. According to these writers, Cromwell's troops had shown little concern for popular rights after they had swept the royalist supporters of King Charles I before them during the English Civil War of the 1640s. The New Model army became an instrument of repression. The apparent reason was that Cromwell's soldiers had hardened into regulars, whose loyalty in time of flux devolved onto their tyrannical Puritan leader— all at the expense of liberty.

Commentary in condemnation of standing armies and in praise of the citizen-soldier may be traced to early sixteenth-century Florence and the writings of Niccolò Machiavelli. Familiarity with Machiavelli's thought in combination with the menacing reality of Cromwell's army led Englishman James Harrington to write a broadly influential opposition tract, *The Commonwealth of Oceana,* published in 1656. Machiavelli had warned in his classic work, *The Prince* (1513), "that no state is safe unless it has its own arms. . . . Your own arms are those composed of your subjects or citizens or dependents, all others are either mercenaries or auxiliaries." Harrington, in turn, carefully defined the independent citizen as the individual who held property, such as a freehold farm. The property-holding citizen had a clear economic stake in the preservation of society, and every property holder had to accept a fundamental duty of citizenship, to keep and bear arms for the defense and preservation of public liberty and personal property.

To Harrington and other seventeenth-century opposition commentators who followed, "the . . . ideas of propertied independence and the militia" were inextricably tied together, as political scientist J. G. A. Pocock has observed. Since "independent proprietors," those with a demonstrable stake in society, should naturally provide for "the public defense," they would never become a "threat to the public liberty or the public purse." If they did, they would be attacking the very polity in which their property gave them a clear stake, which would have been contradictory behavior.[2]

Long-term political and social stability thus depended on those who had property and, therefore, were citizens. For citizens to protect liberty, argued Harrington and others, they had to be ever vigilant against those potential tyrants like Cromwell who were hungry for power. They had to display public virtue, the essential quality of good citizenship. In *The Creation of the American Republic, 1776–1787,* historian Gordon S. Wood has described such behavior as "the willingness of the people to surrender all, even their lives, for the good of the state." Public virtue "was primarily the consequence of men's individual private virtues."[3] Without citizen virtue, nations would never be safe from the covetousness of the few who, for the sake of power, would enslave the many. "In free countries, as People work for themselves, so they fight for themselves," explained radical whig pamphleteer Thomas Gordon in *Cato's Letters* (1721). Every virtuous freeholder would willingly sacrifice his personal interests, even to the point of death, to defend property and liberties; for if these were lost, "he loses all the Blessings of Life."[4]

England's opposition writers worried endlessly about propertied citizens who would not meet the demands of public virtue and vigilance. Those frantic for power could always corrupt the system. They could bribe freeholders into passivity with fancy titles, sinecures, and even more grants of property. Or excessive prosperity and luxurious living could lull propertied citizens to sleep. Such an example could be found in Robert Molesworth's widely read *An Account of Denmark* (1694). He told the story of a standing army's destruction of a constitutional order because pleasure-seeking aristocrats refused to act as a check on that force's rapacity. The corrupting hand of personal greed and the desire for luxury had replaced public virtue as the highest value among citizens in Denmark, as had happened in the ancient republics of Athens, Carthage, and Rome. Invariably, the outcome was disastrous for liberty, resulting directly in political tyranny.

The most virulent tool of impending tyranny, claimed the radical whig writers, was a standing army. For them, a standing army was a military organization *separate* from the citizenry and not committed to the service of society. Unlike the militia, it did not consist of citizens; it consisted of trained regulars, soldiers for hire (mercenaries) who had no necessary propertied stake in society. Attacking property and liberty was something that only poverty stricken ne'er-do-wells would consider doing. Such rootless persons had nothing to lose and much to gain in the use of force and the destruction of the liberties of propertied citizens.

A standing army in any polity, the whig writers insisted, was an obvious indicator as well as agent of corruption. The presence of military hirelings suggested that property holders, as they wallowed in luxury, had blinded themselves to their obligations of citizenship by handing matters of community defense to hired substitutes. Those who grasped for power could use the many offices, places, and contracts needed to maintain a standing army as a resource to reward self-serving, propertied citizens willing to condone the actions of potential tyrants.

Like a spreading cancer, a standing army could destroy society from the inside. Its maintenance would demand heavier and heavier levels of taxation, eventually threatening the right to property itself as the foundation of independent citizenship. In time, citizens would be facing *political slavery*, the worst of all possible fates according to the opposition writers. Even if a

standing army did not cause rot from within, it could always become a ruthless force in the hands of an aspiring tyrant to be
turned against the people, as the whig writers viewed the case
with Oliver Cromwell.

The existence of a standing army thus connoted to whig
ideologues that luxury, corruption, power, and tyranny were to
various degrees threatening property, liberty, and life itself. An
active militia, by comparison, indicated that citizens were taking their obligations seriously and behaving virtuously. How
well the Lexington and Concord confrontations fit this construct
is especially interesting. Brute military power on the part of
Gage's regulars had not overcome the vigilant militia of the
Massachusetts citizenry. Liberty, even if all but snuffed out by
power-hungry imperial leaders in Britain (as provincial leaders
so often proclaimed before and after 1775), still had a fighting
chance in America—and had prevailed on April 19, 1775.

Ideological Transmission

Over the years, historians have investigated the ways in which
the opposition whig political writers of seventeenth- and eighteenth-century England influenced the ideological formulations
and outcomes of the American Revolution. In his *Ideological
Origins,* Bailyn considered the content of the political pamphlets produced in the colonies at the time of the Revolution.
He concluded that England's radical whig writers dramatically
influenced the ideological world view of Revolutionary Americans. The opposition writers, Bailyn argued, transmitted to the
colonists "a world regenerative creed" that underscored the
pressing necessity of defending liberty at all costs rather than
succumbing to the conspiring forces of tyranny in a darkened
world.[5]

Provincial Americans (or perhaps more accurately, those favored few who were well educated and had access to opposition
pamphlets) thus absorbed, according to Bailyn, the tenets of English radical whiggism. Provincial leaders, who increasingly
found themselves in the position of opposition as they chal-

lenged Britain's imperial policies, readily identified with the viewpoints of those who worried about the abuse of power by potential tyrants.

A major concern of provincial patriot leaders related to virtuous citizenship and involved balance in government. A *balanced* government was one in which the three acknowledged social estates—the monarchy, aristocracy, and democracy—mixed and blended their particular interests as represented by the King and by the House of Lords and the House of Commons in Parliament. If any one of the three gained too much power in relation to the other two, that aggrandizing estate could threaten the political liberties of the others. Whig opposition writers interpreted much of seventeenth-century English history as a struggle to contain the absolutist cravings of the Stuart kings. Charles I paid with his head in 1649. James II had to flee the realm during the "Glorious Revolution" of 1688–89, and Parliament finally emerged as a political body capable of controlling willful monarchs.

Such alleged abuses of power in England did not stop with the ousting of the Stuart kings. As the eighteenth century unfolded, radical whig opposition writers fixated on the King's chief advisers, or the fourth hand in government. Sir Robert Walpole, who headed the King's cabinet between 1721 and 1742, came to personify the newfound villains. The task was now to counteract these administrators, who reputedly used electoral bribery, patronage, and other forms of political influence to manipulate Parliament. The King's ministers thus replaced the Stuart absolutists as the chief conspirators against liberty. Certainly after 1763, with reinvigorated imperial control directed toward the colonies, such an ideological perspective helped cause provincial Americans to feel the alleged hand of oppression descending on them.

In England, as Bailyn and others have pointed out, the radical whig pamphleteers had little influence on governmental policies. Despite their persistent warnings, Parliament maintained and supported a peacetime standing army. This body did so within the context of language contained in the Bill of Rights, the grand document of the Glorious Revolution. The

Bill of Rights mandated that any regular military establishment must be clearly subordinate to civil authority. Specifically it stated: "That the raising or keeping of a standing army within the kingdom in time of peace, unless it be with the consent of Parliament, is against the law." Likewise, all citizens were to have the right to bear arms in defense of the state.

Ideologues who cheered the demise of James II and the promulgation of the Bill of Rights hoped that virtuous citizens formed into militia companies would be central to national defense. Reality, however, was something else. Militia units did exist, yet Parliament relied most heavily on a well-trained standing army (along with superior naval forces). Parliament exercised civil control through yearly appropriations and the annual Mutiny Act, first adopted in 1689, that legitimized the standing military establishment and prescribed its code of discipline. Propertied citizens generally did not fret about the implications of a standing army in their midst, and the establishment remained the backbone of imperial defense, although with sharply reduced troop strength when not at war.

One important reason that English subjects did not object to standing military forces, even with curtailed numbers in peacetime, was that the empire was persistently at war between 1689 and 1763, contending mostly with France and Spain over control of territories in Europe and America. At the same time, a conscious effort was underway to limit the destructiveness of war, a pattern that historian Walter Millis (*Arms and Men*) has attributed to the rising spirit of "eighteenth-century rationalism." Since warfare was an extension of diplomatic efforts to maintain a balance of power among competing nations, Millis argued that the new notion was to separate productive civilians from the impact of organized human brutality, to make war "the king's rather than the community's business."[6] If Millis is correct, then trying to make warfare more rational in the Age of Reason effectively reduced the need for propertied citizens to become involved in military conflicts.

The desire to separate war and its destructiveness from society ties into another major reason for Britain's primary reliance on standing forces. The skills and training required for engaging in combat were turning soldiers into highly specialized laborers. Whether the desire for separation spurred specialization, or vice versa, will likely never be determined. The result, however, as Millis has asserted, was that armies increasingly came to be "composed of a class apart: the professional, long-service soldiers and seamen who could be hired, cajoled, or pressed into doing the nation's fighting, with a minimum of interference in the civilian's pursuit of profit or pleasure."[7]

Although Millis treats the functional specialization and separation of soldiers and war making from society as an important characteristic of Enlightenment rationalism, that very specialization and separation worried the radical opposition whigs. Clinging to their conception of the inevitable corrupting influence of standing forces, they balked at the social makeup of Britain's soldiery. The rank and file rarely contained freeholding citizens. Common soldiers came from the poorer elements, described graphically by Millis as "the sweepings of jails, ginmills, and poorhouses, oafs from the farm beguiled into 'taking the king's shilling,' adventurers and unfortunates who might find a home" in the ranks.[8] Millis, however, may have overstated matters. More recent findings by historian Sylvia R. Frey, based on her sampling of soldiers under British arms during the War for Independence, indicate that "the majority of British conscripts and German mercenaries did not come from the permanent substratum of the poor, but were members of the working classes who were temporarily unemployed or permanently displaced, and thus represented the less productive, but by no means useless, elements of society."[9]

However low the social origins of the soldiery, military life in peace and war was harsh. Regular forces in Europe, according to historian John Keegan, were embedded in "a military slave system" and "kept in obedience by harsh discipline and an almost complete denial of civil rights to its members."[10] Some terms of service were for life, and discipline was severe (insolence toward officers and desertion often resulted in death sentences or penalties of 1,000 lashes well laid on). Still, a soldier's existence was an alternative to filching in the streets, rotting in prison, or starving or freezing to death for want of food and clothing. Service in the standing military establishment thus became a means of helping the British care for their poor population, whether temporarily or permanently lacking work, in an era when the modern social service state did not yet exist.

Getting individuals from the poorer classes into rank-and-file service and, hence, cleaning the streets, represented one part of the social equation; the other related to the officer corps, drawn by and large from the ranks of the nobility and gentry. Training in, and the practice of, the military art had long since become a legitimate calling for sons who were not the firstborn and, therefore, would not share directly in the inheritance of landed estates and aristocratic titles. As an alternative, these younger sons of favored families could purchase commissions and move up the officer-grade ranks to colonel, so long as they had the financial means. The price of commissions varied but frequently lay beyond the resources of the middle classes. Often, aspiring officers needed influential patrons in government who could help them (usually for generous fees) find commissions to purchase. Demonstrated military competence, regardless of social background, rarely played a role in the promotion of company- and field-grade officers. Service in the officer corps was a respectable source of status and potential advancement for the elite sons of Britain.

In its organization, then, the standing army provided employment for the sons of the well-to-do while preparing those with few or no advantages to serve as battlefield cannon fodder. Rigorous training and discipline taught the rank and file loyalty, if not blind obedience and unflinching courage in the face of concentrated enemy fire. Furthermore, officers assumed that harsh discipline was necessary to control down and outers in the ranks. The rigid disciplinary code governing military life was not for the ulterior purpose of producing mindless automatons who could be turned against the citizenry by some potential tyrant crazed for power. The likelihood of such a threat to civil society was extremely remote, given that the army's officers had so clear a propertied stake in society.

Although radical whig pamphleteers persisted in issuing warnings about luxury, corruption, and irresponsible citizenship, Britain's eighteenth-century standing military forces became more firmly entrenched as time passed. During the Seven Years' War (1756–63, later known in its American phase as the French and Indian War), the military establishment demonstrated its effectiveness by defeating Spanish and French armies. By the Peace of Paris of 1763, France renounced all claims to Canada, thereby removing what every good English subject viewed as the "French menace" from the North American continent. To regain Cuba, Spain had to give up its claim to East and West Florida. In 1763, the British military establishment, with its impressive string of recent victories, could fairly claim to be among the mightiest in the world.

Only in the British North American provinces, it seems, were people paying serious attention to the antistanding-army concerns of the radical whig writers. There the fear of a ministerial conspiracy against liberty would soon fuse with the antistanding-army ideological strain and help produce conditions pointing toward open rebellion by the American settlers.

The Provincial Militia Tradition

During the decade before the triumphant high tide of the first British empire in 1763, British ministers had contemplated cracking down on American colonists and bringing an end to the so-called era of salutary neglect. Between 1700 and 1760 the legislative assertiveness of provincial assemblies and an attrition in the prerogatives of royal governors had increased. Such trends suggested to the King's ministers that the colonists had lost sight of their subordinate status in the empire. Even before the Peace of Paris, the ministry of John Stuart, Lord Bute (youthful George III's mentor and confidant) had made the decision to maintain regular forces in North America. Thus, amid all the victory celebrations came the startling announcement from London that there would be a peacetime lodgment of 8,000 to 10,000 royal troops. An astounded Philadelphia whig wrote: "While we were surrounded by the French, we had no army to defend us: but now they are removed, and [with] the English in quiet possession of the northern Continent . . . we are burdened with a standing army and subjected to the insufferable insults from any petty officer." The decision was enough to make conspiracy-minded provincials suspicious of the ministry's true intentions, especially with the French menace removed from the landscape.

Actually, the redcoats were to form a frontier constabulary to stand between aggrandizing white settlers and incensed Native Americans being pushed off tribal lands. The regulars were to keep the peace and to prevent Indian uprisings like Pontiac's Rebellion of 1763–64. This clash was both bloody and financially costly, precipitated in part because of Indian concerns about holding onto their territory without traditional French support. Also, as historian Fred Anderson has shown in *Crucible of War, 1754–66,* new British trade policies would have curtailed tribal access to prized European goods. Don Higginbotham (*The War of American Independence, 1763–1789*) has offered a balanced conclusion on ministry intentions as of 1763: "While defense against the Indians or a resurgence of Bourbon ambitions figured implicitly in the decision to keep an army in North America, the chief function of the redcoats was actually to prevent war, not to wage it."[11] Most historians agree: The royal army was not coming in through the back door with the intent of deployment against colonial recalcitrants who might resist imperial policies.

England's political leaders were not plotting political slavery for the Americans. Their concerns after 1763 focused on achieving efficiency and economy in the administration of the vastly expanded postwar imperial domain. During the Seven Years' War the English national debt had jumped from £75,000,000 to about £137,000,000 sterling. No imperial leader wanted to see that figure, staggering for its time, rise any higher. To keep white settlers separated from Native Americans would be cost effective because it would aid in avoiding the expense of prolonged local Indian wars. Over the long term, the ministry reasoned, the presence of the troops would save money, even though someone would have to feed, house, and pay for them.

The task of maintaining frontier harmony, furthermore, could not be entrusted to provincial militia because most units were virtually moribund, if they were still functioning at all. Colonial militia were as likely as anyone to spark a general conflagration, based on their traditional support of white land claimants. Regular troops were the only alternative, the ministry concluded, even if that necessitated a standing army present in the American provinces during peacetime.

Despite the nonfunctional state of most provincial militia units, Americans took great pride in their system of armed defense built on the concept of the virtuous citizen-soldier. As early as 1632, points out historian John Shy, the assembly of Virginia had ordered every fit male to carry a weapon to church so that "he might exercise with it after the service."[12] During the next 130 years the militia system kept adapting to problems of the moment. Although early militia, especially those in New England, had been essential in defense against hostile Native Americans, militia units during the 1730s and 1740s in the South played a large part in guarding the white populace against individual slave depredations and group uprisings. Over time the militia became the exclusive province of free, white, adult, propertied males, usually between the ages of 16 and 60. Indians, slaves, free blacks, indentured servants, apprentices, and indigents came to be excluded from militia service. A primary function of the militia thus turned out to be protecting the propertied and the privileged in colonial society from the unpropertied and unprivileged.

Although militiamen developed a record of sorts in tracking down recalcitrant slaves and devastating small bands of Native Americans, citizen-soldiers did not earn much of a record in full-scale combat. During the imperial wars of 1689–1763, few encounters brought the militia glory. Candidates for front-line combat, as opposed to home defense, came from the poor and indigent classes, those who ironically had been excluded from militia service. Virginia, for example, in supporting British regiments during the Seven Years' War, chose not to move its militia out of the province; rather, the planter-elite assembly passed legislation that placed the burden of service on "such able bodied men, as do not follow or exercise any lawful calling or employment, or have not, some other lawful and sufficient maintenance."

Persons from the poor and indigent classes became the prime candidates for long-term duty and front-line combat. Although no one called them such, in effect they were colonial regulars—substitutes for more favored, property-holding militiamen. What is so striking is that the pattern of service obligation was coming to resemble that of eighteenth-century England. In both societies the horror of open-field combat had been set aside as an appropriate calling for the "poorer sort" of persons (with upper-class leadership), while the middle classes filled militia ranks.

The middle-class character of the militia rank and file has led some historians to view the institution as another seedbed of future democratic flowerings. Since militiamen were invariably persons of some substance, propertyholding must have been widespread. What has been forgotten is that militia laws by the early eighteenth century rather systematically excluded the indigents and the unprivileged (a mushrooming proportion of the population by the 1750s) from service. Furthermore, the common practice of having militiamen elect their own officers has abetted impressions about the institution's egalitarian character.

Available evidence, however, suggests that the majority of the ranking officers were persons of at least modest wealth and distinction, when compared to their neighbors. As befitted the deferential character of late colonial society, the rank and file accepted the leadership of their socioeconomic "betters" in the officer-grade ranks. Favoritism toward the well-to-do did not change one basic point, however. Whether or not the militia system was a source of incipient democracy, the lack of solid training and combat experience on the part of popularly elected officers and rank-and-file freemen was one reason for the militia's uneven combat record.

The presence or absence of democratic characteristics may be a misplaced consideration. Richard H. Kohn has argued in *Eagle and Sword, 1783–1802* that "the militia was not a system at all. . . . In reality," he has contended, "it was a concept of defense: the idea of universal obligation for defensive war, a people in arms to ward off an invader."[13] The function of the militiaman was to protect hearth and home, not to engage in regular, sustained warfare. In *Citizens in Arms*, historian Lawrence D. Cress has pointed out that "pervasive localism" characterized the range of concerns of most colonists. If need be, they would assemble and fight as militia to protect their immediate interests. Those deemed most expendable in society—the down and outers—became the designated candidates to be sent off to engage in full-scale combat at some far distant geographic point. That was the reality of provincial troop participation in the French and Indian War, if not in earlier colonial wars as well.[14]

The failure to make this critical distinction served to confuse regular army officers about American fighting prowess. General James Wolfe, whose brilliant tactics resulted in the fall of Quebec during September 1759, described provincial soldiers as "the dirtiest, most contemptible, cowardly dogs you can conceive. There is no depending on them in combat." To another officer, they were "nastier than anything I could conceive." Regular army officers repeatedly characterized American soldiers as lazy, shiftless, hardly even fit for latrine duty. As John Shy has reminded us, however, these provincial soldiers were not militia, but rather outcasts from middle-class society, unfortunates who had been lured or legally pressed into service through promises of bounty payments and decent food and clothing. New England supplied the vast bulk of provincial troops engaged in conquering Canada. "It was the Yankee," concludes Shy, "who came to be regarded as a poor species of fighting man. This helps explain the notion of the British government in 1774 that Massachusetts might be coerced without too much trouble."[15]

General Gage, another French and Indian War veteran, wrote shortly after Bunker Hill in 1775: "In all their Wars against the French, they never Showed so much Conduct, Attention, and Perseverance as they do now." As with other army officers and the British ministry, Gage did not distinguish between short-term militia and longer-term expeditionary service and those who made up the respective ranks. At Lexington and Concord, Gage's regulars did not fight against unfortunates who had been dragooned into service and whose primary goal, with little or no property to protect, was to stay alive. They had run into propertied freeholders operating locally, actually defending hearth and home. That was the unique strength of the militia system. Whether this same system could be effective in sustained, broad-scale warfare was problematic at best.

Several salient points stand out about the provincial militia tradition. The ideal was universal military obligation, training, and service, which implied knowledge of, and the right to bear, arms in defense of liberty and property. In actuality, the military component of the concept of citizenship in late colonial America extended as far as the outer limits of propertyholding went. Major combat and elaborate offensive operations, such as those conducted during the Seven Years' War, had drawn most heavily on the unprivileged and downtrodden who had been converted into quasiregulars in arms (for the duration of the war instead of for life). Stated differently, military practice in the late colonial period was being Anglicized or Europeanized, as were so many other facets of provincial life.

The merging of British and American practices represented an important trend, given the high regard accorded anti-standing-army ideology in America. Despite reality, provincial patriot leaders clung tenaciously to the precepts of the militia tradition after 1763. Ignoring long-term provincial regiments, they spoke as if militia were the sole units of colonial defense while constantly juxtaposing the virtuous citizen-soldier with the standing-army regular of the parent nation. In the spirit of the opposition whig writers, they proclaimed the superiority of armed militiamen as martial agents, never conceding the point that well-trained regulars might be more than a match for vigilant citizen-amateurs. Like the British generals, they had over-rated themselves and underrated their opponents. Unlike the British, Lexington and Concord seemed to prove them right. However, their rebellion was going to be much longer and more enervating than they could have imagined back in April 1775. By late 1776, patriot leaders would be consciously reverting to the French and Indian War pattern of seeking out the unproper-tied in their midst for long-term military service in the quest to defend liberty and implant republicanism in America for the propertied members of society.

The Tyranny of Standing Armies

In 1774, one distressed American writer gave ample summary to a whole lexicon of provincial perceptions about why the specter of tyranny seemed so real. He stated that it was "the MONSTER or a standing ARMY" in America that symbolized what was wrong. The army's presence was but one element in "a plan . . . systematically laid, and pursued by the British min-istry, near twelve years, for enslaving America." The standing army was that which the Crown had lodged as a frontier con-stabulary in 1763. In a number of ways, this force, in conjunc-tion with Royal naval vessels patrolling vigorously for smug-glers in American waters, was like a poisonous thorn in colonial flesh, precipitating in turn a rapid decline in healthy imperial re-lations. The question of who should pay for these troops with-out adding to the home government's soaring national debt was one of the major reasons for Parliament's Stamp Act of 1765 and Townshend duties of 1767. In response to these taxation schemes, Americans had declared they would resist taxes not specifically levied by their local assemblies. To do otherwise would be to succumb to taxation by a legislative body in which the colonists lacked direct representation.

Another vexing problem centered on the matter of provid-ing housing for British regulars. Parliament adopted a new Quartering Act in 1765. Troops were to be billeted in public and uninhabited private facilities when barracks were not available. The act was silent on the subject of using private inhabited homes, although everyone agreed that this practice was illegal. The major point of contention was that of indirect taxation. The colonists were to absorb the costs of quartering the troops, based on provincial taxes and appropriations made by their assemblies. American leaders loudly objected on the grounds that this plan represented a forced form of taxation, as mandated by King and Parliament.

The dispute took a particularly nasty turn in New York, a colony in which many troops were stationed because of its central geographical location. In defiance of Parliament, the New York assembly passed its own Quartering Act, prescribing the province's financial liabilities and limiting them to a year. In turn, Parliament, sensing yet another slap at its legislative sovereignty, suspended the New York assembly until that body would conform to the 1765 Act. The legal wrangle continued until 1769 when Parliament finally backed down and amended its original law to allow individual provinces to legislate for themselves in providing billets for the regular army. The dispute generated a legacy of bad feelings on both sides, all of which strengthened the escalating provincial sense of alienation from the parent government.

One of the most dramatic events involving the King's standing military forces occurred in Boston on March 5, 1770. This incident quickly gained the title "Boston Massacre" and involved a squad of regulars firing on the working populace of that port city. The roots of the massacre may be traced to the unusual turbulence characterizing Massachusetts political life during the 1760s. Heated resistance to imperial legislation, such as the Stamp Act, and local crowds—the British thought of them as mobs—blocked royal officials from implementing Parliament's plans. During August 1765, a long night of crowd turbulence forced the local Stamp Act distributor to resign that post. Crowd violence continued in the days ahead, sometimes directed against royal officers assigned the responsibility of executing imperial legislation, sometimes against local customs officers charged with collecting trade duties, and sometimes against press gangs off British naval vessels out searching for "forced" crew members.

By the late 1760s, the Bostonians had earned quite a reputation among imperial leaders in England as a disrespectful and lawless people. This city seemed to serve as a festering source of turbulence which, in turn, influenced anti-imperial behavior in many other American communities as well. Francis Bernard, the beleaguered Massachusetts royal governor, summarized these perceptions when he wrote home to England that since 1765 Boston had been "under the uninterrupted dominion of a faction supported by a trained mob." He believed that only the presence of regular troops could "rescue the government" and restore stability. Fear of local reprisals, however, kept him from specifically calling for standing military intervention.

Bernard's desire became reality in 1768. The new Secretary for American Affairs, the Earl of Hillsborough, also subscribed to the dictum that provincial political stability depended on bringing the Boston "rabble" under control. In the late spring, General Gage, then in New York, received orders from Hillsborough to send four regiments to the Bay Colony port. Much to the enraged but controlled dismay of the local patriots, the regulars began disembarking on October 1, 1768. For those colonists who believed in conspiratorial plots, the Crown had finally revealed the real intent of the British frontier constabulary. The purpose was the suppression of American rights.

Between 1763 and 1768, provincial writers offered little commentary about the peacetime lodgment of British regulars in America. Since the troops were out of sight for most eastern settlers, except in the area of New York City, they were also largely out of mind. As of October 1, however, the regulars were intimidatingly present in the major port city of New England. Their red coats and muskets served to symbolize the suppression of liberty and to infuse antistanding-army ideology with vibrant meaning. A local minister, Andrew Eliot, caught the tenor of the moment when he exclaimed: "Good God! What can be worse to a people who have tasted the sweets of liberty! Things have come to an unhappy crisis; . . . all confidence is now at an end; and the moment there is any bloodshed all affection will cease."

Eliot wrote as if the letting of blood was inevitable. He presumed that well-trained, highly disciplined troops represented brute power, waiting to be unleashed on innocent civilians who wanted nothing more than to preserve political liberty. The populace, however, was not that innocent, nor were the troops that brutal. Local whig leaders, however, disdained such objective thought. They kept a "Journal of the Times" that made the most of isolated confrontations between hard-nosed, off-duty soldiers and taunting civilians. Although some of the wealthier merchants seemed pleased with the hard money the soldiery was infusing into the local economy, the vast majority of Bostonians had nothing good to say about the redcoats, despite a pattern of relatively decent troop behavior under trying circumstances. Rather, they agreed with the local whig who described these "new guardians of liberty" as puppet-like automatons who would gladly "scatter with the [French] pox some of their loose money."

When the troops were not out whoring, charged local patriot leaders, they were allegedly getting drunk and always ready for a brawl. For the Bostonians, the swaggering, mindless redcoats seemed to violate every canon of the Bill of Rights of 1689, even though the troops operated under strict regulations never to use their weapons unless ordered to do so after a civil magistrate had first read the Riot Bill. (In English law the only time that officers could order up volleys without a prior reading of the Riot Bill was when the populace had been declared by the King and Parliament to be in a state of open rebellion.)

That bloodshed came when it did surprised and shocked many inhabitants. By early 1770 the ministry had shown how divided it was in its own thinking about keeping regulars in Boston during peacetime, since two regiments had been withdrawn in 1769. From the day of the arrival of the first troops, however, troop baiting had emerged as a popular local sport. A

The Machiavellian Moment: Florentine Political Thought and the Atlantic Republican Tradition (Princeton, N.J., 1975), 333–505.

3 Wood, *The Creation of the American Republic, 1776–1787* (Chapel Hill, N.C., 1969), 69.

4 Gordon, *Cato's Letters,* no. 65 (February 10, 1721).

5 Bailyn, *Ideological Origins,* 138. See also Caroline Robbins, *The Eighteenth-Century Commonwealthman: Studies in the Transmission, Development and Circumstance of English Liberal Thought from the Restoration of Charles II until the War with the Thirteen Colonies* (Cambridge, Mass., 1959), passim; John Phillip Reid, *In Defiance of the Law: The Standing-Army Controversy, the Two Constitutions, and the Coming of the American Revolution* (Chapel Hill, 1981), passim; and various works discussed in Robert E. Shalhope, "Toward a Republican Synthesis: The Emergence of an Understanding of Republicanism in American Historiography," *William and Mary Quarterly,* 3d Series, 29 (1972), 49–80.

6 Millis, *Arms and Men: A Study in American Military History* (New York, 1956), 13.

7 Ibid., p. 14. See also Michael Roberts, *The Military Revolution, 1560–1660* (Belfast, Ireland, 1956), which dates the revolution in military practice to an earlier period in time.

8 Millis, *Arms and Men,* 15.

9 Sylvia R. Frey, "The Common British Soldier in the Late Eighteenth Century: A Profile," *Societas: A Review of Social History,* 5 (1975), 126. See also Frey, *The British Soldier in America: A Social History of Military Life in the Revolutionary Period* (Austin, Tx., 1981), 3–21.

10 Keegan, *A History of Warfare* (New York, 1993), 343.

11 Anderson, *Crucible of War: The Seven Years' War and the Fate of Empire in British North America, 1754–1766* (New York, 2000), 470–71; Higginbotham, *The War of American Independence: Military Attitudes, Policies, and Practice, 1763–1789* (New York, 1971), 33.

12 Shy, "A New Look at the Colonial Militia," in *A People Numerous and Armed: Reflections on the Military Struggle for American Independence* (New York, 1976), 24.

13 Kohn, *Eagle and Sword: The Federalists and the Creation of the Military Establishment in America, 1783–1802* (New York, 1975), 7.

14 Cress, *Citizens in Arms: The Army and Militia in American Society before the War of 1812* (Chapel Hill, N.C., 1982), 5–8. For evidence that provincial Americans drew on the poorer classes for troops to fight in the colonial wars, see Harold E. Selesky, *War and Society in Colonial Connecticut* (New Haven, Conn., 1990), 144–94; James Titus, *The Old Dominion at War: Society, Politics, and Warfare in Late Colonial Virginia* (Columbia, S.C., 1991), 41–45, 59–61, 78–100; and Gary B. Nash, *The Urban Crucible: Social Change, Political Consciousness, and the Origins of the American Revolution* (Cambridge, Mass., 1979), passim. For a different perspective, see Fred Anderson, *A People's Army: Massachusetts Soldiers and Society in the Seven Years' War* (Chapel Hill, N.C., 1984), 26–62, 230–39.

15 Shy, "A New Look at Colonial Militia," in *A People Numerous and Armed,* 32.

CHAPTER TWO

The Republican War, 1775–1776

A Republican Order as the Goal

Republicanism was the central concept giving form and meaning to what Americans sought through the act of civil war. Their goal was the formation of a republican society. Then, as now, definitions of that term varied. The central thrust, however, was toward a socioeconomic and political order predicated on liberty and harmony in human relationships. In his *Thoughts on Government* (1776), John Adams argued "that there is no good government but what is republican." Succinctly, the Massachusetts patriot explained that "a republic is 'an empire of laws, and not of men.'" For Adams, republicanism transcended particular governmental forms; it encompassed an attitude of profound respect for the law and human liberty, working against tyranny and unnecessary privilege. As historian Bernard Bailyn has explained, republicanism represented to the Revolutionary generation a "faith . . . that a better world than any that had ever been known could be built where authority was distrusted and held in constant scrutiny; where the status of men flowed from their achievements and from their personal qualities, not from distinctions ascribed to them at birth; and where the use of power over the lives of men was jealously guarded and severely restricted."[1] To achieve republicanism was to establish an even handed and impartial sociopolitical order in which citizens might prosper and enjoy the blessings of life, liberty, and property.

The indispensable being in the search for a republican order, according to whig ideologues, was the virtuous citizen, who had to be fully committed to the worthiness of the quest. In 1775, especially after Lexington and Concord, the qualities of virtue and commitment appeared to stand out everywhere. Historian Charles Royster (*A Revolutionary People at War*) has characterized this period as that of the *rage militaire*, based on what a Philadelphia citizen described as the "passion for arms" that "has taken possession of the whole continent."[2] Except among the neutrals (no one has effectively estimated the size of this group) and those who remained loyal to the Crown (this group fluctuated in size throughout the war but probably represented about one-fifth of the colonial population), a spirit of determined enthusiasm in resistance to tyranny pervaded the countryside. Testaments to the critical nature of the republican mission poured forth, as evidenced by numbers of militia companies coming out of hibernation and training with renewed vigor.

At the war's outset, most patriots accepted by faith that militia could stand up to regulars and thereby secure a republican polity. Public virtue and moral commitment was all that was necessary for militia success. During May 1774, the Maryland Provincial Convention explained "that a well-regulated Militia, composed of the gentlemen, freeholders, and other freemen, is the natural strength and only stable security of a free Government." Hence it urged the local population to organize itself with haste. Charles Lee, a retired British officer living in Virginia (soon to become one of Washington's most controversial lieutenants), assured anyone who may have doubted the fighting efficacy of militia that citizen-soldiers could be more tenacious than regulars. "A Militia, by confining themselves to essentials," Lee observed, "may become, in a very few months, a most formidable infantry." If civilians were just willing to serve, opined Lee, "this continent may have formed for action, in three or four months, an hundred thousand infantry." Even if better trained, Britain's army could not cope with such numbers. "History tells us," concluded Lee, that free states in ancient times were all "subjugated by the force or art of tyrants. They almost all, in their turns, recovered their liberty and destroyed their tyrants" through effective militia action. New Englander Elbridge Gerry was more pointed; he wrote, "On the Discipline of your militia depends your liberty."

Popular confidence in citizen-soldiers and the militia as indispensable to achieving republicanism ran high through most of 1775. Success, of course, depended on the depth of commitment of citizen-soldiers—best described by their willingness to sacrifice themselves and their immediate interests for the benefit of posterity. Commentators repeatedly noted that Americans-in-arms were not only virtuous but ready for the long-term fight. One address, written in February 1776, expressed matters this way: "Our Troops are animated with the Love of Freedom—We confess that they have not the Advantages arising from Experience and Discipline. But facts have shown, that native Courage warmed with Patriotism, is sufficient to counterbalance these Advantages."

Similarly, a French observer reported to his superiors from the Boston area late in 1775 that "[e]verybody here is a soldier; the troops are well dressed, well paid, and well commanded. They have 50,000 men under pay and a large number of volunteers who desire none. . . . They are stronger than others thought. It surpasses one's imagination. . . . Nothing frightens them." Despite his flurries of hyperbole, the Frenchman was fully convinced that qualities of dedication, vigilance, and virtue characterized the patriot soldiery. Moreover, as historian David Hackett Fischer has emphasized (*Paul Revere's Ride,* 1994), these were not bumpkins in arms. The ferocious militia response at Concord and in subsequent operations that spring owed much to local military preparedness; enough organization was in place to sustain at least a short-term militia campaign.[3]

In poetry and prose, rebellious Americans exhorted one another to action. One poet, leaving behind his "dear Clorinda," poured forth his republican soul:

> My bleeding country calls, and I must go.
> Distress'd it calls aloud, to arms, to arms;
> The trumpet sounds, I now must go and leave your charms:
> I've drawn my sword, I'll go forth with the brave,
> And die a freeman, ere I live a slave.

Melodramatic verse, indeed, outdone only by the more prosaic advice of "an elderly lady" to "young men" about to enter wartime service in New Jersey. "Let me beg of you, my children, that if you fall, it may be like men," she exhorted them, "and that your wounds not be in your back parts."

Charles Royster has stressed that American citizen-soldiers of 1775 felt more than courage, moral confidence, and virtue. Many of them believed that America's republican quest represented a divinely ordained mission. Typical was the New Jersey soldier who rejoiced "that the ALMIGHTY Governor of the universe hath given us a station so honorable and planted us the guardians of liberty." For such persons, tyranny was more than synonymous with political slavery; it was the work of Satan. The contest truly was between sin and the forces of darkness and liberty and God's righteousness. As Royster has stated, many citizens saw in the impending military contest "the greatest test of the chosen people. In it they bore the weight of both their heritage and God's promise for the future."[4]

Whether by Christian precept, whig doctrine, or some combination of these two in conjunction with Enlightenment rationalism, the concept animating most provincial Americans in 1775 was republicanism. Theirs was a special calling, since citizens firmly believed that liberty was being snuffed out across the globe. Standing orders of the day issued to the rebel army surrounding Boston summarized the patriot mood and the calling best: "Let us therefore animate and encourage each other, and show the whole world that a Freeman contending for LIBERTY on his own ground is superior to any slavish mercenary on earth."

With this sense of noble purpose, the patriot enthusiasts of 1775 decided to test the very vitals of republicanism and their worthiness in aspiring to that ideal. The War for Independence was to be the measuring rod of the depth of commitment that free states demanded of virtuous citizens. The question was whether the provincials had the fortitude to endure sustained warfare against Britain's powerful armed forces and to emerge bloodstained but triumphant. That they rather uniformly and willingly did has been the historical myth. Most did not.

Regulars Versus Republicans: The British at Bay

Dr. James Thacher, a patriot witness to events around Boston following Lexington and Concord, recorded this scenario in his diary: "Such was the enthusiasm for the cause of liberty, and so general and extensive the alarm, that thousands of our citizens who were engaged in the cultivation of their farms, spontaneously rushed to the scene of action, and the army was established without the effort of public authority." As such, one of the most remarkable armies ever assembled sprang up almost instantly and entrapped Gage's regulars on the peninsula of Boston. By the end of April the rebel camp held over 10,000 enthusiasts, and the Massachusetts Provincial Congress persuaded many of them to stay on until the end of the year. Their nominal commander was Artemas Ward, described by acerbic Charles Lee as "a fat old gentleman who had been a popular *church-warden*." In actuality, Ward had seen martial action against the French and Indians, and he drew upon that experience in attempting to hold the irregular collection of patriots together.

Establishing some semblance of an army was no simple task with 10,000 independent-minded volunteers. Discipline was lax, with citizen-soldiers coming and going from camp as they

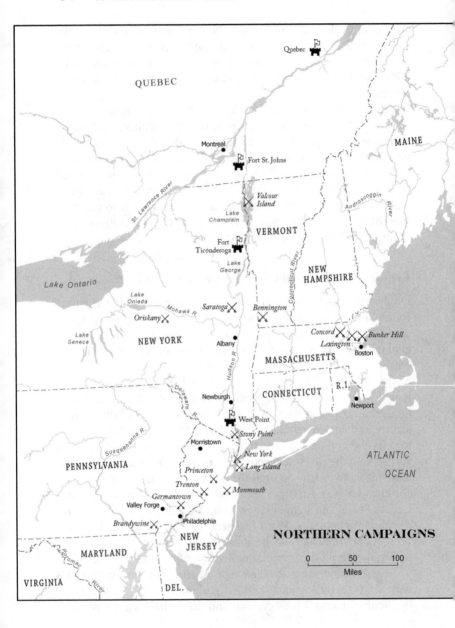

NORTHERN CAMPAIGNS

pleased and taking orders quite casually, if at all. Ward himself had minimal authority over patriots from other provinces; he issued general orders but only after meeting with a council of senior officers. Moreover, the troops lacked tents and equipment, particularly muskets and field artillery. Also, these enthusiasts had little sense of camp sanitation. Ward's assignment was enervating, but he managed to keep enough units in some semblance of order to discourage any offensive movements by General Gage.

Most patriot soldiers saw little wrong with the chaotic character of New England's republican army. These early citizen-soldiers seemed to revel in the contrasts between themselves and British regulars. The differences connoted that liberty was more vibrant than trained might. The general lack of discipline, the haphazard election of junior officers, and the continuing public response that further swelled the ranks all seemed to justify assumptions that tyranny was on the run. Many of these early soldiers were freehold farmers, artisans, and tradespeople who had rushed from their homes and families to the scene of action. Their numbers reassured each in the belief that the King's regulars could not stand up to middle-class, property-holding citizens filled with moral fervency and virtue.

The story of Israel Putnam's rush to the martial field further supported this mood. Putnam, a prosperous Connecticut freeholder and Seven Years' War veteran, was reputedly behind his plow when he learned about the first shots at Lexington Green. Like the Roman Cincinnatus, the future Continental general cut his horse from the traces, armed his laborers, and rode off to defend the sweet fruit of liberty. Nothing, it seemed, could overcome such intensely felt commitment.

The righteous confidence born of high enthusiasm served the cause well in the next few months, as the patriots chalked up an impressive early record. The capture of Fort Ticonderoga on Lake Champlain on May 10, 1775, was a case in point. Determined Benedict Arnold, then an officer in the Connecticut militia—and, as James Kirby Martin (*Benedict Arnold, Revolutionary Hero*) has pointed out, also a republican enthusiast at this stage of the war—suggested the venture in order to seize heavy artillery pieces badly needed around Boston.[5] Massachusetts commissioned him to lead the raid, but Ethan Allen of Vermont, acting under Connecticut orders, got under way first. Catching up with Allen's Green Mountain Boys, Arnold disputed Allen's right to command, and the two shared an uneasy truce when they stormed into the lightly garrisoned fort. Totally surprised, the British offered little resistance. Enterprise and élan had secured more than 60 serviceable cannons. Furthermore, despite the bickering over command, Arnold and others reduced enemy posts north of Ticonderoga, thus clearing the way for a possible invasion of Quebec Province in Canada, a conceivable fourteenth colony in rebellion.

The action that most exemplified the dominant assumption that citizen-soldiers could withstand the withering fire of any regular onslaught occurred on June 17, 1775, at Breed's Hill, across the back-bay from Boston. Near the end of May, Gage received reinforcements, including Generals William Howe, John Burgoyne, and Henry Clinton. These three urged the British commander to take Dorchester Heights, located south of Boston and an excellent site for artillery placements, assuming the rebels could secure the ordnance pieces to bombard the town. On the evening of June 16, however, the patriots diverted Gage's focus by digging in on the Charlestown peninsula north of Boston. The New Englanders planned to fortify Bunker Hill, but for some inexplicable reason they threw up their most extended works on Breed's Hill, lower than Bunker and closer to the enemy in Boston.

Seeing the works early on June 17, the British commanders quickly prepared for action. They wrangled over tactics. Instead of choosing flanking maneuvers and attempting to cut the rebels off by taking the narrow neck of land connecting Charlestown peninsula to the mainland, they opted for a massed frontal assault. The redcoats were to advance in formed ranks straight toward the American lines. Gage thought such an assault would teach the rebel citizen-soldiers respect for the prowess of British arms. The North American commander detailed 2,500 troops to be rowed across the bay, with General Howe in immediate command. That afternoon, the British found themselves advancing into what would be the bloodiest battle of the entire war.

On and around Breed's Hill, the Americans under William Prescott and Israel Putnam waited patiently. Well entrenched, the rebels allowed the regulars to get within yards of them and then, at the last moment, they loosed a volley that shattered the first British advance. Reeling, the British columns reformed and came on again, only to be thrown back with equal violence. Stunned by the carnage, Howe later admitted to *"a moment that I never felt before,"* the prospect of extermination in battle. With the outcome and British martial honor at stake, Howe ordered a third assault.

Many have commented on the iron discipline of the eighteenth-century regular soldier. Thoroughly trained rank-and-file redcoats feared concentrated enemy firepower less than the certainty of discipline for disobeying orders. The regulars who rallied for a third attempt at that hill were more than disciplined: they were awesomely brave. Although inconceivable to deeply committed whigs, the redcoats probably took regimental pride and the cause of their King as seriously as the patriots took their own. Now the regulars moved up the slope again, this time without the extra weight of full field packs. They had to step on and over the bleeding, mangled bodies of their comrades. Again, patriot fire erupted and staggered them. Then American ammunition began to give out. The regulars bore in with their bayonets and drove the defiant patriots from their works. Finally, with the battle over, Howe's exhausted soldiers had the bloodied landscape all to themselves.

The British had won in the technical sense of having forced the Americans to retreat, but they had not proved the superiority of well-trained regulars. They had suffered 1,054 casualties, slightly over 40 percent of those committed to battle. That was a staggeringly high casualty figure in an age of small-scale armies. American casualties reached 411 (30 percent of the rebels engaged). The victory was "dear bought," wrote a shocked Henry Clinton, "another such would have ruined us." Howe, who took over command of British forces in North America after the recall of Gage in October 1775, never forgot the bitter lesson he had learned about the fighting abilities of *entrenched* citizen-soldiers. That lesson represents one explanation for his dilatory movements in the field during the massive British campaign effort of 1776.

The patriots, who at first were sullen about losing, soon added the engagement to the list of examples of the fighting prowess of virtuous citizen-in-arms. "Bunker Hill, along with Lexington and Concord," historians Robert W. Coakley and Stetson Conn have claimed in *The War of the American Revolution,* "went far to create the American tradition that the citizen-soldier when aroused is more than a match for the trained professional."[6] Unfortunately for that tradition, the war did not end in 1775.

Over and above patriot self-assurance, there were other reasons why American citizen-soldiers stood up so well early on in the war. The British ministry and its military leaders, as John Shy has emphasized in *Toward Lexington,* did not expect a full-scale regional revolt in 1775; nor were British forces strong enough or deployed well enough to meet an effective irregular challenge.[7] Like the vaunted British navy, the army, since the Seven Years' War, had atrophied from lack of use. The British machinery of war needed to recover from its decay. Moreover, when the patriots fought in these early days, they generally dictated the terms. On the Lexington and Concord road, they harried exposed columns; at Ticonderoga, they picked off a weak and isolated post by surprise; and at Bunker Hill, they took advantage of terrain and a serious British tactical error (not seizing the neck of Charlestown Peninsula). In the first breaths of warfare, it seemed that republican ardor was carrying the patriots to victory. Success was coming so easily that Americans would have greater difficulty in responding effectively when the tide of war suddenly changed.

The Adoption of a Continental Army

The civil war could not be fought exclusively in New England, or at least patriot New Englanders hoped not. Broad-scale popular defense of liberty required the involvement of as many colonies as possible. In May 1775, the Massachusetts rebel leadership thus asked the Second Continental Congress to "adopt" the citizen's army around Boston. On June 14 the delegates agreed to take charge and also voted to raise 10 companies of Pennsylvania, Maryland, and Virginia riflemen to support the citizen-soldiers already in the field. By these actions, Congress had transformed the New England force, at least on paper, into a Continental army.

To usher in the existence of an intercolonial army required putting a command structure in place. As their first step, the delegates named George Washington, a dignified and reserved Virginia planter of great landed wealth, commander in chief. Although he had fought in the French and Indian War (Washington had survived the slaughter of General Edward Braddock's army in 1755), the 43-year-old Virginian had never commanded large numbers of troops. Yet Washington believed firmly in the worthiness of the American cause and was willing to dedicate himself completely to winning the war. His appointment resulted from the active support of New Englanders in Congress, such as John Adams, who favored having a southern commander. Through Washington, their idea was to ensure interregional support for what was still a fray in New England. Unknown to them in 1775, they had selected a person whose strength of character and depth of commitment to the goal of establishing a republican order would have a profoundly positive influence on the success of the cause.

The Congressional delegates also named the nucleus of a Continental general officer corps. They offered commissions to four major and eight brigadier generals. Because of the composition of the soldiery at the time, most of the commissions went to New Englanders. Not surprisingly, Artemas Ward became a major general, as did Israel Putnam and wealthy landholder Philip Schuyler of New York, both of whom had considerable experience in the colonial wars. The fourth major generalship went to Charles Lee, a person of substantial intellect but irascible temperament. Lee had an excellent military record in Europe and was an ardent republican and a staunch advocate of the citizen-soldier as the essential component of America's forces. During the early days of the contest, he rendered valuable service. Of the original brigadiers, Nathanael Greene, the lame Quaker from Rhode Island who had studied manuals on the art of war, became the most indispensable. Other appointments supplied the army with its first quartermaster, commissary, and adjutant generals. The initial adjutant general was another British veteran officer and adopted Virginian, Horatio Gates.

Even as Congress undertook the task of establishing a central army, many issues needed resolution. To whom the army belonged was still unclear. When Massachusetts asked the delegates to adopt the patriot soldiery surrounding Boston, the Provincial Congress was nervous about "having an Army . . . established here, without a civil power to provide for and control them." Since the objective was to have a Continental force with troops from all the colonies, it could not be maintained and operated by rebel leaders in one province. Congress did represent all the rebellious provinces, yet it was to remain an extralegal body with unclearly defined authority throughout much of the war (until the final ratification of the Articles of Confederation in March 1781). Out of expediency and the need for broad-scale planning, coordination, and participation, Congress agreed to take charge. The issue of whether the army was of Congress or of the states, however, did not receive clear resolution, which caused the new commander in chief innumerable difficulties in the days ahead.

To have had 13 sovereign heads to report to instead of one would have made Washington's assignment impossible. In many ways, the Virginian resolved the broad issue early by placing higher priority on Congressional dictates than on requests for military support coming from the states. Even more important, he insisted on proper military deference to Congress as the source of civil power under which he and the army drew its lifeblood. At times, Washington's insistence on military subordination to civil authority exasperated more than one Congressional leader, who sometimes tried to dump insoluble civil problems, such as logistical support, back onto the army. Washington, however, consistently sought to keep military power within prescribed bounds, even when state and Congressional politics adversely affected the war effort.[8] Above all else, Washington did not want to see the republican cause undermined by a military dictatorship, which turned out to be one of his greatest contributions to the Revolution.

Throughout the war, dealing with Congress was its own kind of vexing problem for Washington and others. The delegates, attempting to function as a deliberative, policymaking, and coordinating body, also tried to handle matters of administrative detail. In 1775, Congress began doing routine army business by creating *ad hoc* committees to make recommendations and by asking particular states to attend to this or that item. Pressing requests for support and for policy decisions had a way of getting bogged down, ignored, or lost. In 1776, the establishment of a Congressional board of war somewhat eased the pattern of interminable administrative confusion, since army needs now were to be handled by one standing committee. However, Congress made no serious attempt to move beyond the haphazard, inefficient pattern of administration (for which it gained a well-deserved reputation) until 1781, when the delegates finally established separate executive departments relating to war, finance, and diplomacy. By that time, the worst days of the war had nearly passed.

The Congressional administrative maze seemed to have no end, nor did the wrangling among Continental officers over rank. The ink had hardly dried on the first commissions of June 1775 when disputes broke out over why this or that person should outrank some other. Contentions over status and rank thus besieged Washington and Congress about as much as the British adversary, as historian Jonathan G. Rossie has shown in

The Politics of Command in the American Revolution.[9] In early 1777, Congress tried to settle these disputes once and for all with its Baltimore resolution: "In voting for general officers, a due regard shall be had to the line of succession, the merit of the persons proposed, and the quota of troops raised, and to be raised, by each state." If virtue meant subordination of self-interest to the greater good of the cause, many officers did not seem to comprehend its meaning. They put as high a priority on personal honor as on disinterested service, which adversely affected the ideal goal of unity in the cause.

Still another divisive issue—only before Independence—had to do with the purpose and function of the Continental army. The establishment of an intercolonial military force made clear to English leaders that the provincials had entered a new phase of heightened resistance and were preparing for full-scale war, should reconciliation prove impossible. During 1775, reconciliationists in Congress, individuals who hoped to settle differences with England short of declared independence, worried about what the British ministry would think about Congress's adoption of the New England force. They did not want this action to impede imperial reunification, should reconciliation still be possible. Pressure from this large bloc in Congress resulted in the "Declaration of the Causes and Necessity for Taking up Arms," written in July 1775, which was then forwarded to England. The reason for the military establishment, the Declaration stated, was not "to dissolve that union which has so long and so happily subsisted between us." Rather, the new Continental army would function solely to *defend* American lives, liberty, and property until "hostilities shall cease on the part of the aggressors, and all danger of their being renewed shall be removed, and not before."

Through the Declaration, Congress provided ammunition for the myth of Americans being forced into war by an arbitrary and capricious enemy. Still, the fact cannot be dismissed that establishing a Continental army was an aggressive, warlike act in itself, no matter how the reconciliationists sugar-coated the message for leaders in England. After all, warfare had not spread beyond a portion of New England and eastern New York in the early summer of 1775, and Congress could have chosen less extreme methods to protect the provinces while still seeking reconciliation.

George Washington soon appreciated that, in accepting command, he had to reckon with a veritable host of difficulties. His purpose was to manage an army that was to maintain its citizen-soldier character and to act only to defend American rights (until Congress said otherwise). The civil authority that would have the most important voice in formulating military policy and actions was unclear; moreover, Washington could not be sure whether the army was to seek reconciliation or secure independence, at least until Congress and the 13 provinces made up their minds. His officers were already wrangling over status and rank—in effect, the squabbling was akin to the Arnold-Allen bickering writ large—and, worse yet, when he reached camp at Cambridge on July 2, he found a cantonment that came closer to epitomizing martial chaos than an organized army. That Washington was able to deal with these and numerous other administrative problems that beset the Continental army during the next eight years stands as a testament to his unusual strength of will. Serving as commander in chief of the new republican force would have very quickly broken most leaders.

Initially, the most serious problem of all, as the new commander viewed it, was the lack of order and discipline in camp. "Discipline is the soul of the army," he stated flatly. "It makes small numbers formidable; procures success to the weak and esteem to all." As historian Marcus Cunliffe pointed out in *Soldiers and Civilians, 1775–1865,* Washington's ideal model for an effective army was the British standing force that he opposed.[10] From the outset, the commander insisted that everyone in camp respect the distinctions between officers and enlisted soldiers. In this regard, Washington found the "leveling" tendencies of the New Englanders to be particularly vexing. He complained in one letter that "their officers generally speaking are the most indifferent kind of people I ever saw. I dare say the men would fight well (if properly officered), although they are an exceeding dirty and nasty people."

Regional prejudice aside, the Virginian committed himself to overcoming the informal, individualistic bravado that characterized most units. Washington was a realist: he doubted how long virtue and moral ardor would hold up in intense campaigning against trained regulars. He suspected that the *rage militaire* would give out quickly should the enemy begin to enjoy significant martial success. His immediate objective became that of turning the citizen-soldiers into well-trained and disciplined fighters—functioning cogs in the machinery of war rather than the strutting individualists of militia muster days. Sustaining the rebellion depended upon thorough training and rigorous discipline, as much as anything else, in Washington's mind.

The new commander and his closest aides thus wanted an army made up of toughened regulars. Washington's personal involvement in the French and Indian War had persuaded him that heavy reliance on amateur citizen-soldiers in long-term campaigns was folly. As he once boldly stated: "To place any dependence upon militia is assuredly resting upon a broken staff." Positive that "seasoned soldiers performed better than seasonal ones," as historian Caroline Cox (*A Proper Sense of Honor*) has succinctly written, Washington tried not to question the presumed virtue and moral commitment of citizen-soldiers, but he was sure that rigorous training, regimen, and discipline were essential to sustaining troops in combat.[11] Militia, with their short-term enlistments, could come out, fight, and go back home when they pleased. They could be (and often were) erratic and prone to run in battle. Their very independence, thought Washington, made them an unsteady base on which to lean in combating His Majesty's redcoats.

From a similar angle, Nathanael Greene perhaps summarized attitudes best among Washington's closest general officers when he wrote that militiamen represented "people coming from home with all the tender feelings of domestic life." As such, they were "not sufficiently fortified with natural courage to stand the shocking scenes of war. To march over dead men, to hear without concern the groans of the wounded, I say few men can stand such scenes unless steeled by habit and fortified by military pride." Only training, discipline, and combat experience (qualities setting off the regular from the amateur soldier) could make for an effective army, concluded Greene.

Historians have hotly debated the issue of whether regulars or militia were more essential to winning the war. Claude H. Van Tyne, in his classic study, *The War of Independence,* argued that the war "proved the utter failure of the militia system."[12] Don Higginbotham has presented a more moderate viewpoint in stating that "the militia . . . for all its frailties, made its finest contributions to the nation in the Revolution."[13] Higginbotham's position makes more sense. The most significant problem facing Washington in 1775 was how to bring into being an effective Continental fighting machine in the face of the colonial militia tradition and so many ideological pronouncements about the inherent tenacity of virtuous citizen-soldiers.

Washington knew he could not abandon the militia tradition; he would have to work with it. However, he hoped to modify the system by employing militia on the periphery of his main force, "fighting a partisan war against enemy parties of a few dozen to a few hundred, and . . . against tories," as historian Mark V. Kwasny has stated in *Washington's Partisan War.*[14] Meanwhile, the new commander intended to develop a large body of trustworthy regulars in combining the best of both the amateur and regular traditions. As Cunliffe phrased it, the new commander "recognized that he would have to depend largely on scratch units and that he could not hope for more than a nucleus of seasoned Continentals. His aim was to make this nucleus as large as possible, and to enlist battalions for as long as Congress would allow and Americans would consent to serve."[15]

The key point is that Washington was realistic enough to begin constructing an army out of the materials at hand. No matter how much free-wheeling citizen-soldiers might object, even to the point of going home, instilling camp discipline was the first vital step. During the summer and fall of 1775, prompted by general orders and court martial hearings, the republican force begrudgingly accepted a superficial sense of decorum. Soldiers, for example, found drunk or asleep while on duty had been winked at in the past. The winks became fewer and the floggings more frequent. The commander also came down hard on unsanitary camp conditions. Disease was by far the greatest enemy attacking eighteenth-century armies. Washington put particular stress on clean kitchens and proper waste disposal. Whenever possible, he used tact and persuasion to guide the changes; failing that, he was not squeamish about the lash. (The Congressional Articles of War of 1775 allowed a maximum of 39 stripes, although Washington thought that many crimes, such as striking an officer, were worth at least 500.) By late autumn, the commander felt that he was making headway in disciplining his citizens-in-arms. (Of course, lapses occurred—in October a captain was caught shaving one of his men!)

While Washington labored to establish "a respectable army," as he once phrased his greatest task, the British remained inactive around Boston. Replacing Thomas Gage with 46-year-old William Howe made little difference. Dark-complexioned and handsome, Howe had a good military record, which included innovative leadership in training regulars in light infantry tactics. Yet he made no moves to break out of Boston.

In January 1776 Washington began tightening the ring of patriot forces around Boston. He wanted to storm that port city and drive the British into the sea, but his ranking officers persistently opposed the idea. Then his talented Chief of Artillery, 25-year-old Henry Knox, brought the ordnance pieces taken at Ticonderoga into camp after a harrowing overland trek in the dead of winter. The logical decision was to place the cannons on Dorchester Heights. Twelve hundred men worked through the night of March 4 to fortify the Heights. Now the guns could be unleashed against Boston at any time.

This feat demanded a response from Howe. After a severe late winter storm aborted a planned British attack on the Heights, Howe conceded that he was maintaining untenable ground. On

March 17, a fleet of almost 200 vessels carried away His Majesty's redcoats, with an estimated 1,000 local loyalists also on board, to Halifax, Nova Scotia. Without having fired a shot, the Continental establishment could claim a great victory. Howe's retreat only added to the misleading impression among patriot soldiers that virtue and moral commitment would surely win out over rigorous training and discipline. The British, however, were already planning a massive campaign effort with the objective of reconquering the rebellious colonies by the end of 1776. The republican-minded patriots of 1775 were about to encounter one of their most harrowing trials by military fire.

The British Military Counterthrust

Back in October 1774, General Gage, writing from Boston, had warned that "[i]f force is to be used at length, it must be a considerable one; for to begin with small numbers will only encourage resistance and not terrify." Lord Dartmouth replied that sending thousands of troops to America "would be impossible without putting the Army on a war establishment, and I am unwilling to think that matters have come to such a pass yet." Within nine months, as official reports of Lexington, Concord, Ticonderoga, and Bunker Hill reached England, Lord Frederick North's ministry realized that imperial authority was facing much more than a whimsical rebel challenge. Two other points were clear: the ministry lacked a strategy for subduing the patriots; and although formidable looking on paper, the army and navy were in a state of peacetime lethargy. The military establishment had to shake off its cobwebs, and the ministry had to formulate a strategy for conquering the eastern edge of a large continent, since political accommodation was becoming less likely with each passing week.

Great Britain appeared to have most of the advantages going into war, especially with respect to available troop strength. Population in the 13 colonies stood at 2.5 million in 1775 (including 500,000 African Americans, most of whom were slaves). Britain's population was closer to 11 million with some

48,000 soldiers on the muster rolls in 1775 (the actual number available and fit for duty was considerably lower). Likewise, the Royal Navy on paper had 139 war vessels; however, many were old and rotting, and few had enough sailors for extended service. An enlistment campaign finally got under way late in the year, but English subjects did not seem particularly interested in signing up. The ministry finally had to resort to pardoning criminals and shortening the length of enlistments (for the war rather than for life) to secure soldiers.

As a general rule, Britain's recruiting experience of late 1775 held up throughout the war. The average citizen had little inclination for regular military service. The tradition of reserving long-term military duty for down and outers as well as rigid discipline and the harsh conditions of camp life militated against any popular rush to arms, certainly much more so than feelings of sympathy for the American cause. In reality, no one really expected the middle classes to come forward. The well-established practice of separating military concerns from society thus severely limited Britain's natural manpower base in 1775 and thereafter. Also, within the spirit of the age, the ministry sought to keep the effects of the war as far removed from the home populace as possible. The goal was to make sure that the contest did not directly touch the general citizenry, and almost as a *quid pro quo,* the ministry expected these same civilians not to turn against or impede the war effort.

Only one alternative existed for assembling an army with haste. As Don Higginbotham has described the process, "the Crown, refusing to call upon the productive elements in society, resorted to the familiar practice of hiring soldiers from the continent."[16] All told, six German principalities ultimately supplied some 30,000 soldiers. Over half (17,000) came from Hesse-Cassel, where the landgrave dragooned these unfortunates into service in return for handsome British subsidies paid into his treasury. The war in America meant nothing to the German soldiers, which was of no concern to the British ministry. The Hessians, as they came to be called, represented what the Crown believed to be the necessary advantage in troop strength to crush the American rebellion.

All but unprepared at the outset for the needed military buildup, Lord North's ministry responded aggressively with its massive campaign effort of 1776, the most gargantuan land and sea offensive undertaken by Britain during the eighteenth century—and not to be matched, as an overseas expeditionary operation, until the 1942 allied invasion of North Africa. The ministry's objective was to shatter rebel militancy in one campaign; this decisive approach would work to avoid the expenses associated with long-term warfare and assure that the American rebels would not have time to ally with such traditional British enemies as France and Spain.

Besides the King and Lord North, the principal figure in formulating policy and putting together the campaign effort was Lord George Germain, who replaced Lord Dartmouth as the American Secretary in late 1775 and stayed in office until early 1782. Until recently, historians have had little good to say about him, largely because Germain was courtmartialed and cashiered from British military service on charges of cowardice at the Battle of Minden in 1759. However, Piers Mackesy, in *The War for America, 1775–1783,* has shown that Germain was primarily the victim of petty political infighting that carried over into his court martial. Mackesy's assessment is that he was a capable administrator, a man who was thoroughly loyal to his patron George III and often effective as war minister.[17]

Germain's administrative acumen was evident in preparations for the 1776 campaign. That effort stretched Britain's often inept and generally corrupt bureaucracy to its limits. Effective coordination among the Admiralty, War, and American offices was often lacking, but a flotilla of unparalleled proportions set sail for America by the early summer. Land and naval forces were well-supplied, well-clothed, and exceptionally well-armed. Their bivouac point was Staten Island, across the bay from New York City, where William Howe (having sailed south from Halifax) landed with some 10,000 soldiers at the end of June. By mid-August, another 20,000 troops had traveled across the Atlantic on some 370 transport vessels and been placed at Howe's disposal. In addition, Howe's talented brother Admiral Richard, Lord Howe, had command of more than 70 naval vessels and 13,000 sailors in the vicinity. With 45,000 soldiers and sailors confronting New York by August 1776, Great Britain had obviously overcome its bureaucratic and manpower difficulties and was now in a position to achieve a strong martial foothold in America.

Success depended on strategy, and there matters were, at best, confused. The grand problem was that of regaining political control over the 13 provinces through the application of military power. This task may very well have been beyond the standard military means of the day, given the characteristic separateness, diffuseness, and sheer geographical size of the rebellious colonies. Attempting to regain control of much of the eastern edge of a continent stretching more than 1,000 miles from Maine to Georgia was beyond ordinary eighteenth-century military assignments in this age of formalized warfare, especially because the erstwhile colonies lacked a strategic vital center which, if captured, would have destroyed the rebellion. Conquering one city, such as the nominal capital, Philadelphia, or even one region, such as defiant New England, would not guarantee total American submission. Pursuing the accepted military strategy of capturing posts and territory thus had many deficiencies as the likely means for restoring lost political allegiance.

Historian Eric Robson's study, *The American Revolution in Its Political and Military Aspects, 1763–1783,* raised the issue of whether Great Britain ever had a realistic chance of winning the war, given the nature and scale of eighteenth-century military activity. Robson framed two fundamental questions: Why did the British lose? Why did the Americans win?[18] What he found was that the parent nation faced nearly insurmountable bureaucratic, strategic, tactical, and logistical obstacles. In addition, condescending attitudes toward the rebels was a serious problem. As one English officer stated in 1779: "The contempt every Soldier has for an American is not the smallest. They cannot possibly believe that any good Quality can exist among them." Throughout the war, British political leaders, military officers, and soldiers clung to their sense of military superiority;

as a result, many of them missed the point that reconquering such a vast territory was an all but unattainable task for the conventional small-scale forces of their era.

Home officials, however, were not thinking in such problematic terms. Their fundamental strategy in 1776 was to concentrate troops in and around New York City, an excellent seaport and base of operations. New York would initially serve as the point from which the surrounding countryside could be subdued. In time, the King's forces could move northward and take the Hudson Highlands region, severing New England from the other states and isolating for conquest the area that had been the hotbed of patriot defiance. The British legions could also move southward and westward across New Jersey, providing a land base not only for food supplies but also for loyalists to rise up and help reinstate royal political authority. Then the net could be cast ever wider, until the patriot will to resist had become completely ensnared.

Still, a major issue, the *intensity* with which the campaign was to be conducted, was unclear. Germain preferred a virtual scorched-earth policy with the paramount goal being the early entrapment or annihilation of Washington's army. He reasoned that the rebellion would not be extinguished until the main rebel force no longer existed. The Howe brothers favored a less truculent approach to the 1776 campaign. Historian Stephen Conway has categorized the Howes as "conciliationists," as compared to "hard liners" in the British officer corps.[19] They accepted the ground rules of formalized warfare, which treated combat as more akin to a chess board experience. Moreover, they can be identified with the whig leaders in England who felt some sympathy for American grievances. The Howes believed that needless brutality, even if it ended the rebellion, would only further alienate the Americans and set the stage for yet another civil war in the years ahead. They agreed with their colleague Henry Clinton, who said that the principal goal of the campaign was "to gain the hearts and subdue the minds of the people." The Howe brothers intended to use persuasion in conjunction with demonstrated military might, employing their martial resources to prod the rebels into renewing their allegiance to the Crown.

When the Howes arrived in the New York vicinity, they carried instructions with them to act as Crown-appointed peace commissioners. Even though they lacked the authority to negotiate a settlement until the colonists surrendered, they hoped that the presence of their massed forces would be enough to bring submission. To pursue peace and war at the same time was inevitably clumsy for commanders in the field. Yet the Howes tried to accomplish that; and Germain, back in England, could do nothing to push them into a military reign of terror, which may have been the only operational approach that would have ended the rebellion in 1776.

The New York Campaign

After the British evacuation of Boston in March 1776, the Continental army moved to New York City, the logical point for the beginning of the British counterstrike. If troop strength was far short of what Washington would have liked, enthusiasm for the cause remained buoyant, as historian Allen Bowman has demonstrated in *The Morale of the American Revolutionary Army.*[20] Philip Vickers Fithian, a chaplain on duty with the New Jersey militia in New York, wrote home about patriot soldiers eager for combat. Nothing, he claimed, was too much to endure for liberty, not even army food. In Pennsylvania, Private Aaron Wright personified the spirit of virtuous commitment. He detested strict discipline, arbitrary officers, and citizens uninterested in or only lukewarm about the cause. Once, when a junior-grade officer resigned, then asked for reinstatement, Wright bristled: "You shall not command us," he told him, "for he whose mind can change in an hour, is not fit to command in the field where liberty is contended for."

Amid preparations to resist the British counterthrust, virtuous soldiers continued to attest to their steadfastness in the republican cause. William Young of Pennsylvania referred affectionately to "our American land" and begged Jehovah to afflict the unrighteous enemy with every kind of ill-fortune. Private Joseph Plumb Martin of Connecticut probably offered a succinct summary of soldiers' attitudes prior to the start of the 1776 land offensive. He recalled that he had formed "pretty correct ideas of the contest between this country and the mother country. . . . I thought I was as warm a patriot as the best of them." Martin disliked "arbitrary government." His "correct ideas" did not go beyond this point, except that he and his comrades heartily applauded the news they received in July that Congress had approved the Declaration of Independence.

Comparisons between whig virtue and imperial tyranny had started to become too neat, adding to unnecessary overconfidence among rebels in and out of the army. Committed patriots reveled in the words of the Declaration of Independence and its indictment of the King. After all, the Crown had kept among them "in Times of Peace, Standing Armies, without the consent of our Legislatures." The King had rendered "the Military independent of and superior to Civil Power" in America. Worse yet, he had "abdicated Government here" by "waging War against us." Then there was the prospect that George III was "transporting large Armies of foreign Mercenaries to complete the Works of Death, Desolation, and Tyranny" that he had begun so many years before. For those citizen-soldiers who cheered so enthusiastically at the first public readings of the Declaration, all that stood in the King's tyrannical path was their republican army, a military force that was not for hire—units consisting of short-term enlistees, militia, and volunteers who believed that they could repel any force because of the urgency and righteousness of their cause.

George Washington was less sanguine. Reenlistments for the 1776 campaign had come in very slowly, and the Continental army lacked even a small hard core of well-trained and seasoned veterans. Although Washington could count a force of nearly 28,000 in mid-August 1776, only about 19,000 were actually fit for duty. Most were raw militia or half-trained Continentals.

Washington's tactical situation was not much better. Since New York City was on the island of Manhattan, the British fleet could land Howe's army almost anywhere it pleased. The commander in chief had to deploy his soldiers knowing that he risked being outflanked. Washington felt he had little choice except to split his units between Manhattan and Long Island, divided by the East River. His strongest fortifications had to be on Brooklyn Heights, which Washington understood to be essential to the defense of New York. The presence of enemy artillery there could reduce that port city to submission or to ashes (much as critical ordnance placements on Dorchester Heights had rendered the British defense of Boston virtually impossible). In making these deployments, Washington's reserves on Manhattan would have a difficult time backing up his advanced forces on Brooklyn Heights. Moreover, General Howe could wreak havoc upon the divided Americans if the Royal navy seized control of the East River. That maneuver would effectively entrap Washington's main units on Long Island between British naval and land forces, leaving the reserves on Manhattan to be defeated later in mopping up operations. These rebel dispositions, mandated because of Congressional insistence that New York City must be defended, regardless of the perils, were fraught with grave risks.

After a year of military delusion—a period during which the British were arguably caught off balance—the myriad weaknesses of the patriot military establishment became all too apparent when William Howe finally got the summer offensive rolling. On August 22, the British landed at Gravesend, Long Island; and on August 27, they swept north in a multipronged attack. Although the patriots fought well in the center, a surprise flanking maneuver smashed the whole of the rebel line, driving it back to the Heights. The retreat quickly turned into a rout with the Hessians bayoneting trapped American soldiers begging for quarter. The day's devastation revealed some 1,500 rebel casualties, compared to fewer than 400 for the British.

Washington, with his back against the East River, drew more soldiers from New York City into the Brooklyn entrenchments when he should have ordered an evacuation to reunite his army. He was not yet ready to concede New York. Even more curious, given the rebel army's untenable position, the Howes showed little military dash. Pressure by land and water could have resulted in the surrender of thousands of Continental troops. Rather than storming the Brooklyn entrenchments, however, William Howe dawdled and, in uninspired fashion, prepared for conventional siege operations. Admiral Richard failed to maneuver his ships into the East River. Washington, realizing that entrapment loomed, called a council of war, which wisely decided on evacuation. With the assistance of John Glover's Marblehead (Massachusetts) mariners and the cover of a heavy evening fog, the rebels managed to extricate themselves late on the night of August 29.

Why the Howes failed to bag their prey—and squandered their best opportunity to do irreparable damage to the patriot resisters—has produced much historical speculation. Among the explanations for Admiral Richard's dilatoriness, commentators have cited unfavorable winds, tides, or blindness in sensing the obvious advantage. As for William's lack of aggressiveness, some have claimed that his Bunker Hill experience dissuaded him from pursuing the Americans into their trenches. Others have suggested that Howe worried incessantly about troop strength and feared the impact of heavy casualties in a general engagement. The very presence of so many Hessians demonstrated that Britain could not easily replace combat losses. Howe did believe that maintaining a substantial numerical advantage was essential to wearing down the Americans. In his study of British planning and strategy, Ira D. Gruber (*The Howe Brothers and the American Revolution*) has emphasized the whiggish disposition of the brothers. Acting as much as advocates of peace as of war, they may have "been following a strategy of careful advances, designed to create the impression of British invincibility, destroy the colonists' faith in the Continental army, . . . and produce a genuine reconciliation."[21] Regardless of the reasons, the Howe brothers let Washington's army escape. The American commander never again allowed his forces to get into such a dangerously exposed posture.

In the weeks that followed the Battle of Long Island, Washington kept retreating while William Howe, characteristically slow in pressing his advantages, nipped at the heels of the rebels. Manhattan clearly offered little safety because of successive British landings that forced Washington to withdraw his beleaguered force progressively northward toward Westchester County. As the patriot soldiers retreated, they left behind some 6,000 comrades in Forts Washington and Lee, perched high on the palisades on opposite sides of the Hudson River. After inflicting an inconclusive beating on Continental units at White Plains on October 28, Howe doubled back, gaining control of the ground between Washington and the rebel forts. On November 16, a determined force of Hessians overwhelmed Fort Washington on the New York side. The British sustained 452 casualties; however, 2,000 Americans fell into enemy hands, many of whom later died in the squalor of British prison ships in New York harbor. Two days later, in an astonishing operation that saw the British scale the New Jersey palisades undetected, a large detachment under Charles, Lord Cornwallis, caught the rebel force under General Nathanael Greene off guard at Fort Lee. Greene barely got his troops out but lost the bulk of his matériel. For the confident citizen-soldier, the defense of New York had turned into a genuine catastrophe.

When Fort Lee fell, Washington was already in New Jersey. After White Plains, he had crossed the Hudson with 5,000 troops, leaving another 8,000 in the lower Hudson Highlands region under Charles Lee. The only option for the commander in chief was to direct a harrowing retreat. Although still moving slowly, Howe had decided to follow up on the Fort Lee debacle with a full-scale invasion of New Jersey. Washington's forces had already endured a tremendous pounding. The burden of the sick and wounded, as well as the problem of massive desertions, resulted in a distressing manpower toll. So full of virtue and commitment just a few months before, the fleeing remnants of the Continental establishment were thoroughly dispirited. Their sense of superior purpose simply wilted in the face of massed, disciplined, forward marching regulars. Personally frustrated when frightened New Jersey militiamen failed to come to his support in adequate numbers, Washington led his battered columns through New Brunswick, Princeton, and across the Dela-

garrisons in New Jersey offered just such an opportunity, and the patriot general especially targeted Trenton.

Before attempting something dramatic, however, Washington had to address a fundamental problem. His troop strength was marginal, and a great many of those soldiers still with him would melt away on December 31 when their enlistments ran out. He anxiously awaited the arrival of Charles Lee's regiments. Lee, however, was advancing lackadaisically through northern New Jersey, spending about as much time criticizing his commander in chief as moving toward the Delaware. He may not have been cooperating on purpose, expecting that, if Washington failed to mount some form of a counteroffensive, Congress would sack him in favor of none other than Lee himself. A British patrol intervened at Basking Ridge when it stumbled upon and captured Lee at a local tavern. General John Sullivan of New Hampshire took command and promptly linked up with Washington. Several hundred Pennsylvania militia also came forward, all of which gave the commander nearly 6,000 effectives—more than enough for strikes across the Delaware.

The Americans moved out stealthily on Christmas night 1776. Only Washington's main body of 2,400 troops, one of three planned columns, got across the icy Delaware with the assistance of John Glover's mariners. One force was enough. Warned that something might be afoot, Johann Rall, a seasoned commander, had taken security precautions. However, despite the persistent tale that his men were drunk from Christmas celebrations (most were not), bad luck and bad weather—a snow squall masked part of the patriot advance—allowed the rebel attackers to catch the Hessians off guard. Without fortifications, they could hardly defend themselves. About 600 got away, but some 900 were captured and another 100 killed.

Then, after resting and disposing of the prisoners back in Pennsylvania, Washington crossed into New Jersey again on December 30. Near Trenton, he skirmished sharply on January 2 with Lord Cornwallis at Assunpink Creek. The fighting broke off in the evening, with the Earl sure that he would "bag the fox" at daybreak. Washington, in response, left his campfires burning and slipped away toward Princeton, where, on the next morning, he smashed a British brigade coming up to join Cornwallis. Only exhaustion stopped the patriot force from descending on New Brunswick and the lightly guarded British paychest there. Instead, Washington and his redeemed army pushed north toward the cover of the Watchung Mountains and Morristown, New Jersey, where what remained of Washington's Continental force spent a relatively safe winter and attempted to regroup for continued warfare.

Success and Failure

So close to having fulfilled their campaign objectives, the British had come up short of the mark. So close to collapse, the Americans had survived. Through its massive campaign effort, Great Britain had nearly overcome the obstacles that were blocking them from ending the rebellion. Failure to pursue Washington until his force was beaten beyond revival was the critical mistake. Trenton and Princeton proved that a rebel army, however desperate for troops, was still in the field and capable of inflicting biting wounds. Moreover, should sufficient numbers somehow be obtained, some sort of rebel force would be in place to contest the British in future campaigns. In this sense, Britain's effort, predicated on the concentration of forces at New York, had failed, and for one fundamental reason: the unwillingness or inability of the British general officers to follow through to total victory when annihilation was possible.

Also of long-term significance was William Howe's decision to abandon his distant Jersey outposts and draw a much narrower ring around New York. This action effectively undercut New Jersey neutrals and tories, great numbers of whom had identified themselves, having taken loyalty oaths to the King. Their military protection gone, they found themselves subjected to the less than temperate justice of local patriots. As historian Paul H. Smith has documented in *Loyalists and Redcoats,* British field generals time and again undermined the loyalists or used them ineffectively by not holding the ground that British forces had taken.[24] Britain, with so much potential support among the divided Americans, simply did not use this reservoir of human strength intelligently. By not effectively utilizing thousands of people who were willing to fight, grow foodstuffs, or reinstitute civilian government, the British further weakened their effort by having to maintain a cumbersome dependence on human and logistical resources from across the Atlantic. Over the long run, this pattern helped exhaust the British cause.

As was so often the case, rather than learning from mistakes and correcting them, there were excuses. "Now as to the Hessians, they are the worst troops I ever saw," complained a British officer in dismissing the Trenton setback. As for Commander in Chief William Howe, he settled into comfortable quarters in New York City and reveled in the honor of the knighthood that the Crown bestowed on him for his Long Island victory. He began planning for the 1777 campaign and enjoyed the pleasures of his pert blonde consort, Mrs. Joshua Loring. (Her understanding husband did not mind; he was savoring the rewards of the lucrative post Howe awarded him as commissary of prisoners.) Like the patronizing officer who faulted the Hessians, Howe did not accept the point that bringing the Americans back into the empire rested upon much more than just winning occasional battles. It depended on making effective use of those triumphs, of going for the jugular; and the British high command had not done that. As a result, the former parent nation had little to show for its effort in 1776, except for control of New York City and its immediate environs and Newport, Rhode Island, which Clinton had captured in December for use as a naval and foraging base.

For Washington, the climax of the 1776 campaign at Trenton and Princeton may be described as a dazzling display of innovative generalship. Outmaneuvered and outfought from August until December, and with the patriot army disintegrating around him, he had responded with a tactical masterpiece that left the enemy stung and frustrated. Washington had engineered one of the most astonishing campaign turnabouts of the era.

Militarily, months of British planning and effort had come undone, "destroying," as Ira D. Gruber has written, "the illusion of British invincibility, . . . and spoiling the Howes' hopes for an end to the war and a start toward a lasting reunion."[25] The British never again came so close to crushing the rebellion as they did in 1776; never again did the Americans come so close to losing.

Washington, however, had little time to celebrate his success. The campaign of 1776 had simply confirmed what the commander in chief feared: that enthusiasm and brave talk of virtue were not enough to sustain the military effort, that the patriot army, resting so squarely on the militia tradition, had reached the limits of what a highly motivated but short-term, half-trained, insufficiently organized, partly disciplined, and poorly equipped force could accomplish against seasoned regulars. Washington had long since concluded that fighting and winning a war for the sake of human liberty through republican forms and means was a fool's consistency. Virtue and moral commitment were simply not enough. Some form of well-trained American standing army had to be brought into being if the cause was going to succeed and ultimately achieve its objective of establishing an independent republican nation in North America.

Popular morale and support for the cause, so seriously damaged during the New York campaign and consequent retreat across New Jersey, needed a healthy revival as well. No doubt Washington would have agreed with the Pennsylvania soldier who proclaimed, even after the Trenton victory, that only divine intervention could save the cause. "If Salvation comes to our guilty Land, it will be through the tender mercy of God," the soldier lamented, "and not through the virtue of her people." Widespread ardor for the war did not burst forth again after Trenton and Princeton. It never again reached the lofty levels of enthusiasm that had been prevalent before the Battle of Long Island. Too many eager patriots had learned that enemy bayonets were profoundly indifferent to what they considered the justness, sincerity, and purity of their cause. The most pressing issue in early 1777 was how Washington and other rebels intended to endure, given that so many sunshine patriots were now more committed to staying home than to rushing to arms. With this attitude representing the new reality, the republican phase of war and the *rage militaire,* with the virtuous citizen-soldier as the emblematic centerpiece, had come to an end.

Notes

1 Bailyn, *Ideological Origins,* 319.

2 Royster, *A Revolutionary People at War: The Continental Army and American Character, 1775–1783* (Chapel Hill, N.C., 1979), 24. See also Royster, "'The Nature of Treason': Revolutionary Virtue and American Reactions to Benedict Arnold," *William and Mary Quarterly,* 3d Series, 36 (1979), 163–93.

3 Fischer, *Paul Revere's Ride* (New York, 1994), 152–57, *passim.*

4 Royster, *A Revolutionary People at War,* 9.

5 Martin, *Benedict Arnold, Revolutionary Hero: An American Warrior Reconsidered* (New York, 1997), 62–79.

6 Coakley and Conn, *The War of the American Revolution: Narrative, Chronology, and Bibliography* (Washington, D.C., 1975), 29.

7 Shy, *Toward Lexington: The Role of the British Army in the Coming of the American Revolution* (Princeton, N.J., 1965), 375–424.

8 See the valuable discussion in John Todd White, "Standing Armies in Time of War: Republican Theory and Military Practice during the American Revolution," (Ph. D. dissertation, George Washington University, 1978), 147–290.

9 Rossie, *The Politics of Command in the American Revolution* (Syracuse, N.Y., 1975), esp. 135–53. See also Richard H. Kohn, "American Generals of the Revolution: Subordination and Restraint," in Don Higginbotham, ed., *Reconsiderations of the Revolutionary War: Selected Essays* (Westport, Conn., 1978), 104–23.

10 Cunliffe, *Soldiers and Civilians: The Martial Spirit in America, 1775–1865,* 2d ed. (New York, 1973), 147–49. See also Cunliffe, *George Washington: Man and Monument,* rev. ed. (New York, 1982), 60–101.

11 Cox, *A Proper Sense of Honor: Service and Sacrifice in George Washington's Army* (Chapel Hill, N.C., 2004), 12.

12 Van Tyne, *The War of Independence: American Phase* (Boston, 1929), 115.

13 Higginbotham, "The American Militia: A Traditional Institution with Revolutionary Responsibilities," in Higginbotham, ed., *Reconsiderations,* 103.

14 Kwasny, *Washington's Partisan War, 1775–1783* (Kent, Ohio, 1996), 186.

15 Cunliffe, *Soldiers and Civilians,* 148.

16 Higginbotham, *The War of American Independence,* 130.

17 Mackesy, *The War for America, 1775–1783* (Cambridge, Mass., 1964), 46–57.

18 Robson, *The American Revolution in Its Political and Military Aspects, 1763–1783* (New York, 1955), 93–174. See also Millis, *Arms and Men,* 22–33.

19 Conway, "To Subdue America: British Army Officers and the Conduct of the Revolutionary War," *William and Mary Quarterly,* 3d Series, 43 (1986), 381–92.

20 Bowman, *The Morale of the American Revolutionary Army* (Washington, D.C., 1943), 45–56. See also Mark E. Lender, *The New Jersey Soldier,* New Jersey's Revolutionary Experience, no. 5 (Trenton, N. J., 1975), *passim.*

21 Gruber, *The Howe Brothers and the American Revolution* (Chapel Hill, N.C., 1972), 156.

22 Lender, "Small Battles Won: New Jersey and the Patriot Military Revival," *New Jersey Heritage,* 1 (2002), 33–35.

23 Fischer, *Washington's Crossing* (New York, 2004), 373–75.

24 Smith, *Loyalists and Redcoats: A Study in British Revolutionary Policy* (Chapel Hill, N.C., 1964), 10–43, 168–74.

25 Gruber, *The Howe Brothers,* 156.

CHAPTER THREE

Toward an American Standing Army, 1776–1777

The Nature of the Continental Army

Since the Revolution, the myth has persisted that provincial Americans, like the great Cincinnatus of republican Rome, exercised their obligations of citizenship by voluntarily leaving plows or bellows, shouldering muskets, and following Washington in defense of liberty and property. Afterward, having humbled the tyrannical British, they returned to their civilian callings, expecting no more than thanks from a grateful new nation. Over time, these citizen-soldiers became idealized as the legendary "embattled farmer" or the enduring and proud "ragged Continental." To this day, this conception of the citizen-soldier epitomizes for most Americans the spirit of the Revolutionary generation. Perhaps the strength and endurance of the image explains why many historians, until recently, have not challenged but have accepted and enshrined the legend.

The roots of the myth may be traced to several sources. These include the antistanding-army ideology of the eighteenth century, historical commentary written during the war itself and thereafter, and the loquacious musings of Fourth of July orators. Politicians through the generations, likewise, have borrowed selectively from the past in exhorting their followers to support some program, cause, or supposed truth, often in the name of the dedicated and committed Revolutionary generation. Historians themselves have repeated ingrained tradition, seemingly more willing to let national legend stand rather than to investigate extant records and deal with the interpretive consequences.

During the nineteenth century, for example, no historian had greater influence than George Bancroft. His *History of the United States from the Discovery of the American Continent* was a massive treatise in praise of national destiny. Like many of the Revolutionary generation, Bancroft viewed the enshrinement of liberty in America as part of God's "grand design" for redeeming the corrupted world. The citizen-soldier was essential to that design. Leaving "behind . . . their families and their all," they "came swift as a roe or a young hart over the mountains" to the fields of battle. Troops from all the states displayed a love of human rights that reached deeply into the freemen's well of voluntarism. "The alacrity with which these troops were raised," Bancroft concluded, "showed that the public mind heaved like the sea from New England to the Ohio and beyond the Blue Ridge."[1]

Early in the twentieth century, Charles K. Bolton published his influential monograph, *The Private Soldier under Washington*. Still a classic survey of the world of the soldiery, Bolton declared that the rank and file "were not a rabble recruited from the low ranks from which a city mob is drawn." Although some may have fought for reasons other than patriotic ardor, idealism motivated the bulk of these dedicated freedom fighters. A suggestion by a French officer with Washington that American Continentals really amounted to paid mercenaries, the author stressed, was not worthy of a serious reply.[2] Bolton, however, barely looked into the social composition of the Continental soldiery before formulating his generalizations.

Bancroft and Bolton typified those early patriot writers who lent credence to the popular image before an establishment of professional historians came into being in the United States. That image, however, has not changed very much since an identifiable professional group appeared in the early twentieth century. Writing in the 1950s, Howard H. Peckham (*The War for Independence*) concluded:

> The American in arms was a citizen-soldier. He had volunteered because he had an idea of how his political life should be ordered. He introduced a new concept into war: patriotism.... The American's own honor was at stake. He was fighting to determine the destiny of his country and therefore of his children. Once he received some military training, he usually could defeat the professional soldier and the mercenary because he had higher motivation, more initiative, and greater hope. These embattled farmers and artisans fought as men possessed— possessed of a fervent and ennobling desire to be free men.[3]

Joining this strain of patriotic historiography has been Edmund S. Morgan, whose widely read *The Birth of the Republic, 1763–89* claimed that it was "doubtful that the British could ever have won more than a stalemate" because the Revolution was decidedly "a people's war." "It was this experience at Concord and at Bunker Hill," opined Morgan, that "would tell again whenever a British army attempted to sweep through the country."[4] More recently, historian John Resch has claimed, based on his study of one farming community, that "enlistments from Peterborough [New Hampshire] represented a cross section of the town's society. . . . For Peterborough the Revolution was a people's war not a poor man's war."[5]

By comparison, Charles Royster (*A Revolutionary People at War*) has acknowledged that popular participation fell off dramatically in the wake of the New York campaign. However, the reason was that "Revolutionaries outside the army assumed that they could rely on popular defiance throughout a vast continent when their army was not near or even if there were no Continental army." Royster seems to be saying: Broad-scale participation was important; yet if it had all but collapsed by late 1776, that did not matter; citizens would again become involved if they had to, since they understood that "the absence of an army would have conceded the collapse of public virtue."[6] By implication, their apparent *willingness* to be involved meant that they *really were,* even if the historical record demonstrates that innumerable patriots disdained service, once the glory days of war had passed.

In this context, it is important to recall that Thomas Paine, in his first *Crisis* paper, written in 1776 during the patriot retreat across New Jersey, denounced "the summer soldier and the sunshine patriot" as the bane of the Revolutionary cause. "These are the times that try men's souls," Paine wrote urgently. "Tyranny, like hell, is not easily conquered; yet we have the consolation with us, that the harder the conflict, the more glorious the triumph." Paine employed biting language in urging wavering persons to remain virtuous and not to disavow the military obligations of citizenship. He reminded them that the success of the republican quest depended on citizens willing to make personal sacrifices over and over again. Paine understood that the *rage militaire* had passed—or been beaten out of the confident patriots by the mighty British campaign. The purpose of his forceful prose was to stem the tide. Yet Paine's immortal words made little difference in the months ahead. Very few propertied, middle-class citizens, after feeling the reverberations of the 1776 campaign, wanted anything to do with service in the Continental army.

Even as early as the autumn of 1775, Washington's chief problem was to field enough soldiers to give the Continental establishment the appearance of more than a shadowy likeness of an army. Enthusiasm for sustained participation had been fading even at the height of the *rage militaire,* possibly because of Washington's emphasis on thorough training and camp discipline, possibly because of killer camp diseases, and possibly because of boredom. The lack of committed involvement was one of the essential reasons why, in the end, the British came so close to winning (when they should not have) and the Americans so close to losing the war (when the geographic size, diffuseness of population, and lack of a strategic vital center made the conquest of the 13 provinces a virtually impossible task for military forces designed to wage mostly formalized warfare).

The dimensions of that paradox can be comprehended only by looking at the related problems of troop strength and popular commitment that Congress, Washington, and other patriots faced and the ways in which they attempted to address these critical issues.

A New Model Rebel Army

The challenges that confronted Washington at Cambridge during the summer and fall of 1775 were very much interrelated. Training, discipline, hygiene, and dedicated rather than wrangling officers were all necessary qualities of a respectable military machine. Even though Washington strove to bring about orderly conditions from the moment he took command, he knew that he could not build a worthy army unless Americans could be convinced that it was their duty to serve in the ranks for more than brief periods of time. In Washington's mind, short service terms undercut the ability of any army to perform capably. He believed that erratic service as a function of short-term enlistments was a major problem with militia. Worse yet, an army unsure of its size, strength, or fighting capacity at any given time was not the kind of establishment around which effective long-term campaign plans could be developed and executed.

That citizen-soldiers came and went from Cambridge, virtually as they pleased, disturbed Washington, as did the matter that so few apparent patriots wanted to enlist for the 1776 campaign. Although recruiting occurred throughout the colonies and Washington (in October 1775) commenced an extensive effort to secure one-year enlistees from among those in camp, not many stepped forward. By December, fewer than 4,000 of the early enthusiasts had signed up for the next year, and entire militia units had marched home. If the British had possessed a clear sense of how short of troop strength the Continental army really was in early 1776, they would have been wise to make every effort to break out of Boston.

Ennobling appeals to the patriot populace, moreover, did not seem to have much impact. In and out of camp, recruiters reminded potential enlistees of "the bountiful rewards of the industry of our worthy forefathers" and "the future grandeur of the western world." They asked "whether we will see our wives and children, with everything that is dear to us, subjected to the merciless rage of uncontrolled despotism." They reminded the populace that "we are engaged . . . in the cause of virtue, of liberty, of *God.*" It would take only "a few more noble exertions, . . . a few more spirited struggles, and we secure our liberties; a few more successful battles, and we are a free and happy people." With the great deed accomplished, "happy" would be "the man who can boast he was one of those heroes that put the finishing stroke to this arduous work," hence bequeathing this "estimable patrimony to his grateful children."

Other recruitment pleas during the fall of 1775 stressed that "never was a cause more important or glorious than that which you are engaged in." The fate of humanity, claimed these writers, depended on the outcome: "For if tyranny should prevail in this great Country, we may expect liberty will expire through the world." The message was simple: "Persevere, ye guardians of liberty." However, few guardians signed up, even in the midst of the *rage militaire.*

Why the citizen-soldiers of 1775 preferred to go home rather than to reenlist involved a host of individual explanations. All potential enlistees, no doubt, had sound reasons in their own minds. For some, it may have been relatively low pay, compared to what they could be earning as civilians. For others, the issue may have been unattended responsibilities at home or the stringencies of camp life. Many of these early soldiers were middle-class property holders with crops that needed harvesting. They faced the prospect of personal financial disaster if they neglected their farming operations, if they did not care for their stock, or they left fields unplowed and unplanted in the spring. They could be seasonal soldiers, and some willingly performed irregular—and even gallant—militia service after 1775. That way, the "glorious cause," as many called it, would not interfere too directly with the accepted seasonal rhythms of eighteenth-century life.

David Ramsay, a leading South Carolinian and contemporary historian of the era, offered a variety of explanations in his *History of the American Revolution,* first published in 1793. For some, "they were . . . soon tired of military life.—Novelty and the first impulse of passion had led them to camp; but the approaching cold season, together with the fatigues and dangers incident to war, induced a general wish to relinquish the service." These and others who had not known the travail of military life were "but feebly impressed with the military ideas of union, subordination, and discipline." Washington's emphasis on discipline, Ramsay contended, drove many away. "Even in European states," he wrote, "where long habits have established submission to superiors as a primary duty of the common people, the difficulty of governing recruits . . . is great; but to exercise discipline over freemen, accustomed to act only from the impulse of their own minds, required not only a knowledge of human nature, but an accommodating spirit, and a degree of patience which is rarely found among officers of regular armies."[7]

Washington's frustration in trying to reenlist patriot citizens became even more intense as he learned about the fate of the rebel invasion of Canada. During the summer of 1775, the Continental Congress sanctioned a two-pronged assault on Quebec Province. The expedition was an obvious violation of Congress's "Declaration" against offensive warfare—in hopes of reconciliation. Yet the delegates wanted Quebec to throw in its lot with the patriots, which seemed strange to many of its French-speaking inhabitants, who were more than aware of the anti-Catholic phobias of their more southerly neighbors. Securing Canada as the fourteenth colony in rebellion would have enlarged the American phalanx against Great Britain, making any invasion by His Majesty's armies down through the Lake Champlain–Hudson River corridor much more difficult. For some Congressional delegates, too, taking Canada would provide a broader base from which to launch the dawning dream of a New World phoenix rising up out of the ashes of the old.

The determined patriot detachments proceeded north in the late summer of 1775. One group moved over the border from New York under the capable guidance of General Richard Montgomery, while Colonel Benedict Arnold launched his epic march to Quebec through the wilderness of Maine. In December, with Montreal in hand but with short-term enlistments set to expire at year's end, the two commanders gambled on an all-out attack on the walled city of Quebec. Early on the morning of December 31, the rebels advanced under the cover of a driving snowstorm. Everything went wrong. Montgomery was shot dead; Arnold was seriously wounded; and hundreds of other troops became casualties or prisoners, including the roughhewn but talented leader of Virginia riflemen, Daniel Morgan. Even though Arnold persisted in a hopeless siege of Quebec, the plan for taking Canada never recovered from this staggering blow. In June 1776, a large reinforcement of British regulars drove patriot forces, devastated by smallpox, out of Canada once and for all.

Devoted patriots deeply mourned Montgomery's loss and praised Arnold for their heroism. Arnold became America's Hannibal. Whigs proclaimed Montgomery, a former British regular officer who had settled in New York and married into the wealthy Livingston family, a true martyr of classic proportions. He became yet another of the rebellion's sainted farmer-soldiers. The slain general was "An American Patriot! . . . A General from the Plough! Such was Cincinnatus, in the greatest days of Roman virtue." Like the oft-mentioned Roman hero, Montgomery had "bid farewell to his peaceful retirement" and taken up the sword in the cause of liberty. Here again was patriot imagery at its best, with all of the allusions to classical Rome that virtuous republicans so loved, dwelling on glory rather than defeat—and, conveniently, ignoring Montgomery's background as a regular army officer.[8]

Washington and Congress, although chagrined about Montgomery's death (he was one of the most promising Continental generals), clearly understood one of the reasons for the failure at Quebec. Facing expiring enlistments, Montgomery and Arnold had rushed into battle and may not have acted at the most propitious time. As Washington stated after recalling Montgomery's loss, "the evils arising from short, or even any limited enlistments of the troops, are greater, and more extensively hurtful than any person . . . can form any idea of. . . . It takes you two or three months to bring new men in any tolerable degree acquainted with their duty," the commander explained. It took even more time to establish "such a subordinate way of thinking as is necessary for a soldier; before this is accomplished, the time approaches for their dismissal, and you are beginning to make interest for the continuance for another limited period." To woo the perpetual short-term enlistee, then, Washington argued, "you are obliged to relax your discipline," thereby undercutting any possibility of maintaining a well-trained establishment. The Americans could not have it both ways; winning the war against British regulars required discipline and, in Washington's mind, a core of malleable, long-term enlistees. Rigorous training, discipline, and long-term enlistments did not suit the temperament of that many patriots, despite brave words and easy talk about public virtue and abiding commitment to the cause.

Washington had to find the means to solve this problem. The impact of the failed assault on Quebec City, along with the struggle to sign up enlistees for the 1776 campaign, convinced him, carrying forward on his thoughts of 1775, that Congress must agree to a full "new modeling" of the Continental army. Trying to train and discipline free spirits was not enough. Congress would have to approve policies supporting a regular military establishment—the nucleus of a standing army that would serve for the duration of the war, would be well paid, and would not buckle under to either harsh camp life or concentrated enemy offensives. Furthermore, officers needed to have reason for pride in command as well as incentives for staying in the service. The latter problem became more pressing in 1777 and 1778; the former was paramount even before the patriot cause felt the full brunt of the British offensive of 1776.

In the minds of a few republican ideologues more interested in consistency than in overcoming the British martial challenge, Washington's thinking represented a frontal assault on antistanding-army ideology and the concept of a virtuous citizenry capable of overcoming any military threat. Washington, the supreme realist, firmly grasped the huge challenge that His Majesty's forces represented. He needed a cadre of soldiers that could be counted on day in and day out, that could be deployed when and where they were needed, not when and where they felt like fighting.

Reports from Quebec had also mortified Congressional delegates, including many who would normally have preferred relying on militia. In 1776, bespectacled James Wilson of Pennsylvania typified this latter group. As historian John Todd White has pointed out, Wilson saw the nation as having "a choice between two evils." Besides being expensive, an army of short-term soldiers provided no continuity or stability, and service (especially with rigorous camp discipline) would never be attractive enough to assure sufficient troop strength. That had already been demonstrated in the midst of the *rage militaire*.[9] On the other hand, an American standing army could threaten the very liberties that rebel leaders hoped to ensure. As a worried Samuel Adams explained, in "a Standing Army, . . . Soldiers are apt to consider themselves as a Body distinct from the rest of the Citizens. They have their Arms always in their hands. Their Rules and their Discipline is [sic] severe. They soon become attached to their officers and disposed to yield implicit obedience to their Commands. . . . Such a Power," concluded Adams, "should be watched with a jealous Eye."

Adams, Wilson, and others worried openly about the risks of "new modeling" the Continental establishment. They recalled Oliver Cromwell's highly efficient, thoroughly disciplined Puritan army which had, in time, become an agent of oppression in maintaining Cromwell in power. Cromwell's force had helped to inspire James Harrington's *Oceana* and a handful of other opposition whig tracts warning against the dangers of standing armies. The Congressmen thus faced an essential dilemma. With the citizen-soldier more interested in going home (or staying there), or only performing short-term militia service, the choice was whether to develop a standing military establishment capable of contending with Britain's war machine or to trust the Revolution's fate to ever fluctuating numbers of citizen-soldiers who did not want to stay in the field for any length of time.

Ultimately pushing fears of societal corruption or the potential for an internal military coup aside, Congress finally accepted Washington's reasoning. The weight of events during the first nine months of 1776 confirmed the logic of the commander's appeals and persuaded the delegates to approve a standing regular force. John Todd White has pointed out at least four factors that moved Congress toward Washington's position: 1) news that the King was hiring thousands of Hessian mercenaries; 2) the arrival of a sizable royal force in Canada that drove the Americans out of Quebec Province; 3) the massive British concentration of forces on Staten Island; and 4) the overall failure of short-term enlistment appeals, in combination with the relatively mild military code of 1775, to attract even close to what patriot leaders considered sufficient troop strength for the Continental army.[10]

The delegates swallowed the bitter pill of reality during the late summer and fall 1776, when Great Britain's New York land offensive was beginning to take its heavy toll. Besides putting greater muscle into the Articles of War (Congress raised the legal limit on lashes from 39 to 100 and increased the numbers of crimes for which the death penalty could be exacted), the delegates voted Washington the substance of the "respectable army" that he wanted. There were to be 88 battalions of 738 officers and men each, to serve for a minimum of three years or for the war's duration, if more than three years. The delegates also assigned state troop quotas according to population distribution. Thus more populous Massachusetts was to enlist 15 battalions, while Delaware and Georgia were to supply one each. In December 1776, Congress empowered Washington to recruit 16 more battalions, without state affiliations, and a number of cavalry, artillery, and support units. The projected army numbered 75,000 on paper, which contrasted sharply with Washington's 6,000 effectives on the eve of the Trenton counterthrust.

Hindsight, of course, has demonstrated the naiveté of patriot hopes for (or the ability to support logistically) an army of this size. It should be recalled, however, that Congress adopted this legislation in September, before experiencing the full effects of the 1776 campaign. Furthermore, the delegates had rough estimates of available American manpower. Accepting the base of nearly 2 million whites, allowing for as many as 500,000 loyalists, and conservatively figuring that one in every four or five of the remainder were adult males between the ages of 16 and 50, there probably were some 350,000 potential soldiers in the population. (During the 1760s Benjamin Franklin had estimated the number of white males in the same age group at 250,000, using a smaller population base.) Even if the figure of 350,000 is slightly high, an army of 75,000 would have enrolled no more than one-fourth to one-fifth of the eligible males at any one time. This would have left the remainder available for civilian occupations, including the production of food and the procurement and production of war matériel and other vital goods.[11]

Congress recognized that an army of 75,000, or even one half that size, was unlikely without sufficient financial inducements. Specifically, the inclusion of bounty provisions in the recruiting laws was an admission that appeals to virtue had not spurred enough enlistments. That had already been proved by the end of 1775, at the height of the *rage militaire*. Even though potential enlistees listened to patriotic appeals "with patience," to use Washington's description after the 1776 campaign, the numbers who actually signed up were "no more than a drop in the Ocean." The commanding general saw only one way to solve the problem: "The allowance of a large and extraordinary bounty." Unpalatable as such an idea was to republican sensibilities, Congress conceded Washington's argument that "such People, as compose the bulk of an Army," would not be "influenced by any other principles than those of Interest." As such, the delegates voted each potential recruit a bounty payment of $20 (that sum increased steadily during the war) upon enlistment, a yearly clothing issue, and a hundred acres of land for those who served for the duration. After much debate, the minimum term of service was set at three years, although individuals would be encouraged to sign up for longer periods. Washington kept pressing for full duration commitments, but he readily conceded that three years was far more desirable than the shorter terms that so far had bedeviled the cause.

The argument can be made that the British offensive of 1776 frightened Congress into accepting the concept of a standing army for hire as opposed to a republican force. The reality of military circumstances certainly was an important factor, as was the necessity of a response to the astonishing collapse of citizen enthusiasm in regard to actual service. Likewise, the crushing blows that Washington's forces sustained during the autumn of 1776 established the point that a disciplined army carried more sustained punching power than one depending on public virtue and zealous commitment. The commander now had the authority to construct a military establishment that would approach the Old World model, to seek out and hire those who could be trained as a resolute core of regulars fighting on behalf of the cause of republicanism. Washington was doing more than building on practices that had become common during the French and Indian War. He was seeking to Europeanize the Continental military establishment, ironically for the purpose of ensuring the liberties of all citizens. The questions that were uppermost in early 1777 were: Could Washington find enough potential troops and, if he did, would he be spawning a military monster in the Cromwellian mold that would come back to haunt the very cause and citizenry for which it was being hired to defend?

William Howe's Campaign of 1777

John Taylor was the kind of person the patriot cause needed in its darkest hours. He was solid—a good whig, a respected faculty member of Queen's College (now Rutgers) in New Brunswick, New Jersey, and a man with convictions about the military obligations of citizens in a republic. He willingly strapped on his sword as a militia colonel and participated in the patriot military revival in New Jersey during 1777. In April, while on duty near Princeton, he watched the training of some of the army's new regulars. What he saw bothered him. The "yeomanry," Taylor wrote despondently to a friend, the country's "original safeguard," were staying home; Continental regiments were being filled with people he did not trust. They were "mostly foreigners," he claimed. They were "really mercenaries" with "no attachment to the country except what accrues from the emoluments of service." The rebellion and, therefore, the republican cause were in trouble. "Hope for the best," he concluded, "but at the same time fear the worst."

What Taylor had witnessed at Princeton was part of the process of building and training Washington's new American army. Primarily at Morristown, but at other locations as well, Continental officers were hastily attempting to bring together a force capable of withstanding another major British offensive, one that Lord North's ministry hoped would complete the goals of 1776 and end the civil war once and for all. Washington had few reasons to be optimistic. During the early winter of 1777, soldiers in camp had dwindled to below 3,000. By May, his following was back up to 10,000, with 7,363 present and fit for duty. His total numbers, concentrated mostly in the Watchung Mountains northwest of William Howe's major outposts at Perth Amboy and New Brunswick, represented little more than one-third of the effective troop strength available to Howe.

Although Washington lacked a sizable army, he had the advantage of the hilly terrain; moreover, he and his lieutenants were in complete agreement regarding what the Continentals should accomplish during the campaign season. Their objective was to stay alive as a fighting force in the field while strengthening themselves and hurting the enemy as much as possible in the meantime. As historian Russell F. Weigley has argued, Washington understood that he must maintain "the strategic defensive," parrying and thrusting when necessary but avoiding full-scale engagements that might threaten the army's continued existence. The New York campaign had taught him that large battles with a "tactically superior enemy" were ill advised, especially when his troops were neither so numerous nor proficient in open-field maneuvers.[12] However reluctantly, the naturally aggressive Washington, as historian Dave R. Palmer has shown (*The Way of the Fox, 1775–1783*), took on the role of Fabius Cunctator, the Roman Delayer who wore out the Carthaginian enemy by simply maintaining a defensive presence in the field.[13] During the spring of 1777, the commander in chief ordered raiding parties to harass the British in the New Brunswick–Perth Amboy vicinity. Besides pestering the enemy and maintaining the high ground, he had to wait for the British to offer some form of action.

Even while Washington held back, his small-scale tactics made life dangerous for British units trying to forage in the rich New Jersey countryside. Rebel parties, Continental and militia, played havoc with enemy foraging detachments; ultimately, the King's troops had to keep relying on supplies shipped from the British Isles at enormous cost. (This trans-Atlantic supply effort also drained the resources of the Royal navy, which had to protect the supply ships from rebel privateers.) These raids were a major inconvenience for the British and a logistical coup for the patriots. Moreover, Washington's troops acquired much-needed operational experience during this "defensive" phase of the war.

The burden of proof during 1777 was on the British, especially if they wanted to hold down on further additions to their national debt or avoid the prospect of an enlarged war, should the rebels secure allies. Success depended on coordinated operations, specifically between Howe's main force in New York and His Majesty's forces in Canada, now under the command of General John Burgoyne. The logical plan—the so-called Hudson Highlands strategy—was to secure the Hudson River corridor and cut New England off from the remaining states. William Howe, vacillating endlessly about what course to follow, finally made up his mind that Philadelphia had to be taken;

in the process, he hoped to destroy Washington's army in a climactic set-piece battle.

Why Howe chose Philadelphia as his target when he knew Burgoyne was pushing south from Canada has perplexed generations of historians. Possibly Howe could not imagine that Burgoyne would face such strong partisan resistance, or Howe may have viewed the well-connected, dandyish Burgoyne as a potential rival for New World military glory, should the latter be too successful. On the positive side, Howe clearly wanted another crack at the main Continental army after the embarrassments of Trenton and Princeton. He, too, had learned from previous errors that a nearly shattered army was not *ipso facto* moribund. Even if Howe did not demolish Washington and his Continentals, he would still have Philadelphia, a base from which to subdue the surrounding countryside. Also, seizing the rebel capital might signal the beginning of an overall patriot collapse—much as taking a European capital would all but resolve an Old World conflict. In the end, Howe may have considered all or only some of these possibilities before not doing what Germain and the ministry wanted. He did not work in synchronized fashion with "Gentleman Johnny" Burgoyne.

In May 1777, Washington moved the bulk of his forces south from Morristown to Middlebrook, New Jersey, holding the high ground a few miles northwest of New Brunswick. Try as Howe might, he could not lure the Continentals out of their mountainside stronghold and into a decisive engagement. Memories of Bunker Hill likely dissuaded the British commander from assaulting the Middlebrook site. Washington's tactical positioning was masterful. Not only did Howe not dare attack him, but with the Continental army intact and with militia units working actively in support, Sir William decided there would be too many risks in marching overland to Philadelphia. The rebels could nip at his flanks or, worse, beat him to the Delaware and cause havoc in any attempted crossing. Also, the patriots might choose to slip behind the British force and disrupt communications and supply lines back to New York. Eighteenth-century generals rarely took such chances, and Howe was no risk taker. Because of the positioning of Washington's army, the British commander concluded that the only safe way to get to Pennsylvania was by sea. So, frustrated and delayed by his own indecision and futile attempts to lure the rebels into a conclusive battle, Howe evacuated New Jersey in late June and set sail on July 23 with 15,000 redcoats, leaving a reserve force of 7,300 in New York City under Henry Clinton.

Back in London, Lord George Germain went along with Howe's campaign design rather than demanding that he move forces up the Hudson River in support of Burgoyne. Reluctantly, the American Secretary approved the plan; yet he still urged Howe to take Philadelphia quickly enough to dispatch troops northward to aid Burgoyne. This advice was futile. Now committed fully to his own objective, Howe debarked his troops on August 25 at Head of Elk at the top of Chesapeake Bay, some 50 miles southwest of Philadelphia. Adverse winds and difficult channels had kept the British army at sea for a critical month in the middle of the campaign season. Even if Howe had wanted to help Burgoyne, crucial time had been lost, and Burgoyne's army was nearly 300 miles away—too far to receive meaningful assistance.

Meanwhile, Washington, who could not believe that Howe was moving south by sea rather than north up the Hudson, arrived in Philadelphia with 11,000 soldiers. Pressured by Congress to defend the patriot seat of government, he diverged from his Fabian posture and got ready for a general engagement. Howe also prepared; and the two armies clashed on September 11, when Washington moved to block the British approach to the city at Chadd's Ford on Brandywine Creek. Howe had one wing of his army demonstrate across the ford, keeping the center of the Continental line occupied, while a second wing swung wide, as on Long Island the year before. Those units smashed through the American line right under luckless General John Sulli-van and carried the day. The Continentals sustained an estimated 900 casualties, compared to Howe's 550.

Outgeneraled again, Washington was still game. Some of his units had fought well at Brandywine, a sign that training and discipline were making his army more competitive. Having temporarily stripped off the mask of Fabius, Washington prepared to re-engage. A torrential rainstorm that soaked the Continentals' powder destroyed one attempt. Before the rebel counterattack could come, however, Sir Charles Grey, one of Howe's subordinates, executed a surprise night raid on Anthony Wayne's division on September 20. The redcoats used their bayonets well, leaving behind nearly 300 victims in what became known as the Paoli Massacre. Within another few days, Howe had maneuvered his opponent out of position northwest of Philadelphia, which caused Congress to flee to York, Pennsylvania. The British marched triumphantly into the city on September 26.

Not backing off, Washington soon dashed any British hopes that the loss of the rebel capital would bring peace overtures. Early on October 4, the Americans attacked at Germantown, a thriving community north of Philadelphia where Howe had stationed many of his troops. Washington's battle plan proved too complicated. The rebels struck in four columns, converging from several directions, but a dense morning fog disoriented them, and, at one point, they started shooting each other. Although caught by surprise, the British rallied and drove off the Continental forces. Howe's dead and wounded amounted to 520; Washington lost 650 troops. To make matters worse, the enemy captured over 400 patriots.

The results of Germantown were a terrible disappointment to Washington; Howe was elated. In retrospect, the moods should have been reversed. From a strategic point of view, Howe had frittered away a most critical campaign season in which he had nothing concrete to show for his efforts, except for losses to his army and large numbers of elated loyalists in eastern Pennsylvania. In taking Philadelphia, the British had captured an empty shell whose loss did little to deter continued rebel resistance. The Continentals would fight on, raiding Howe's communication lines outside the city and grimly defending Forts Mercer and Mifflin, which blocked the Delaware River below Philadelphia. Even after Germantown, Washington hoped that holding these forts would prevent the Royal navy from freighting supplies to Howe, letting his redcoats starve in the prize. The British finally secured the river and thus assured their supply lines into Philadelphia, but only in mid-November after weeks of fierce combat.

The costs of Howe's delays and Washington's willingness to fight were incalculable for the British cause. Howe had conducted his campaign at the expense of Burgoyne's northern army, which pointed toward formal diplomatic accords between the patriot Americans and France that, in turn, rendered Great Britain's task of winning the war problematic at best. Although Howe enjoyed great success in particular battles during 1777, he had failed the test of strategic vision. Philadelphia did little more than provide his army with comfortable winter quarters. That was a staggering price to pay for the loss of Burgoyne's army and France's formal intervention on behalf of the Americans.

The Saratoga Campaign

Far to the north in September 1777, Burgoyne's struggling units faced unremitting harassment. Growing numbers of New England militia were backing up an experienced core of regular Continentals under Horatio Gates, who had just taken over command of the army's Northern Department from Philip Schuyler. The rebels smelled blood, and they had almost entrapped Burgoyne's slow-moving force of 7,000 British and Hessian soldiers, initially supported by numerous Indian allies. Gentleman Johnny still held out hope that he could punch through the New York wilderness to Albany before winter, but he desperately needed assistance from the south. A diversionary force finally moved north from New York City under Henry Clinton, but it represented too little support coming too late and never got near Burgoyne's beleaguered army.

Actually, the impending Burgoyne debacle was an ironic culmination to the Canadian campaign of 1776. The Montgomery/Arnold assault on Quebec had resulted in a ministerial decision to rush 10,000 regulars to Canada. During the spring of 1776, the rebels countered by sending hundreds of soldiers northward. They were no match for the British relief force. By mid-June, while under the command of John Sullivan, they withdrew from Canada as smallpox ravaged these courageous souls. As summer turned to fall, it appeared as if the redcoats, Canadians, and Indians under Quebec's royal governor and ranking general, Guy Carleton, would have no problem sweeping as far south as Albany before winter.

Carleton decided to float his army southward onto Lake Champlain, aiming at Fort Ticonderoga. However, he wasted much of the summer constructing his fleet, which included 20 gunboats and a few larger war vessels, some of which had to be disassembled on the Richelieu River near Montreal, carried overland around rapids, and reassembled at St. Johns. Meanwhile, indomitable Benedict Arnold oversaw the construction of a small patriot flotilla to defend Lake Champlain. The two fleets clashed on October 11 at Valcour Island. Arnold's outnumbered and outgunned craft fought courageously before slipping away under cover of darkness and fog. The resolute determination of the patriot fleet, even when defeated in detail over the next few days, and the lateness of the season convinced Carleton that pressing the advantage would be unwise. He retreated to Canada to wait out the winter season. By doing so, Carleton "had succumbed to the brazenness of such fighting rebels as Arnold," as James Kirby Martin has written. He thus "afforded" the patriots "an opportunity to offer combat another day," as they did in resisting Burgoyne's powerful force during the 1777 campaign.[14]

Lobbying in England during the winter of 1776–77 netted Burgoyne overall command of the Canadian army. His detachments left St. Johns on June 15, 1777; soon they had taken Fort Ticonderoga, beaten a patriot rearguard at Hubbardton, Vermont, and swept on to Skenesborough, where they rested for three weeks. To Burgoyne's right in the Mohawk Valley, a flanking column under Colonel Barry St. Leger was also faring well. With 1,700 regulars, Indians, and loyalists, St. Leger had Fort Schuyler under siege by early August, where 750 rebels gamely refused to surrender. The American situation looked hopeless; and Washington, then positioning his Continentals to defend Pennsylvania, could not help, except for sending a few reinforcements northward.

Suddenly, the scales of war shifted. As the main British force resumed its southward advance, patriot defenders felled trees across roads and blocked fords with boulders. Burgoyne's movement slowed to a crawl. His columns included some 2,000 women and children, plus an excessively large baggage and artillery train. Burgoyne's personal "necessities," consisting of his silver dining service, fresh uniforms for all occasions, and many cases of his favorite champagne, filled 30 wagons. After Gates replaced Schuyler, many more New England militiamen, allegedly put off by Schuyler's aristocratic bearing, flocked to the scene. Unwittingly, Burgoyne may have also aided the patriot rally when, out of fear that he would lose his Indian allies, he did not punish those natives who participated in the murder of Jane McCrea, the fiancee of one of his loyalist officers. Word spread among New Englanders that Burgoyne actually encouraged such atrocities, which may have caused some rebel militia to muster their arms and join Gates's ranks.

The British advance started to falter in mid-August. On August 16, New Hampshire militia under General John Stark crushed two Hessian columns sent to capture rebel stores at Bennington, Vermont. The action cost Burgoyne 900 troops. St. Leger also ran into serious trouble. His Indian allies had stopped a militia attempt to relieve Fort Schuyler at the bloody battle of Oriskany on August 6—killing or wounding American General Nicholas Herkimer and half of his men. Then Benedict Arnold, heading another relief column, cleverly repaired the damage. He sent a half-witted loyalist into St. Leger's camp, spreading stories about huge numbers of rebel soldiers sweeping in their direction. The Indians panicked and fled, leaving St.

Leger only with regulars and loyalists. Rather than confront Arnold, the British colonel raised the siege of Fort Schuyler on August 22 and withdrew to Canada. Burgoyne was now alone.

The first of the two-part Battle of Saratoga occurred on September 19. Burgoyne found his southward march blocked by rebel entrenchments on Bemis Heights, six miles north of Stillwater, New York. His attempt to push through the patriot line that day faltered when Daniel Morgan's riflemen and troops under Arnold savagely attacked his detachments at Freeman's Farm, well in front of Bemis Heights. The British sustained 556 casualties, compared to 280 for the Americans. Burgoyne, how-ever, won a technical victory because his troops held the ground at Freeman's Farm, where he formed his own defensive line and regrouped for further combat.

Over the next few days, the most dramatic action occurred between Gates and Arnold. Arnold felt deeply slighted when he learned that Gates, in his official after-action report to Congress, had neglected his subordinate's praiseworthy role at Freeman's Farm. Gates, although never near the battle himself, did not want to share any glory with Arnold, and he eventually relieved the offended Arnold of command. When Burgoyne finally moved part of this force forward again on October 7, patriot troops sallied forth once more. While the battle was still in doubt, Arnold, on his own authority, mounted his horse and rushed to the front. He rallied the patriots and led the way in shattering the redcoat line. When the day had ended, Bur-goyne's position was all but hopeless. This time Gates reluc-tantly gave Arnold, who had been seriously wounded while charging into a Hessian redoubt, proper public credit.

Burgoyne, who had lost over 600 troops on October 7 com-pared to 130 American casualties, retreated eight miles north to Saratoga (modern-day Schuylerville), New York. With his de-pleted command hopelessly surrounded by ever-growing num-bers of militia, a dejected Burgoyne formally surrendered on October 17, 1777. A British officer noted poignantly in describ-ing the scene that "we marched out, according to treaty, with drums beating and the honors of war, but the drums seemed to have lost their former inspiring sounds, . . . then it seemed by its last feeble effort, as if almost ashamed to be heard on such an occasion."

Unknown to this officer, Saratoga turned out to be a very solemn drum beat for Great Britain's attempt to reconquer the rebellious American provinces. The lack of coordinated planning by Germain, Howe, Burgoyne, and Clinton, among many others, had made a shambles of the British campaign. If there was one source of hope left for the British, it was that the Americans still had to demonstrate that enough of their numbers had the fortitude to endure militarily in the cause. At the end of 1777, that crucial issue remained in doubt.

The American Search for Manpower

Two important characteristics of the Saratoga battle related directly to the Continental manpower problem. First, militia had turned out in substantial numbers. They played an important role in sealing Burgoyne's fate, although the Continentals carried the brunt of the fighting on September 19 and October 7. Militiamen were always valuable as harassing auxiliaries, if they chose to come out. In 1777, for example, Washington had not been as lucky as Gates. The Pennsylvania militia gave the Virginian only minimal assistance against Howe. Staunch loyalist feelings among southeastern Pennsylvanians, as well as the strongly held doctrine of pacifism among Quakers, were primary reasons for such a scanty turnout, making Washington's situation that much more perilous in comparison to that of Gates. Inconsistent militia support, which varied by region, continued as a problem for the patriot cause throughout the war.

Second, Gates worked out a controversial arrangement with his British adversary, whereby Burgoyne's troops would be marched to Boston and shipped back to England, all in return for unconditional surrender. Once home, they were to sit out the remainder of the war. Most persons could quickly figure out that their return to England would free other soldiers on duty in Britain for service in America. Congress, on Washington's advice, rejected Gates's terms of capitulation. Ultimately, Burgoyne's "convention army," as it came to be known, marched southward from Boston to the interior of Virginia. Along the way, patriot recruiters convinced many Hessian and British veterans to enlist in Continental ranks.

The reality of the matter was that Washington, Gates, and others fought the campaign of 1777 with minimal numbers of troops, even with militia in the field. Had recruiters not offered enlistment bounties and promises of regular pay, decent food, new clothing, and free land after the war, Washington may not have had enough of an army to challenge Howe and his minions. Throughout the war, the American commander struggled to build up a central core of long-term regulars, and the task of doing so was continuous and enervating.

Recruiting campaigns represented the basic means of obtaining long-term enlistees. Although Washington and Congress issued instructions on who might serve (they preferred healthy free-born citizens between the ages of 17 and 50), they could not afford to be too fastidious. The army and the 13 states participated together in the process of recruiting. The army employed the traditional European practice of "beating up" for enlistees. A sergeant or a junior officer whose commission likely depended on raising his own squad or company would travel through an area with a few drummers to attract a crowd. Often they would set up a table at a tavern, where they regaled potential recruits with liquor and the glories of military service. The procedure was laborious, suited to armies that could spare soldiers and take unlimited time to find recruits. The Continental army could afford neither.

Civilian recruiting efforts tended to be more complex. State officials conducted their own appeals, and a number appointed their own state recruiting officers. Many states also offered bounties, over and above Congressional allocations, and they frequently angered neighbors by "poaching" for enlistees across state boundaries. State bounties also upset troops who had enlisted without them, which in 1779 forced Congress to vote these Continentals a gratuity payment of $200 per person. State authorities often had recruiting problems when funds designated for bounties ran low. As such, although state-directed efforts did produce a trickle of recruits, as did "beating up" on the part of the army, the results were generally disappointing.

There was little doubt, especially after the campaign of 1776, that recruiting based on voluntarism alone could keep the Continental establishment functioning at even minimum levels of strength. Memories of hardship, defeat, rigid discipline, and disease remained too vivid. Horror stories circulated everywhere and scared off thousands of potential recruits. At Morristown in early 1777, many officers openly questioned whether the newly planned regiments, so fine in theory, would ever exist. In the first weeks of the new year, only about 1,000 of the veterans of 1776 chose to reenlist. The recruiting situation was so chaotic in early 1777 that Washington wondered, even as late as May, about whether he would dare challenge Howe in the circumspect way that he did. As Charles H. Lesser's invaluable compilation of Continental manpower reports (*The Sinews of Independence*) has shown, Continental strength, based on returns from all departments, did not reach a peak for 1777 until October, when 39,443 (including militia) were in the ranks.[15] This number represented 35,000 fewer soldiers than Congress had projected, as well as more than 8,000 short of peak strength the year before (48,017 in October 1776). Even with the new financial incentives, voluntarism had begun to wither well before the war was two years old. Moreover, the pattern worsened as the war continued. Each year, as a general rule, fewer and fewer patriots wanted to have anything to do with Continental military service.

Maintaining minimal troop strength was an endless problem for Congress, the states, and the army command. In searching for any and all recruits, they enlisted every "able-bodied and effective" civilian they could find instead of accepting only propertied freeholders of the ideal republican type. Early in 1777, for instance, New Jersey granted exemptions from militia service to all men who hired substitutes for Continental duty and to masters who would enroll indentured servants and slaves. In the following year Maryland permitted the virtual impressment of vagrants for nine months of regular service. Stated differently, the majority of recruits who fought with Washington after 1776 represented the very poorest and most desperate persons in society, including ne'er-do-wells, drifters, unemployed laborers, captured British soldiers and Hessians, indentured servants, and chattel slaves. Some of these soldiers were in such desperate economic straits that states had to pass laws prohibiting creditors from pulling them from the ranks and having them thrown in jail for petty debts. Very few of the new Continentals were independent farmers and tradespeople. Their service after 1776 mostly came as militia offering occasional support as partisans on the periphery of the Continental establishment.

A number of recent quantitative studies have verified that Washington's new regulars were largely from the poor and dependent classes in Revolutionary America, whose numbers had been growing dramatically for at least two decades before the rebellion. These soldiers were not normally engaged in the defense of home and family because they rarely had either. As historian Charles Neimeyer has concluded in *America Goes to War,* they "were part of a larger group of free (and unfree) waged (and unwaged) laborers . . . of various racial and ethnic elements" whose service was "much more crucial to the outcome" of the Revolutionary War "than has been previously supposed."[16]

Post-1776 Continentals were most often in their teens or early twenties, although a small handful were lads of 14 and younger. The army considered the young "very proper for the service," as one South Carolina recruiter indicated, because "they have little, and some no property," and thus had few economic ties or marital bonds in the civilian world. Lack of property and economic standing, however, was not just a function of age; the families of most recruits were also quite poor.

Historians Edward C. Papenfuse and Gregory A. Stiverson found that "poverty was endemic" among Maryland troops of 1782, with half of those with traceable economic status coming from family units holding less than £45 in assessed wealth.[17] Mark Edward Lender ascertained that in New Jersey, at least 90 percent of the Continentals with traceable economic back-grounds represented the poorest two-thirds in society and that 46 percent of the soldiery or their families for those underage owned no taxable property whatsoever. Fifty-seven percent were landless, not an attractive condition in that state's largely agricultural economy.[18] Historian John R. Sellers's investigation of Continentals from Massachusetts and from Virginia revealed distinctly similar patterns, especially in confirming the poverty-stricken family backgrounds of Washington's new regulars.[19] Among the post-1776 Continentals, poverty—before, during, and after Continental service—was a unifying characteristic. What is certainly clear is that when Washington's soldiers marched off to war after 1776, they left behind them little in the way of property to defend.

Besides unemployed wage laborers and transient groups, the unfree also became fair game for Continental service. Going beyond indentured servants, as many as 5,000 African Americans, many of them slaves, eventually became part of the Continental ranks. Massachusetts led the way in 1777 by declaring blacks (both slave and free) eligible for the state draft. Shortly thereafter, Rhode Islanders began recruiting two African American battalions. Other states, mostly in the North, soon followed, so that "[b]y the end of 1777," as Sylvia R. Frey has observed in *Water from the Rock,* "free blacks and slaves were serving in mixed regiments in a number of states."[20] Most of the slaves entered the ranks as substitutes for masters who were in some way avoiding Continental service.

The South, however, remained somewhat obdurate in adopting such practices. Although Maryland and Virginia eventually permitted slaves to substitute for whites, the lower South persistently refused to do so, even in the face of a successful British invasion of Georgia in late 1778. To let slaves fight for liberty was simply too threatening to the social fabric of that region. Despite the lower South, General Philip Schuyler perhaps best summarized the pattern when he asked why so many "Sons of Freedom" were so willing "to trust their all to be defended by slaves." Irony aside, the answer was simple: Increasingly after 1776, when middle- and upper-class property holders felt pressure from recruiters or from state-legislated conscription programs, they turned to those who did not always have the right or freedom to decide for themselves whether military service was an appropriate test of disinterested citizenship.

For those bound in slavery or temporary servitude, Continental service could offer them access to personal freedom—in return for duration commitments. Redemptioners were often economically straitened German migrants who, upon reaching America, sold their labor for several years to pay for their voyage across the Atlantic. Johan Carl Buettner was a typical redemptioner. He reluctantly agreed to six years of servitude with a New Jersey Quaker farmer who paid the costs of his passage. One day, Buettner heard about the possibility of joining a Continental battalion to be made up principally of German redemptioners. The only requirement, in committing to duration service, was that he share his meager (actually mostly nonexistent) soldier's wages to help compensate his master. For risking his life, he would also receive several acres of land and his personal freedom at war's end. Buettner signed on, "less concerned about the freedom of North America," he later wrote, "than about [obtaining] his own [liberty]."

Enemy deserters and prisoners of war were also welcome in the army's ranks. Early Congressional pronouncements barred such persons from joining up; but troop shortages remained so acute after 1776 that even Washington warned that unless the army be allowed "to moulder away, . . . we must look for Reinforcements to other places than our own states." The commander in chief personally pardoned at least one English prisoner on the condition that he enlist in a Continental unit. Apparently, this practice was common. Because of incomplete records, the matter of how many enemy deserters and prisoners were in the ranks has not been established. Nathanael Greene claimed that he had a large number of British deserters, including many Irish, fighting in his southern Continental force during 1781. They evidently took perverse delight in turning their musket fire upon their former employers. Moreover, recruiters regularly enrolled Hessians, such as those from Burgoyne's convention army, and Congress started to issue regular appeals to these German mercenaries, promising them land and a new start in life once the war was won.

Loyalists arrested on charges of aiding the British, especially in the middle states, often received a choice of accepting Continental service or going on trial for their lives. Patriot courts in Morristown, New Jersey, for instance, sentenced at least 105 loyalists to hang; although four of them held to principle and went to the gallows, the court reprieved all who consented to "enlist in the American army for . . . the war." The pattern was similar in criminal dealings, epitomized by the story of John Saunders, who received a sentence in 1777 of two public floggings for stealing horses in the Morristown vicinity. After the first beating, the dazed Saunders agreed to enlist in the Continental army; the judge, a generous man, canceled the second flogging.

By the spring of 1777, rebel leaders fully comprehended that troop quotas resting upon abstract notions of public virtue would go largely unfilled. Washington called openly for conscription: "The Government must have recourse to coercive measures; for if the quotas required of each State cannot be had by voluntary enlistment, in time, and the Powers of Government are not adequate to *drafting*, there is an end of the Contest, and opposition becomes vain."

Congress recommended the draft to the states on April 14, 1777. However, the states that adopted conscription laws also provided huge loopholes in the form of substitute and fine provisions, which protected the most economically favored patriots from Continental duty. Hundreds of well-to-do property holders paid fines rather than face service. Drafting days also saw a brisk trade in willing substitutes, most of whom came from the poor or unfree classes. The result was that persons of lesser economic standing like Joseph Plumb Martin enlisted for the duration as a substitute. When a group of reputed patriots learned that he might be available for hire, they quickly had a bidding contest for his services. "I forgot the sum," Martin recalled later, but "I thought, as I must go, I might as well endeavor to get as much for my skin as I could." Regardless of the amount paid him, "[t]hey were now freed from any further trouble, at least for the present, and I had become the scapegoat for them."

Hundreds of others, apparently embedded in straitened personal circumstances, felt the same way. In New Jersey, somewhere between 20 and 40 percent of the state line of 1778 consisted of substitutes for draftees. In New Hampshire, the town of Epping sent only substitutes forward when the local militia held its draft in 1777. The draft, inherently at odds with the concepts of citizen virtue and selfless commitment to republicanism, actually functioned to enhance the dramatic movement of middle-class citizens away from service in the post-1775 Continental establishment.

Washington and his closest advisers also accepted the presence of women in the army. So-called camp followers were to be found traveling with almost all eighteenth-century armies. Usually marginally poor, these women came along with husbands or lovers, or because they could not find other ways to survive economically. Popular lore aside, they were not just followers or prostitutes. Women as well as men were "on rations"; in return for half-rations, armies assigned these women a variety of duties, including cooking, caring for the sick and wounded, washing and mending clothes, scavenging the field for clothes and equipment, and burying the dead after battle. In the British army, the accepted ratio was one woman for every 10 men on rations; the ratio was one to 15 in the Continental army. Washington personally never approved of the presence of women in camp, but he never drove them out either. He knew that he would also probably lose their husbands or consorts, which would adversely affect overall troop strength. Thus women came along and contributed, even if the commander in chief preferred to keep them out of sight whenever the army paraded in public.

Besides investigating the presence of women, historian Holly A. Mayer (*Belonging to the Army*) has taken note of various other persons who attached themselves to Continental forces on a permanent or semi-permanent basis.[21] Sutlers, private vendors who sold supplies, food, alcohol, and personal items to the troops, were regularly present in camps. Civilian employees of the Commissary or Quartermaster Departments, and private teamsters and others having long-term business with the army, also gravitated into the social orbit of the soldiers. In time, the Continental army came to resemble a small society unto itself.

This pattern was normal for the professional forces of the eighteenth century, with their predominantly lower-class soldiery, their consorts, and the various hangers-on who derived their livelihoods from the military. Even though they had constant points of interaction with the civilian world, the rank and file and those in their circle, rarely from propertied backgrounds, tended to turn inward during their years of service. This pattern was yet another aspect of the growing divide between civil society and well-trained, long-term soldiers that made republican ideologues leery of standing armies. If improperly led by power-hungry commanders, these troops, with no propertied stake in society, could be employed to destroy the very liberties they had been hired to defend and protect.

The Old Myth and The New Soldiery

Washington struggled to maintain minimal numbers of troops in the field during 1777 and beyond. He did so by ignoring the dictates of republican ideology with respect to citizens-in-arms. Middle-class farmers and tradespeople, John Adams observed in passing, apparently had better things to do than go soldiering for years at a time. He asked why such persons "who could get at home a better living, more comfortable lodgings, more than double the wages, in safety, not exposed to the sickness of camp," would enlist for three years or the duration? "I knew it to be impossible," Adams concluded.

From the point of view of social characteristics, the new Continental soldiery increasingly took on the appearance of a traditional European army while looking less like a republican force. Out of necessity, Washington had to accept whatever troops he could get without worrying about the source. In the growing pool of poor and unfree peoples in Revolutionary society, Washington and Congress found individuals who were willing to perform lengthy service and who could stand the brutal rigors of life in the field, including harsh discipline and the ever-present specter of disease, starvation, and death. Myth to the contrary, these were the "hardy" Continentals, the "rabble" that endured to the end. Their more socially acceptable Revolutionary brethren were most willing to let them do the hard, long-term fighting; then, after the war, selective memory returned citizen-soldiers to center stage, where historical myth has kept them placed ever since.

By late 1776, despite the republican concept of virtuous citizenship, the freeholding American populace was hiring, for all practical purposes, a regular army to fight for it. Washington's new model soldiers, however, did not view themselves as mercenaries. Many of them were simply trapped by the circumstances of their lives, and Continental service offered them positive alternatives. African Americans in slavery, as historian Benjamin Quarles has reminded us in *The Negro in the American Revolution,* usually found the army less oppressive than a civilian world that held them in chains and viewed them with unthinking prejudice.[22] For many slaves there was the promise of postwar freedom in return for long-term service; for the criminal, an end to prison; for the debtor, an avoidance of creditors or a settlement of burdensome debts; for the Hessian, a new start in the freer American environment. Most recruits also had the prospect of gaining free land at the end of the war. Their dreams were of a better life, if only they could survive Continental service. These dreams, while intensely personal, also paralleled and complemented the broader patriot quest for liberty and republicanism, all of which made the bargain between civilians and Washington's hard-core regulars possible. The initial financial inducements, likewise, were of paramount importance for persons with little or nothing in the way of economic resources. For them, Continental service meant personal socio-economic mobility or outright freedom, but only if the new nation kept its part of the contractual bargain.

Lest other myths be formulated, it must be stressed that not all luckless individuals rushed to join the Continentals. For many, the toll of long-term military service and its dangers was too dear a price to pay, even if not signing up meant continued economic or legal bondage. Moreover, some of the down and outers who filled Washington's ranks were just plain scoundrels. They were variants of M'Donald Campbell, a sometime New Jersey militiaman and Continental who also served with the British (he claimed afterward that he was spying for the Americans). At one point, he recalled, he "had formed an acquaintance with a young woman . . . of a very creditable family, with whom I had been too intimate." Her father insisted upon marriage, but Campbell instead fled to the Continental ranks. After the war, he highlighted his notorious career by prospering temporarily as a counterfeiter. Men like Campbell and John Saunders typified those who served during the war simply because the rebellion happened to drift into their way. However, for most of those who formed Washington's small hard core of regulars after 1776, the dirty work of fighting the Revolutionary War meant something much more—the dream of postwar prosperity and a new and better beginning in life.

Still, there was a lurking danger in amassing such an unpropertied regular force within the framework of antistand-ing-army ideology. Don Higginbotham has articulated part of the proposition: "So long as American soldiers were little more than a reflection of American society, the Continental army posed no threat to free institutions."[23] In terms of actual social composition, the post-1776 Continentals were a very distorted reflection. The latent possibility was developing that Washington's new modeled army, once shaped into an effective fighting machine, might turn on the cause of republicanism that it had committed to help bring into existence, should an ungrateful citizenry not remember its contractual promises and obligations.

Stated differently, Washington's new soldiers, as they trained, fought, and sacrificed, were gaining the potential to become a threat to patriot civil society, should they get the impression that more respectable, propertied civilians did not intend to allow them to enjoy the full benefits of a freer, more open republican order at war's end. Conditions portending real trouble between army and society were in the making as the war effort deepened and lengthened after the unsuccessful British campaign effort of 1777.

Notes

1 Bancroft, *History of the United States from the Discovery of the American Continent,* 10 vols. (1834–1874; Boston, 1860), 8: 62–64.

2 Bolton, *The Private Soldier under Washington* (New York, 1902), 13, 235, 238.

3 Peckham, *The War for Independence: A Military History* (Chicago, 1958), 204.

4 Morgan, *The Birth of the Republic, 1763–89,* 3d ed. (Chicago, 1992), 79.

5 Resch, *Suffering Soldiers: Revolutionary War Veterans, Moral Sentiment, and Political Culture in the Early Republic* (Amherst, Mass., 1999), 9–10. For a different assessment also based on Peterborough's records, see John Shy, "Hearts and Minds in the American Revolution: The Case of 'Long Bill' Scott and Peterborough, New Hampshire," in Shy, *A People Numerous and Armed,* 163–79.

6 Royster, *A Revolutionary People at War,* 116.

7 Ramsay, *History of the American Revolution,* 2 vols. (New York, 1968 reprint), 1: 233–34.

8 For other examples of the patriots' affinity for classical allusions, see Gary Wills, *Cincinnatus: George Washington and the Enlightenment* (1984), *passim.*

9 White, "Standing Armies in Time of War," 140.

10 Ibid., 144–45.

11 For an argument that one state had stretched itself to the absolute limit by September 1776 with respect to available persons for military service, see Richard Buel, Jr., *Dear Liberty: Connecticut's Mobilization for the Revolutionary War* (Middletown, Conn., 1981), 53–80.

12 Weigley, "American Strategy: A Call for a Critical Strategic History," in Higginbotham, ed., *Reconsiderations of the Revolutionary War,* 48–50.

13 Palmer, *The Way of the Fox: American Strategy in the War for America, 1775–1783* (Westport, Conn., 1975), 115–43.

14 Martin, "The Battle of Valcour Island," in Jack Sweetman, ed., *Great American Naval Battles* (Annapolis, Md., 1998), 24–25.

15 Lesser, ed., *The Sinews of Independence: Monthly Strength Reports of the Continental Army* (Chicago, 1976), 2–56.

16 Neimeyer, *America Goes to War: A Social History of the Continental Army* (New York, 1996), 159–60.

17 Papenfuse and Stiverson, "General Smallwood's Recruits: The Peacetime Career of the Revolutionary War Private," *William and Mary Quarterly,* 3d Series, 30 (1973), 117–32.

18 Lender, "The Enlisted Line: The Continental Soldiers of New Jersey," (Ph.D. dissertation, Rutgers University, 1975), 110–39. See also Lender, "The Social Structure of the New Jersey Brigade: The Continental Line as an American Standing Army," in Peter Karsten, ed., *The Military in America: From the Colonial Era to the Present* (New York, 1980), 27–44.

19 Sellers, "The Common Soldier in the American Revolution," in S. J. Underdal, ed., *Military History of the American Revolution: Proceedings of the Sixth Military History Symposium, USAF Academy* (Washington, D.C., 1976), 151–61; and Sellers, "The Origins and Careers of the New England Soldier: Noncommissioned Officers and Privates in the Massachusetts Continental Line" (paper delivered at the American Historical Association Convention, 1972). More generally, see Robert Middlekauff, "Why Men Fought in the American Revolution," *Huntington Library Quarterly,* 43 (1980), 135–48; and John C. Dann, ed., *The Revolution Remembered: Eyewitness Accounts of the War for Independence* (Chicago, 1980), *passim.*

20 Frey, *Water from the Rock: Black Resistance in a Revolutionary Age* (Princeton, N.J., 1991), 78–79.

21 Mayer, *Belonging to the Army: Camp Followers and Community during the American Revolution* (Columbia, S.C., 1996), *passim.*

22 Quarles, *The Negro in the American Revolution* (Chapel Hill, N.C., 1961), 182–200.

23 Higginbotham, *The War of American Independence,* 93.

CHAPTER FOUR

On and Off the Road of Despair, 1777–1779

Valley Forge

The Continental army had taken a mauling in 1777 but had not been beaten. A pressing concern in December was to find suitable winter quarters. Washington chose Valley Forge, some 18 miles northwest of Philadelphia. Hilly terrain and the Schuylkill River offered natural defenses. Consequently, if Howe changed character and became aggressive during the winter, the army would be able to defend itself. When local patriot leaders insisted that the American commander use his troops to protect the whole region around Philadelphia, Washington promised them nothing. He wrote sharply in reply to their demands: "It would give me infinite pleasure to afford protection to every individual and to every Spot of Ground in the whole of the United States. Nothing is more my wish. But this is not possible with our present force."

On December 19, the army moved into Valley Forge. The soldiers were in miserable shape. Of these 11,000 hardy warriors, at least 2,000 had no shoes; many more lacked decent clothing in the cold, wet, and wind. Private Joseph Plumb Martin noted that the soldiers' path to Valley Forge could "be tracked by their blood upon the frozen ground." Equally demoralizing, the army had not been paid since August. "Unless some great and capital change takes place," Washington wrote nervously, "this Army must inevitably . . . starve, dissolve, or disperse."

Any expectations of modest comfort in this winter camp failed to eventuate. Just about everything went wrong as the soldiery struggled to build huts in the face of intermittent blasts of snow and biting cold. The Marquis de Lafayette, only 20 years old in 1777 but already a major general and one of Washington's favorites, characterized these huts as "little shanties that are scarcely gayer than dungeon cells." By January 1, most of the men and women in the ranks were finally getting some decent protection from the weather, but they had little food, drink, or warmth. Rum was in such short supply that on Christmas day Washington could not issue the prescribed holiday allotment of a gill per person. Firecake, when flour was available to mix with water, became standard fare. This concoction had enough nutritional value, according to Dr. Albigence Waldo of the first Connecticut infantry regiment, to turn human "Guts . . . to Pasteboard." As early as December 21, many soldiers could be heard chanting: "No Meat! No Meat!" Within days the chant had changed to: "No bread, no soldier!"

The lack of food and clothing has most often been attributed to a breakdown in the commissary and quartermaster departments just prior to the Valley Forge encampment. The calamity during the winter encampment derived as much—if not more—from logistics failures as from any scarcity of actual goods. Those charged with moving food, forage, and supplies from depots, storage areas, or other sources lacked the organization, talent, animals, transport, or worst of all, desire to do so. As historian Stephen R. Taaffe (*The Philadelphia Campaign, 1777–1778*) has noted, some wagoners "simply abandoned their freight whenever convenient rather than push on to camp through the interminable muck."[1]

The situation was indefensible: Inefficiency and corruption characterized both departments, and rank-and-file soldiers were the victims. At one point, the troops went without meat for six days, and on three occasions they had no provisions whatsoever. In December 1777, Congress, which had failed to correct commissary problems, finally ordered Washington to confiscate local foodstuffs to ward off starvation. He was hesitant to do so, however, because he "grasped the central principle of modern warfare: the necessity of maintaining a positive relationship between the army and the people," as historian E. Wayne Carp has stated in *To Starve the Army at Pleasure, 1775–1783.*[2] Equipment, as with food and clothing, also remained in desperate supply, as Congress allowed the vital post of quartermaster general to remain open for three months after General Thomas Mifflin's resignation in November. By February 1778, some 4,000 troops were unfit for duty for lack of shoes, clothing, blankets, soap, and medicines.

The impact of these shortages was disastrous. Between December 1777 and June 1778, some 2,500 souls (nearly one-fourth of the army) perished, easy prey to exposure, malnutrition, typhus, dysentery, and other camp maladies. Droves more deserted. Reflecting on the chant, "no bread, no soldier," many felt the country had reneged on its part of the enlistment bargain. They saw no reason to keep suffering to defend the liberties of civilians who were not supporting them, and in some cases were even profiting by peddling rancid meat and moth-infested clothing to the army. That local civilians even refused to sell them straw to help prevent sick and emaciated comrades from freezing to death also infuriated the troops. In the end, the soldiery received little more respect or concern from the civilian populace than did the army's horses, some 500 of which perished that winter for want of forage. So many dead animals only added to bad sanitation conditions and the spread of disease, since it was difficult to bury carcasses in frozen ground. In *The Valley Forge Winter,* historian Wayne Bodle has described conditions this way: "From the Continental horse yard, . . . the stench of dead animals wafted through the air. In the camp the fear of riot or worse hung almost as palpably as the stench."[3] Had the soldiers possessed the collective bodily energy to do so, they might well have turned against the indifferent, uncaring civilians all around them.

One incident epitomized the senselessness of what was happening. General Anthony Wayne, famous for his daring leadership in battle, tried to make arrangements to get 500 coats for the ill-clad troops under his command. Clothier General James Mease, a Congressional appointee, insisted that only authorized civilian tailors could do the work. While Wayne's troops suffered, Mease took a leave of absence, leaving no one empowered to process the order. When he returned to duty, he refused to issue the uniforms because only yellow buttons were available and Pennsylvania's regimental design specified white buttons. Finally, an apoplectic Wayne had the specifications changed, and Mease released the coats. How many soldiers died from exposure while this farce played itself out has never been determined.

The situation began to improve only in early 1778, when Congress finally grasped the severity of the army's plight. In January, the delegates appointed a "Committee at Camp" to work directly with Washington to expedite the movement of emergency food and other provisions. However slowly, supplies began to trickle into Valley Forge. Two key appointments also helped. Supply matters improved after the wealthy Connecticut merchant, Jeremiah Wadsworth, took charge of the commissary department and Nathanael Greene reluctantly acceded to the quartermaster generalship. In addition, the severe winter weather broke early in the spring, all resulting in many saved lives. Popular lore aside, the winter weather at Valley Forge was not the harshest that Washington's army endured; that dubious distinction befell the Morristown encampment of 1779–80. Still, this observation cannot mitigate the unnecessary suffering that did occur.

As much as any other factor, what made Valley Forge so gruesome was the widespread indifference of patriot civilians toward an army in such desperate need. It is important to ask whether such suffering would have occurred had middle-class Americans filled the Continental ranks. That they did not represents a telling reason why these down and outers who had contracted to fight for the cause of liberty experienced such neglect. So it was not just the commissary, quartermaster, and clothing departments (the traditional culprits) that caused the needless privation. Nor was it necessarily the result of popular ignorance about what was happening, as historian John B. B. Trussell has asserted in *Birthplace of an Army*.[4] It was equally that the general populace did not seem to care (befitting social attitudes of the times), since so many of those who suffered were from the ranks of the "poorer sort" of the people.

The soldiers remembered what happened to them. They had already resorted to various forms of individual protest, including desertion. However, most stayed in the ranks and continued to endure further hardships in subsequent months. Life for them was not necessarily any better outside the army, especially since their dreams of personal liberty, economic self-sufficiency, and human dignity now had come to depend on long-term Continental service—as part of the patriot quest for a republican order in America.

Mounting Anger in the Officer Corps

As the first two years of warfare came to a close, Washington's officers were growing as restless as the soldiery. Their discontent started to spill over into overt protest in the weeks preceding the move to Valley Forge. Grievances focused on two primary issues: appropriate rank and economic survival. As a group, the officers worried incessantly about both matters, and they most often expressed their anxieties in their talk of personal honor. In the "cultural context" of the eighteenth century, Caroline Cox has observed, "[a] gentleman's sensibilities moved along a spectrum from honor to shame, with accomplishments requiring public acknowledgment and criticism public vindication."[5] For the army's officers, Charles Royster has written, "honor not only required a man to uphold his rank, keep his word, and demand the same of others; it also required that he resent any insult." For each officer, "honor kept . . . self-esteem inviolable; and . . . the slightest indignity or affront struck him as an attack on his rights as a gentleman."[6] To receive a promotion for meritorious service was to be treated with honor, to demonstrate respect. To pay the officer at a level commensurate with his personal sacrifice was to accomplish the same. However, Congress, always touchy about maintaining its authority over the military, was often insensitive about the feelings of the officer corps. The result was a deepening rift between civil and military leaders—with dangerous implications for the Revolution.

The tribulations of Benedict Arnold over his rank typified the strained relations of many high-ranking officers with Congress. Because of his service at Quebec, Congress commissioned Arnold a brigadier general early in 1776. A year later, the central body passed over him for promotion and named five new major generals, all previously junior to America's Hannibal. Washington thought Arnold deserved recognition, given his meritorious service. The delegates pointed out that Connecticut already had its complement of major generals, based on its proportion of troops in rank. (The Baltimore resolution of 1777 stipulated that general officer promotions would be based on seniority in rank, merit, and proportion of troops in service from each state.) In dismay over what he described as his sullied honor, Arnold hinted at resignation.

Events then took an unusual turn. Late in April 1777, Arnold, visiting his family in Connecticut, rushed into action to stop a British foray that had sacked Danbury, a supply depot of patriot war matériel. He personally rallied the militia, threw himself into the thick of the fighting (in one heated exchange he had his horse shot out from under him while a musket ball tore open his uniform), and was instrumental in driving away the marauding enemy force. Shortly thereafter, a red-faced Congress recognized his merit by promoting him to major general. To prove their superior hand, however, the delegates did not restore his seniority. A querulous Washington mused: "General

Arnold's promotion gives me great pleasure. He has certainly discovered in every instance . . . much bravery, activity, and enterprise. But what will be done about his rank? He will not act, most probably, under those who commanded him but a few weeks ago."

To deny Arnold proper seniority in rank was a second insult. He decided, perhaps unwisely, to take his case directly to Congress. "Honor," he explained, "is a sacrifice no man ought to make, as I received so I wish to transmit [it] inviolate to Posterity." Arnold's lobbying offended some of the delegates, who considered his presence among them an affront to their prerogatives. They restored his seniority only in November 1777, when they acknowledged his vital leadership role at Saratoga. By that time, however, bitterness over such incidents had begun to fester, eventually setting Arnold on the path to treason. Ultimately, Arnold, whom Washington called his best fighting general, "felt defrauded by a cause that had left him lame and nearly lifeless" after his serious wounding at Saratoga "and compromised in sacred honor and debilitated in personal fortune," as James Kirby Martin has shown in *Benedict Arnold: Revolutionary Hero.*[7] Had Congress acted less rigidly—even less foolishly—in this general's case, the Arnold story might well have ended differently.

Arnold's difficulties over rank and personal honor were not unique. While Congress played politics and used a heavy hand with the likes of Arnold, it also insisted that no one in the military question its right to elevate well-connected foreigners to the highest officer ranks. In July 1777, a celebrated dispute broke out over Philippe du Coudray, a self-assured French artillerist. One of the American commissioners in France had promised Coudray that he would be named Washington's Chief of Artillery at the rank of major general, should he come to America. When he arrived, Coudray presented his credentials to Congress, thereby placing the delegates in a bind. They had no desire to anger Washington and downgrade Henry Knox, nor did they want to undercut the commissioners working for a Franco-American alliance.

At this point, Knox, Nathanael Greene, and John Sullivan sent public letters to Congress, which implied they would resign should Coudray be placed ahead of them in rank. Irate at such military insolence that threatened, as one perturbed Connecticut delegate stated, "the authority, Esteem, or dignity of Congress," the delegates insisted on apologies or resignations. The three generals ignored the demand. The controversy ended only when the pompous Coudray, after insisting on riding instead of walking his horse onto a ferry, fell overboard and drowned.

Such incidents helped spread a festering sore in civil-military relations. To the officers, needless tampering with rank became an assault on personal honor. Congress, pressured from all sides and often succumbing to politics, frequently used poor judgment and generally viewed the officers, in the words of John Adams, as "Mastiffs, Scrambling for Rank and Pay like Apes for Nuts." Such thinking, as historian Richard H. Kohn has indicated, was a major reason why the officers "grew to hate Congress for its weakness and its arrogance."[8] Washington's lieutenants wanted the respect they believed was due them as propertied citizens who now held high military rank. Congress, however, treated them as if they were professional soldiers—and a possible threat to civil society. As Washington wrote at Valley Forge, "[w]e should all be considered . . . as one people, embarked in one Cause, in one interest; acting on the same principle and to the same End." The "very jealousy" of Congress over the army's proper "subordination to the supreme Civil Authority," he concluded, "is a likely means to produce a contrary effect."

This warning, as time passed, had more insight than Washington could have imagined in 1778. Part of the tension over rank and honor may be explained in terms of the social origins of the officer corps. In his study of New Jersey Continentals, Mark Edward Lender found that the officers, as a group, came from the top level of society. Some 84 percent of the New Jersey officers were from the wealthiest third of the population—and none from the lowest third. Thirty-two percent of them fell into the wealthiest 10 percent. Some, like William Alexander

(Lord Stirling), owned thousands of acres, or they had excellent family connections, like Ensign John Ford Morris of Morris County, who received his commission at the age of 16.[9] As one observer reported, the officers represented the type of persons "who would not pass unnoticed in the politest court in Europe."

Outside of New Jersey, the pattern was similar. Officers were largely established local and provincial community leaders or sons of the same. Some were economically successful in their own right, like such upwardly mobile merchant-traders as Benedict Arnold or Alexander McDougall of New York. Others had close relatives in important Revolutionary political offices, such as General Jedidiah Huntington, who had married a daughter of Governor Jonathan Trumbull of Connecticut, or Henry Knox, who had married into an elite, even if loyalist, family. Overall, they were no different in socioeconomic composition and personal accomplishments than their fellow Revolutionaries in state legislatures and Congress.[10]

The officers' well-developed concern about personal honor was a reflection of their generally high community status. To be treated by Congress as little more than grasping mercenaries, instead of dedicated, virtuous citizens of the aspiring republic, was particularly irksome, especially when they had demonstrated their fervor through military service when so many prosperous civilians of the same elevated status had not.

To add to their frustrations, many officers, by the end of 1777 if not before, were getting into serious financial trouble. Full-time military participation had eliminated income prospects from agricultural and commercial pursuits. Rampant inflation was undermining their salaries, and they had to deal with the multifold expenses of purchasing uniforms and related equipage so that they could maintain themselves in the style expected of gentlemen officers in the field. Likewise resenting peculation by civilians who were supplying the army with rancid food and shoddy merchandise, the officers borrowed from British practice and struck upon a solution to their own financial difficulties—half-pay pensions for life to begin at the war's end as just recognition and appropriate compensation for their sacrifices and lost income.

A small group of field-grade officers first approached Washington about pensions in November 1777. Initially, the commander was cool to the idea, doubting whether the country could afford them. He also suggested that Congress would look askance at any such proposal, especially one that contained such an unrepublican notion as awarding "some order of knight-hood" over and above pensions to officers of unusual merit. Once at Valley Forge, Washington began to take the pension concept more seriously. Not only were rank-and-file soldiers deserting, but officers had started to resign. Many of them had complained that the cause owed them more than financial penury, especially when the civilian populace, from the officers' perspective, showed so little interest in the army's welfare. Washington conceded before the end of 1777 and referred a plan to Congress that called for half-pay, saleable commissions, and pensions for widows of officers.

Unsurprisingly, Congressional reaction was largely nega-tive. Half-pay, especially in the minds of the New England del-egates, seemed like an assault on republicanism. Massachusetts delegate James Lovell spoke about "a wish or design to put our military officers upon the footing of European." He wondered why the officers had "forgotten that this was in its beginnings a patriotic war." Others fretted about "a total loss of virtue in the Army," about officers who were not "actuated by the principles of patriotism and public spirit," about future pensioners who would become a privileged class "of People idle" not engaged in "useful industry" but "burdening the country." Worse yet, half-pay would "involve the idea of a standing army in time of peace . . . at the disposal of Congress," which would undercut "the rights of the states" to appoint "regimental officers" or have any influence in military matters.

The concerns of the delegates had a clear ideological base. At the core, they feared that pensions represented too risky a step in new modeling the army. Continental officers were now asking for what British officers already had, which was precisely their concern. Whig ideologues explained that Britain's standing army, with its train of pensioners and contractors, had helped cor-rupt the polity of the former parent nation. Purists among them now openly feared that the Revolution might produce little more than the same putrid system in a different environment.

As for Washington, once committed to pensions, he subordinated any previous ideological reservations. Confronted with mounting resignations, he needed something to raise officer morale and encourage further service. The commander was straightforward with Congress: "A small knowledge of human nature will convince us, that, with far the greatest part of mankind, interest is the governing principle." He also stressed that "motives of public virtue may for a time . . . actuate men to the observance of a conduct purely disinterested." However, the days of "continual sacrifice" without an attention to "private interest" had passed. He concluded that "nothing . . . would serve more powerfully to reanimate their languishing zeal, and interest them thoroughly in the service, than a half pay and pensionary establishment."

By late spring in 1778, the alternatives were clear: adhere to ideological purity and lose a substantial portion of the officer corps, or maintain the officers in the hope that a republican polity would still be viable, even with the "corrupting" influence of postwar pensions. Since the army was essentially all that stood between the cause and its collapse, Congress succumbed to reality. In May 1778, the delegates approved pensions but restricted them to seven years. Also concerned about keeping soldiers in the service, they voted a modest bonus of $80 for all rankers who would extend their enlistment time for the war's duration. Congress rejected vendible commissions and pensions for widows. No pensioner, furthermore, could hold public office. Barring the officers from postwar political positions, as John Todd White has stressed, meant that "they would not be able to dominate legislatures and vote for such things as stronger central government and standing armies in time of peace."[11]

In the short run, the officers accepted these restrictions. Something was better than nothing, but they also remembered that many Congressional leaders had treated them with contempt and indicted their character by calling them mercenaries who were extorting pay from a defenseless and helpless polity.

That only exacerbated their sense of blemished honor. Their indignation would keep growing, and they would be heard from again on the issue of pensions, even to the point of a threatened military *coup d'état* in 1783.

Tables Turned: New Life for the Cause

The Continental army endured the Valley Forge winter and survived. Sheer fortitude and the dream, however faded, of a better postwar existence kept many soldiers in camp, and the prospect of pensions helped assure that numbers of officers would be available for additional campaigning. Three other matters also put the army on a more solid footing. The first focused on what appeared to Washington and his immediate staff as an insidious plot to replace the Virginian as commander in chief. The confrontation has come down to posterity as the "Conway Cabal." The second, relating to training and discipline, had to do with one of the most colorful (and effective) foreigners to offer his services to the patriot cause. His name was Friedrich Augustin von Steuben, a pretended Prussian nobleman. The third factor was the creation of a formal Franco-American alliance. With the alliance came not only the first formal recognition of American independence by a prominent European power, but, equally important, a major alteration in the fundamental nature of the war itself.

Historians have traditionally interpreted the so-called Conway Cabal as an organized plot among disaffected generals and Congressional leaders to remove Washington. Historian Bernhard Knollenberg, in *Washington and the Revolution,* was the first to question seriously whether an actual plot existed.[12] However, Washington and his staff believed the cabal was very real and that it involved Generals Thomas Conway and Horatio Gates because of an intercepted letter from Conway to Gates. Conway, an Irish-born French subject of little discretion but with a solid military record in Europe, reputedly wrote to Gates in the fall of 1777: "Heaven has been determined to save your country or a weak general and bad counselors would have ruined it." These words came at a time when Gates had triumphed over Burgoyne at Saratoga and Washington had failed to stand up effectively to William Howe around Philadelphia. The obvious message was that Gates deserved to be at the head of all Continental forces.

That the letter was to Gates should not have, by itself, implicated him. Still there were good reasons for suspicion. This favorite of New England political leaders, when reporting the Saratoga triumph to Congress, had not gone through prescribed channels by sending his comments first to Washington. Disregarding the commander in chief was enough to make him angry and testy. Then Congress reorganized its Board of War and charged it with monitoring daily military activities. The delegates not only chose Gates for the board but named him president, technically making him Washington's civilian superior even though a subordinate in military rank. Gates's elevation had the enthusiastic support of a small number of delegates who were decidedly anti-Washington and held him personally responsible for Howe's presence in Philadelphia. This group had previously objected, for ideological reasons, to new modeling the army. Then, to complicate matters further, Congress in December 1777 promoted Conway, who little deserved it, to a major generalship. Then the delegates named him inspector general of the army, in charge of all training activities and with the authority to report directly to the Board of War rather than through the commander in chief. These decisions would have been enough to make almost anyone suspicious.

At Valley Forge, Washington and his "family," as he affectionately referred to his immediate staff, considered these actions to be preliminary steps in supplanting him with Gates. Washington had earlier urged Congress not to promote Conway because he was undeserving and his advancement would upset too many high-ranking American officers who were. In a brief flurry of hyperbole, the commander claimed that Conway's promotion "will give a fatal blow to the existence of the Army." When the newly appointed inspector arrived at Valley Forge in late December, Washington received him with an air that was chillier than the freezing weather. Within days, Conway left in a huff, explaining sardonically to Washington that "by the two receptions you have honored me with since my arrival, I perceive that I have not the happiness of being agreeable to your excellency." Conway also stated that he "was ready to return to France and to the army where I hope I will meet with no frowns." For Washington and his loyal aides, Conway's abrupt departure was a godsend.

The "scheme," as Washington called it, soon fizzled. In reply to a caustic note from Washington, Gates wrote in mid-February: "I solemnly declare that I am of no faction; . . . After this, I cannot believe your Excellency will either suffer your suspicions or the prejudices of others to induce you to spend another moment upon this subject." Washington accepted Gates's recantation and replied that he was "burying" the matter "hereafter in silence, and, as far as future events will permit, oblivion." However, the commander never again fully trusted Gates, and his mistrust, along with an unwillingness to help Gates when the latter's career fell into disrepute later in the war, served to build the drama during the Newburgh crisis in the winter of 1782–83.

The Conway Cabal, whether imaginary or real, had consequences besides putting Washington on guard against Gates and a clique of republican purists in Congress. John Todd White has stated that the most significant effect was to force Congress to accept "the principle that Washington was essential to the Revolution." White notes further, "[u]ntil the end of the war, the desire to support and not offend the commander in chief played a key role in congressional military policy."[13] The Virginian came out of the turmoil in a stronger position to manage military matters. Moreover, Congress would listen to Washington more carefully and would not be so quick, for example, to elevate such undeserving candidates as Thomas Conway. That the delegates, despite strong feelings, caved in on the issue of pensions in May 1778 was a sign of their newfound respect for Washington. Even though the army would experience declining popular support with each passing year, Congressional communications would improve. In the long run, better relations with Congress helped in maintaining a proper balance in civil-military relations, especially since Washington could exercise firm control over his standing force when he needed to and because he never failed to keep the potentially coercive power of the army subordinate to the will of Congress.

On February 24, Washington wrote to Gates and accepted his apology; that was the day after General von Steuben arrived at Valley Forge. Unlike Conway and many other foreigners, the "Baron" was well-liked from the start. In his early career, he was a staff aide to Frederick the Great of Prussia but had lost that post, possibly because his family had claimed baronial status that the state had never awarded. Despite a checkered career in Europe, Steuben behaved with great acumen once in America. Like Lafayette before him, he volunteered his services to Congress. The resulting agreement was that, once Steuben proved his worth to the army, he would receive appropriate rank and pay.

The Baron had a magnetic personality. He also possessed a thorough knowledge of Prussian training and drilling procedures. Within a month of appearing at Valley Forge, he began the formidable task of introducing the soldiers to a simplified set of drill procedures, as well as to train them in the use of the bayonet. Furthermore, he began preparing a uniform drill manual, which remained the basis for training American troops until the War of 1812. Heretofore, each company had more or less followed its own procedures, which often meant confusion and ineffectiveness in battle because of the lack of standardized combat maneuvers.

Energetically, Steuben put himself in front of a model company of regulars and set the tone for rigorous drill. He pushed these troops hard. Speaking almost no English and barely recognizable French, he communicated through grunts and instantly understandable swear words. The soldiers quickly adapted to Steuben's prodding. They seemed to revel in his commands, which heightened morale in the midst of so much despair. Steuben also insisted that officers lead the training rather than leaving the matter to overworked noncommissioned officers. There is no doubt that a hardier, more resolute, and better-trained army emerged by the late spring of 1778.

His voluntarism earned Steuben both a major generalship and the post of inspector general. John Laurens, one of Washington's most talented aides, wrote affectionately: "The Baron Steuben has had the fortune to please uncommonly, for a stranger, at first sight. . . . All the general officers who have seen him are prepossessed in his favor, and conceive highly of his abilities. . . . The General seems to have a very good opinion of him." The last comment was a classic understatement. When compared to Conway, having a person who was truly capable in the inspector generalship was to bring the Continental army one large step closer to becoming an effective regular fighting force. In the months ahead, Washington came to depend heavily on Steuben, and the former German captain never disappointed him. As Stephen R. Taaffe has summarized historical opinion, Steuben turned out to be one of the Revolution's "most valuable wartime assets."[14]

Initially, Steuben had come from Paris at the urging of the American commissioners. In 1776 Congress, desperately seeking foreign support (and allies), had sent Benjamin Franklin, Silas Deane, and Arthur Lee to Paris with the assignment of wooing the French. There, the Comte de Vergennes, the French foreign minister, welcomed them to the calculating but unpredictable world of European diplomacy. Vergennes was a skillful diplomat. One of his highest policy goals was reducing Britain's imperial might. The Treaty of Paris of 1763, which ended the Seven Years' War, had cost France its North American empire and had swung the European balance of power heavily in Great Britain's favor. Many French subjects, Vergennes among them, viewed the Anglo-American conflict as an opportunity to strike back and weaken an ancient and imperious foe—to restrengthen France at the expense of Great Britain.

From 1775 through 1777, the French government covertly assisted the American rebels. The objective was to help widen the breach beyond repair, making it possible to enter the war in safety and crush the hated British. One of Vergennes's many assistants, the dapper courtier Caron de Beaumarchais, went to London in May 1775 to search out a wayward Frenchman who was reputedly selling state secrets to Lord North's ministry. His other assignment was to contact prominent Americans still conducting business in England. Beaumarchais began meeting with Arthur Lee of the prominent Virginia clan, and they struck upon a plan to facilitate clandestine French aid, should the government of King Louis XVI concur.

In the spring of 1776, the ostensibly private mercantile firm of Roderigue Hortalez & Cie., fronted by Beaumarchais, began operations. With handsome loans and financial grants from the French government, Hortalez & Cie. purchased war matériel destined for American soldiers. In something over a year, this trading operation collected an estimated 30,000 muskets, 100,000 rounds of shot, 200 cannons with full train, 300,000 rounds of powder, 13,000 hand bombs, 3,000 tents, and clothing for 30,000 troops. Even if a portion of the merchandise was old and shoddy, these war goods proved invaluable to the American cause. The bulk of these items passed through New England to upstate New York, where they reached patriot troops operating against Burgoyne. French loans, cash grants, and war goods thus were essential to effecting the circumstances that brought that monarchical nation openly into the republican war effort.

While providing covert aid, Vergennes kept the American commissioners at a distance in public. He wanted France to maintain a posture of neutrality until the wedge had been driven deep enough for timely intervention. When North's ministry insisted that France stop giving succor to American privateers by allowing them to refit their vessels in French ports, Vergennes complied. What he legitimately feared was a hasty reconciliation of differences with reunited British and American subjects suddenly turning against an overextended France. His public posture helped make it appear that the American commissioners had to do a lot of convincing to gain formal French involvement. In reality, they did not. Vergennes was biding France's time, looking for the proper moment to consummate the Franco-American relationship. Meanwhile, the American rebels needed to prove they would not collapse and surrender when hit by concentrated British military strength. The great victory at Saratoga proved to Vergennes and Louis XVI that the American cause had the capacity to endure.

From the patriot point of view, no better a person than Benjamin Franklin could have represented his country's interests. Seventy years old in 1776, he was already well known in European intellectual circles. Many thought Franklin was America's premier scientific genius. In 1772, the French accorded him membership in their Academy of Sciences, primarily for his work on electricity. Now appearing in Paris and Versailles with his simple clothes, fur hat, unkempt hair, and spectacles, Franklin came to embody the uncorrupted, rustic republican. He thrived in this role, easily making friends for the American cause in France. Witty and urbane as a diplomat, he enjoyed seeing the reproduction of his well-known countenance on such objects as snuffboxes, handkerchiefs, rings, and watches. (Franklin, however, had to wonder whether having his likeness etched on the inside of porcelain chamberpots was a compliment!) The public adoration shown him certainly helped strengthen Franco-American relations in the months preceding the formal alliance.

The alliance pact, embodied in two treaties of February 1778, put trade between the two nations on a most-favored-nation basis and declared French recognition of American independence. Louis XVI agreed to renounce French territorial aspirations in North America, including Canada, in return for a free hand in trying to conquer valuable British sugar islands in the West Indies. The two sides stipulated that no formal peace terms could be drawn up without the consent of the other. This clause seemingly guaranteed France a large voice in any peace settlement and some protection from double-dealing, should England and America suddenly attempt to reconcile at France's expense. The mutual consent clause eventually was a source of considerable embarrassment when peace negotiations began in 1782; but in 1778 the Americans could not have avoided such a clause, since it was Vergennes's form of protection against any lingering possibility of an Anglo-American trap.

This particular cycle of diplomacy reached its climactic point in June 1778 when a French/British naval battle erupted in the English Channel. Formal declarations of war soon followed. A civil rebellion within the British empire now had turned into a world war that, in the long run, would stretch British military resources too thinly across the globe. In the short run, formal French intervention (along with that of Spain in 1779 and the Dutch Netherlands in 1780) forced the British to modify their strategic approach to the war. They could not fight everywhere at once but had to redeploy their forces to defend the most vulnerable parts of the empire. Their new war plan started to become clear in June 1778 when they pulled out of Philadelphia.

When Congress and Washington learned about the French alliance, they rejoiced. The commander designated May 6 as a day for celebrating "throughout the whole Army." Morale had improved at Valley Forge. The army had survived the winter, and the troops were better trained and organized than ever before. Recruiting was underway to rebuild flagging Continental numbers, and the prospect of thousands more troops coming from France cheered patriot hearts. The officers had expectations of postwar pensions, and the commander himself had better relations with Congress. Reasons thus abounded to justify the extravagance of giving each soldier a gill of rum and having everyone participate in a *feu de joie* of musketry. Once assembled on parade, the army was to cheer in unison: "Long Live the King of France. Long Live the Friendly European Powers. To the American States." That the army was still alive—and functional—explains the official attitude of permitting soldiers to drink "more than the common quantity of liquor" and tolerating "some little drunkenness among them." Most significant, the cause had been rescued, or so the celebrants hoped—not, however, by republican patriot enthusiasts but by an autocratic European power eager to humiliate an ancient enemy. Fortunate indeed were the American rebels that the former parent nation had numerous enemies in Europe.

The British Dispersal of 1778

Given that leading patriots had set as their goal a republican sociopolitical order in America, the alliance with France made little ideological sense. New Englander Elbridge Gerry expressed the irony of it all:

> What a miraculous change in the political world! The ministry of England . . . endeavoring to enslave those who might have remained loyal subjects of the king. The government of France an advocate of liberty, espousing the cause of protestants and risking a war to secure their independence. The king of England considered by every whig in the nation as a tyrant, and the king of France applauded by every whig in America as the protector of the rights of man! . . . Britain at war with America, France in alliance with her! These, my friend, are astonishing changes.

Ideological incongruities aside, the alliance drastically altered Great Britain's approach to the war. In one action, Lord North hurried a peace commission to America. Known as the Carlisle Commission, it offered the Americans everything they wanted before 1776 except independence. Congress chose to ignore the commissioners. Open war with France also forced the British to redeploy military and naval forces, with more troops garrisoned at home to guard against a possible French invasion. (Eventually, France did organize a massive expeditionary force; however, horrendous weather and logistical problems destroyed plans for an assault on the island kingdom.) Then there was what Piers Mackesy has called the North ministry's "obsession with the West Indies."[15] In 1778, French troops in these islands outnumbered British regulars by at least four to one, prompting calls for a major reinforcement of the economically crucial British sugar islands. Likewise, with war declared the British could now take every opportunity to seize French West Indian islands, which could balance the loss of the North American colonies, should that be the outcome of the war. In any case, the British would no longer concentrate the bulk of their forces at one critical point, such as they had done during the 1776 campaign.

Rather, dispersal with the purpose of maintaining precious territory in different places became the primary goal.

The new approach was clear in the ministry's instructions to Sir Henry Clinton, who replaced Sir William Howe in the spring of 1778 as British North American commander. Clinton's orders were to evacuate the rebel capital, retreat to New York City and, if necessary, evacuate New York if allied pressures become too great. By the fall of 1778, the ministry was siphoning off troops from Clinton for campaigning in the West Indies and elsewhere. As such, British strategy could no longer focus on trying to destroy the Continental army. Henceforth, the allies, provided they start working in unison, could contemplate offensive warfare. That moment finally came with the Yorktown campaign of 1781, over three years after the alliance came about. Meanwhile, Great Britain prepared itself to fend off strikes wherever they came across the globe, all of which increased the likelihood that the Americans could win the war—if their soldiers could just endure in the field.

Clinton, both a contentious and diffident person who once described himself as "a shy bitch," did not relish his first assignment as commander—extricating the British army from Philadelphia, the sole prize of the 1777 campaign. Thoroughly disgusted, the new chief loaded a flock of up to 3,000 loyalists and some Hessians whom he considered unreliable onto the only available transport vessels, and he prepared to march the rest of his force across New Jersey to New York. Clinton's army of 10,000 set out from Philadelphia on June 18, 1778.

Now able to vacate Valley Forge once and for all, Washington and his rejuvenated force immediately took up the pursuit. Still leery of confronting the redcoats in a general engagement, even though ranking officers like Greene, Lafayette, and Wayne viewed the Continentals as now up to the task, the commander chose to peck away at Clinton's flanks. Confusing the whole issue was General Charles Lee, who had recently been exchanged after more than a year as a British prisoner. At first, Lee argued against bringing on a major battle; then, when Washington assigned his advanced units to Lafayette, Lee took this decision as a personal insult, since he outranked the young Frenchman. Washington yielded and placed Lee in charge of the lead units.

Early on June 28, Lee bore in on the rear guard of the enemy near Freehold (Monmouth Court House), New Jersey. He hoped to catch Clinton's troops off guard. The British commander, however, wheeled his forward elements about and counterattacked with over 6,000 troops. Lee then led a generally orderly retreat, his efforts to make a stand frustrated when some of his brigadiers withdrew soldiers without orders. Although Lee had marched into more trouble than anyone could have predicted, the retreat enraged Washington. When he moved forward with the rest of the army on what was an excessively hot and humid day (numbers of soldiers on each side perished of heat prostration), the commander angrily admonished Lee. However, seeing the gravity of the situation, the commander in chief then ordered Lee and Wayne forward to fight a delaying action—some of the most desperate combat of the war—while he rallied the main rebel line on defensible ground to the rear.

Washington was at his best. As Lafayette described the scene, the Virginian rode "along the lines amid the shouts of the soldiers, cheering them by his voice and example and restoring to our standard the fortunes of the fight." Before darkness ended the action, the Continentals had launched counterattacks of their own, showing their new martial prowess to good effect. Clinton, whose army lost at least 251 killed plus 170 wounded, as well as some 600 Hessians who deserted, slipped away toward New York that night, leaving the field to the Continentals.

Washington claimed victory on that basis, despite 267 casualties and 95 missing in action. In addition, an effective "spin" campaign inflated the magnitude of the victory. Among others, Alexander Hamilton and John Laurens, Washington's fiercely loyal young aides, used their connections in Congress (Henry Laurens, then president of Congress, was John's father) and with prominent patriots to depict the battle as a personal triumph for the commander in chief. It was part of a largely successful effort to silence Washington's critics of 1777 once and for all. In this respect, the achievements of the Monmouth campaign were as much political as military.

Once safely ensconced in New York, however, General Clinton scoffed at American claims. The British commander reasonably argued that he was retreating anyway, and that he had brought his army through the middle of enemy territory without so much as the loss of a wagon. Both sides had a case; and historian Willard M. Wallace's comment (*Appeal to Arms*) that, if there ever was a draw in battle, "Monmouth was it," certainly summarizes the tactical outcome.[16]

However inconclusive, Monmouth did pull together a number of threads. Historians have often depicted the engagement as the "coming of age" of the Continental soldier, the point when American regulars had traded volley for volley with the best troops Europe had—and held their own. Certainly Steuben's rigorous drill program had begun to take effect. Only manpower shortages in the months ahead would keep Washington from attacking Clinton's New York base. Ironically, the American commander could not take advantage of the new circumstances before him, as reflected in Britain's strategy of dispersing its forces to protect highly prized enclaves, even though his army had vastly improved as a fighting machine. Lacking enough soldiers, Washington had to maintain his Fabian-like posture, which served to lengthen a war that, with France's formal involvement, had become almost impossible for the British to win.

On still another dimension, the Battle of Monmouth forced a showdown between Washington and Charles Lee, a man who had once thought of himself as timber to head the army. For years, historians have been largely critical of Lee's performance at Monmouth; but more recent scholarship has credited him with generally sound leadership under highly adverse circumstances.[17] After the battle, however, Lee angrily demanded a court martial to clear himself of insinuations that his retreat had cost the rebels a sweeping victory. The panel of officers, heavily influenced by members of Washington's family, convicted the former British officer of disobeying orders to attack, of unnecessarily retreating, and of being disrespectful to the commander in chief. The first two charges were wrong; but as John Shy has written, to have found Lee guilty of disrespect alone would have constituted "a vote of no-confidence in Washington."[18]

Only a few months had intervened since the alleged Conway Cabal. To have treated Lee with leniency might have invited a continuation of needless turmoil in the highest echelon of rebel leadership. The court martial panel suspended this brilliant but irascible officer from command for a year; and when Congress confirmed the sentence, Lee replied with a string of insults, which resulted in his being dropped permanently from the army's rolls. With Lee gone (and Gates neutralized), Washington's control of the army was even more complete.

While a British prisoner, Lee lacked the means to keep up with fundamental policy decisions on how to conduct the war. When he returned to the army before his downfall at Monmouth, he still strongly advocated the maintenance of a republican force. His writings, some of them made public at the time, contradicted Washington's new modeling course. Lee still advocated a "popular war of mass resistance," as John Shy has stated, "based on military service as an obligation of citizenship."[19] He still argued against any form of a standing army as a fundamental threat to liberty; he certainly did not approve of Steuben's effort to train the Continentals on the "European plan." As Lee warned everyone, "when the soldiers of a community are volunteers [regulars], war becomes a distinct profession. The arms of a Republic get into the hands of its worst members." These pious warnings had a hollow ring in 1778. Washington and his advisers, along with Congress, had followed the path of expedient reality to keep an army in the field. Lee's ideas now seemed hopelessly quaint, throwbacks to the *rage militaire* of 1775. Inside the military, he was the last important critic of the Europeanized Continental line. This, too, made him expendable. With Lee's demise, a primary voice of dissent was gone, which assured that new modeling would have no important critics inside the military establishment as the war continued.

With the British back in New York and beginning to transfer some of their forces to points outside North America, warfare became less intense in the northern region. Clinton continued the well-worn tradition of his predecessor in exhorting the home government to send him more soldiers (which it could do only with great difficulty but with no net gain in his available troop strength). Washington kept planning for an all-out assault on New York City, yet this dream remained unfulfilled. Lacking enough soldiers himself, all Washington could do was nibble at the enemy's outer lines, go into winter camp, and hope for a large increment of manpower the following spring. The Continental army spent a relatively mild winter season dispersed around Middlebrook, New Jersey, in 1778–79, followed by the winter encampment that was so debilitating at Jockey Hollow near Morristown during 1779–80.

After 1778, Clinton's forces occasionally fought limited engagements in the Hudson Highlands and New Jersey. After the British had taken Stony Point overlooking the Hudson River in 1779, for example, the Americans countered on July 15 with a light infantry assault under Anthony Wayne. The Americans recaptured Stony Point in a well-orchestrated bayonet attack, reminiscent of the Paoli massacre of 1777. The one effect of this turnabout was to deter Clinton from pursuing any significant campaigning in New Jersey against the main Continental army. In June 1780, nearly a year later, the British half-heartedly attempted to carry the war into New Jersey, but American forces turned them back at Connecticut Farms (June 6) and Springfield (June 23). Such sporadic fighting was in complete contrast to the massive British efforts of 1776 and 1777. By 1780, however, Lord North's ministry and Clinton were attempting to implement a different strategic plan, this time focused on the South.

Washington kept hoping for a major joint allied campaign effort. The semblance of such an endeavor took place in Rhode Island during the summer of 1778, directed against royal forces controlling Newport as a land/naval base. The joint foray turned into a farce when the French commander, Count d'Estaing, pulled out of the land battle for a potential sea engagement

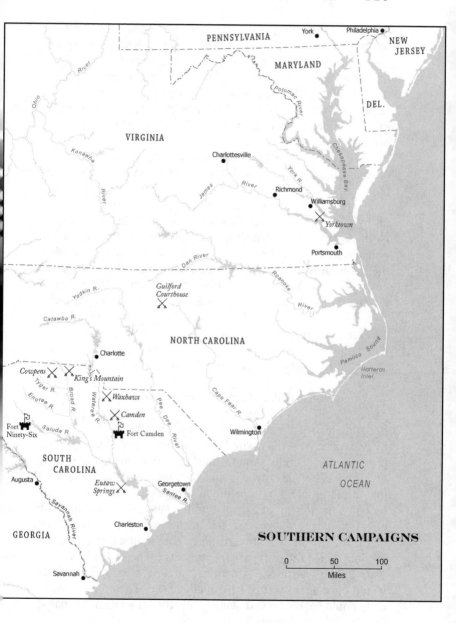

SOUTHERN CAMPAIGNS

against Admiral Richard, Lord Howe. General John Sullivan, who had a history of being caught short in the midst of key engagements, had to retreat from an overextended position, the impact of which was a healthy round of recrimination between the new allies. The Rhode Island fiasco did not augur well for future joint operations, even if the French should again offer the extra balance in troop strength that Washington so desperately needed.

The British retreat of 1778, followed by the inactive northern campaigns of 1779 and 1780, did not mean that Clinton was more faint-hearted than his predecessors. The British dispersal of manpower, made necessary by so many new threats brought on by global war, would alter the primary theater of action in North America. The British ministry, as Russell F. Weigley has pointed out in *The American Way of War,* "decided to exploit their control of the sea to a greater extent than they had previously done and to send expeditions to the South."[20] The idea of the emerging southern strategy was to rally the loyalist population, which the ministry had assumed (somewhat incorrectly) was far more numerous in the South, and to pacify the whole population of that region in piecemeal fashion with a small regular army acting in concert with roving bands of loyalist partisans.

Weigley has called the new British approach "a strategy of partisan war."[21] At its core, Piers Mackesy has argued, was "a fledgling theory of counterrevolutionary warfare," characterized by two objectives: the desire "to restore civil government in one province and thereby demonstrate that royal institutions were not irrevocably destroyed"; and the hope of "deal[ing] with the militia problem by a methodical plan of counterinsurgency based on the raising of Loyalist militia and special forces." The effect would be to "reverse the institutional revolution which had preceded the war" by crushing rebel militia and reinstituting long-since fallen royal governments.[22] The expectation was that, through attrition, Americans in one area after another would once again accept British allegiance. Then the South, in time, could become a vast staging area for yet another campaign devoted to subduing the North.

The southern strategy, with partisan loyalist bands playing the vital part of manpower substitutes for the King's regulars, began on a highly successful note in November 1778 when a British fleet carrying 3,500 soldiers sailed from New York. The target was Savannah, Georgia. Joined by armed loyalists once in Georgia, this expeditionary force quickly subdued the least populous of the American provinces and brought a return of royalist rule to one of the 13 rebel states. Suddenly, as 1779 dawned, the war had taken on a dramatic new dimension.

Growing Internal Division: Army and Society

As the war assumed the character of a virtual stalemate in the North, civil-military relations declined noticeably. The winter at Valley Forge had convinced both ordinary soldiers and officers alike that they would get little more from republican society than they demanded—and quite often forcibly took for themselves. In the army's collective mind set, the civilian populace kept falling short in adequately providing food, clothing, and regular pay. With increasing vehemence, both soldiers and officers protested in dismay and anger. That they did not work in unison may have saved the American cause from some form of military dictatorship. Had they found the means to express their grievances in concert, representative republicanism might not have characterized the final political settlement of the American Revolution.

Officers and rank-and-file regulars did have one point in common: they resented selfish and ungrateful civilian behavior both toward the cause and the army. In particular, the officers complained loudly about civilians being seduced by wartime prosperity and consequent luxury. In 1780, one irate officer spoke out sharply: "It really gives me pain to think of our public affairs; where is the public spirit of the year 1775? Where are those flaming *patriots* who were ready to sacrifice their lives, their fortunes, their all, for the public?" A New Jersey officer had answered that question in 1779 when he explained that it was "truly mortifying to the virtuous soldier" to see civilians "sauntering in idleness and luxury" while they "despise our poverty and laugh at our distress." The problem was "the cruel and ungrateful disposition of the people" who withheld "from the army even the praise and glory justly due to their merit and services." Self-serving citizens, expostulated Major General Alexander McDougall in 1779, always seemed to "expect Spartan Virtue" from the army while they were invariably "wallowing in all the luxury of Rome in her declining State."

Repeatedly, the officers voiced their disgust in such indignant terms. It particularly rankled them, as gentlemen of means before the war, that some civilians were profiteering at their expense and becoming rich while they were dissipating their personal fortunes. In their anger, they remembered that some Congressional delegates had accused them of "extorting" pensions from the central government. They did not forget the seven-year limitation, which they viewed as an insult to persons of virtue who had repeatedly demonstrated their willingness to give their all. They would come back to the pension issue time and again, treating it as a specific measure of the country's appreciation—or lack thereof. Before the war was over, their disgust brought the republic to the brink of a military coup. However, that extreme action developed only when the officers thought themselves desperate, a point that they did not reach in the two years following Valley Forge.

As for rank-and-file soldiers with their more humble dreams of postwar prosperity, protest over their woeful circumstances took a variety of provocative forms. Common soldiers practiced the art of defiance through such diverse methods as swearing, heavy drinking, looting, deserting, and bounty jumping. At the root of such protest was a sense of civilian disregard for them as human beings. Socially, patriot Americans preferred to keep the Continentals at a sufficient distance, largely because they were contemptuous of their lower-class origins. Civilians often ridiculed them as troublemakers, drunkards, and mere hirelings. They were the "lesser sort" and, as such, should be happy with next to nothing. After all, that was what they had before entering the army. James Warren of Massachusetts summarized the perceptions of "respectable" citizens best when he described Washington's troops as "the most undisciplined, profligate Crew that were ever collected" to fight a war. Private Joseph Plumb Martin stated it from a different angle. When he asked for shelter in patriot homes "wet to the skin and almost dead with cold, hunger, and fatigue," he invariably "experienced" both "scornful looks and hard words."

Too often, scholars have categorized behavior best understood as protest in terms of "time-honored military vices," to use Charles Royster's phrase. This type of interpretation has the effect of reducing, if not losing, the impact of what the troops were saying (individually and collectively) about their sense of unpitying treatment by the cause. Writers have commonly described acts of protest as anything but that, since such an admission would have a negative impact on the persistent interpretive myth of consensus and unity in the patriot war effort. As such, many historians have thought, as Royster has written, that soldiers acted defiantly because camp discipline violated "the American soldiers' sense of personal freedom" derived from so much personal liberty in civilian life before enlistment.[23] Whether the down and outers in Washington's ranks ever enjoyed much freedom before serving in the Continental army is open to question, since the poor, indigent, indentured, and enslaved peoples of late colonial America had little or no political or economic voice in expressing their public feelings or controlling their personal lives.

Although some acts of protest may have been in reaction to the travail of camp life or the cruelty of particular officers, much more was in reaction to the lack of popular support, as manifested in rotted clothing, rancid food, and long arrearages in pay. With their swearing, the soldiers seemed to know that they could upset straight-laced civilians who worried about public morality in the republic, but who did not come out for the fight. Heavy drinking, commonly referred to as "barrel fever" among the troops, was a common practice among all Americans and all armies of the eighteenth century. However, in the Continental army it was also a defensive weapon. One general officer, for example, bitterly complained that many soldiers regularly made it "a practice of getting drunk . . . once a Day and thereby render themselves unfit for duty." By doing so, they were only giving back what they had received—a broken promise. Drinking to excess, when they could get supplied by sutlers on the edges of camps, allowed them to avoid duty that so many civilians had come to assume was the rightful obligation of the "poorer sort." Heavy drinking was a way for soldiers to protest sparse levels of support by not being in an effective condition for service—to avoid sacrifice when they alone were expected to carry the burdens of war.

Whether drunkenness, looting, or some other form of defiance, these "situational crimes," as Charles Patrick Neimeyer has written, were "among the smaller, less dangerous steps that soldiers could take to protect their customary rights."[24] Only in time did individual acts of protest take on a decidedly group-oriented quality, ultimately involving larger-scale line mutinies. Individual and group protest rarely resulted in wanton violence against civilians, such as rape or murder. Rather, common soldiers focused on slapping back at the cause or, in some instances, on property seizures and destruction. Their acts of defiance, whether individual or collective, most often varied in number and intensity according to when the army had been supplied and paid. The fewer and more rotten the supplies and the longer the period they remained unpaid, the greater was the likelihood of high levels of individual and group protest.

Beginning with the New York campaign of 1776, when supplies first became a nightmarish problem, common soldier protest started to climb. A Continental sergeant in New York during that campaign described how he and his comrades foraged illegally. Desperate for food, they "liberated" some geese belonging to a local farmer and devoured them "Hearty in the Cause of Liberty of taking what Came to their hand." Next "a sheep and two fat turkeys" approached the soldiers, but "not being able to give the countersign," they were taken prisoner, "tried by fire," and executed for sustenance "by the whole Division of free Booters." When army looting of civilian property continued its unabated course in 1777, Washington threatened severe penalties and emphasized that the army's "business" was "to give protection, and support, to the poor, distressed inhabitants, not to multiply and increase their calamities."

Washington's pleas had little impact. Acts of looting continued unabated as the war dragged on. Incident after incident kept the commander in chief and his staff buried in a daily deluge of civilian complaints. Court-martial proceedings made almost no dent in such activity. The threat of 100 lashes could not stop hungry and angry soldiers from looting, especially when the civilian victims did not seem to be living up to their republican obligations. In 1780 and 1781, Washington was still issuing pleas and threats but to little avail. Not even an occasional hanging for plundering deterred the defiant soldiery.

The pattern of desertion as a form of protest was somewhat different, complicated by what sociologists and psychologists describe as the phenomenon of "unit cohesion." Although soldiers deserted regularly when food and clothing were in short supply or nonexistent, such as at Valley Forge, primary group identification and cohesion increasingly militated against extraordinarily high desertion rates among Continental regulars. Edward A. Shils, Morris Janowitz, and Samuel A. Stouffer, who studied cohesion among troops in World War II, discovered an important prerequisite for keeping soldiers effectively involved in their duties. It was the "primary group"—the squad, platoon, or company—that nurtured cohesiveness.[25] Specifically, soldiers came to know, trust, and depend on one another. When a unit had established personal interrelationships and mutual feelings of dependency, troops were much less likely to desert, regardless of the adversity of conditions.

So it seems to have been with the Continentals. Historian Thad W. Tate discovered that, in the New York, Maryland, and North Carolina lines, about 50 percent of all desertions occurred within six months of enlistment,[26] and a Delaware company, as another example, experienced a loss of almost a third of its strength within a few days of its formation. Mark Edward Lender, in studying desertion rates among Jersey Continentals, found that the rate fell off dramatically through time. In 1777, at least 42 percent deserted; in 1778, 21 percent; in 1779, 10 percent; in 1780, 10 percent.[27] Although the amount of combat also dropped significantly in the North after 1778, the supply situation was as bad if not worse, and pay came ever more infrequently and in increasingly inflated Continental dollars. Unit cohesion thus seems to explain in large part why more soldiers did not strike back through desertion. Another important reason was that by 1779 and 1780 some of these fully cohesive units were on the verge of resorting to collective protest through mutinies.

The study of these patterns also confirms findings about the makeup of the rank and file. Analysis of the desertion phenomenon does not support the proposition of an embattled farmers' army after 1776. If the Continentals had been freehold farmers, the expectation would be for desertions to peak in the late summer or early autumn just before harvest time with soldiers reappearing or reenlisting after the spring planting. According to the available data, the bulk of enlistments came in the winter (as did desertions) after harvesting but before planting time. Fifty-eight percent of all New Jersey desertions occurred between December 1 and April 30, which were also the prime enlistment months. Stated differently, over 40 percent of all New Jersey desertions took place within three months of enlistment; and over 64 percent within the first six months. Group cohesion, rather than the desire to return to field, hearth, and family (which so many of the post-1776 Continentals could not claim as part of their lives) best explains the varying desertion rates.

Desertion decreased through time as a form of rank-and-file protest. In 1780, the secretary of the Continental Congress, Charles Thomson, stated with pleasure that desertions were now "comparatively few." The general pattern was that the first few months of service were those in which the poor and downtrodden asked themselves whether vague promises of a better life in postwar America were worth the immediate sacrifice and possible death. Many concluded that such an equation was unfairly loaded against them. Since they had scant reason to trust civilians and the promises of their leaders, they chose defiance through desertion. Group cohesion, in turn, helped sustain those soldiers who made the adjustment to camp life and served to ease the personal suffering through a long war for a chance at greater freedom and prosperity. For those who stayed and became part of Washington's hard core of regulars, looting, not desertion, was the most widely practiced (and often very necessary) form of defiance.

Still another group protested as individuals through bounty jumping. As Washington once mused, it was "a kind of business" among some soldiers. The procedure was simple: enlist, receive a bounty, desert; enlist somewhere else for another bounty, and desert again. Provided the jumpers showed some imagination and did not reappear in regiments where they might be recognized, theirs was a relatively safe activity. John Welch of the Fourth New Jersey regiment, for instance, enlisted in April 1777, deserted in May, and reenlisted in August. He deserted again in September 1778 and joined yet another time in January 1779, never being caught. Others were not so fortunate. In August 1778, Private Elijah Walker recorded the execution of a remarkably enterprising bounty jumper who had repeatedly enlisted and deserted to gain seven separate bounties before a firing squad ended his career.

The most extreme form of individual protest was desertion to the enemy. Benjamin Quakenbush of the Third New York regiment, for instance, was caught in the act of going over and "Sentenced to run the Gauntlet through the Brigade twice with fixed Bayonets at his Breast to regulate his pace." That he was not shot perhaps reflected upon the desperate shortage of troops. Extreme pain, not death, was the desirable standard of punishment in cases of desertion, looting, and bounty jumping. The hope was that such persons would recover, so that they would be available for future campaigning, since "the execution of all recovered deserters would have wiped out a sizable portion of the army," and "excessive severity would have discouraged enlistments."[28]

While officers and the rank and file alike increasingly prided themselves on their competency as soldiers, they felt mounting alienation toward civilian society, and protested against lack of patriot support for their army, they almost never expressed defiance in concert. Part of the reason lay in the social gap separating the two groups. As befit the deferential character of their times as well as concern for military hierarchy, officers, generally drawn from the ranks of the "better sort," expected obedience from the down and outers in the ranks. Their enthusiasm for the Revolution did not extend to social leveling. Many well-to-do officers feared that the Revolution might get out of hand and lead to real internal socioeconomic upheaval, especially in the form of widespread property redistribution, if the "common herd" of persons gained too much authority, whether legally or extralegally.

The officers around Washington certainly assumed they had the duty to administer harsh discipline to deserters, looters, bounty jumpers, and troublemakers in general. They supported Washington's desire to set the legal limit for lashes at 500, and many sanctioned whippings of more than 100 lashes, despite the Articles of War of 1776. As an example, the officers took with relish to Washington's general orders at Morristown in 1780 that authorized them to inflict 100 to 500 lashes instantly on plunderers; and they could assign up to 50 stripes on the spot, even before court-martial hearings took place. Their concern about protecting property and maintaining social stability, just as much as the need for proper order in the military hierarchy, kept Washington's officers from allying with the soldiery when protesting against what they viewed as society's lack of concern and support for the army.

By late 1779, a fundamental question had to do with whether some issue would provoke a sense of commonality of purpose and unity among Washington's officers and soldiers. Should that happen, the army in its growing bitterness held the potential to become a truly dangerous threat to the very cause that it was upholding and defending. Equally important, a critical question had to do with whether Washington and Congress, bolstered by the alliance with France, could find some means to win the war and obtain acceptable peace terms before some form of internal convulsion, as perpetrated by an army increasingly alienated toward civil society, occurred. Such perplexing dilemmas would not have existed had the war effort been receiving the united support of what many commentators have too often described as a united and fully committed Revolutionary populace.

Notes

1 Taaffe, *The Philadelphia Campaign, 1777–1778* (Lawrence, Kans., 2003), 152–53. See also Mark Edward Lender, "Logistics and the American Victory," in John Ferling, ed., *The World Turned Upside Down: The American Victory in the War of Independence* (Westport, Conn., 1988), 100–02.

2 Carp, *To Starve the Army at Pleasure: Continental Army Administration and American Political Culture, 1775–1783* (Chapel Hill, N.C., 1984), 82–83.

3 Bodle, *The Valley Forge Winter: Civilians and Soldiers in War* (University Park, Pa., 2002), 149–50.

4 Trussell, *Birthplace of an Army: A Study of Valley Forge* (Harrisburg, Pa., 1976), 33–35.

5 Cox, *A Proper Sense of Honor,* 28. See also 37–71.

6 Royster, *A Revolutionary People at War,* 88.

7 Martin, *Benedict Arnold, Revolutionary Hero,* 422–23.

8 Kohn, "American Generals of the Revolution," in Higginbotham, ed., *Reconsiderations of the Revolutionary War,* 109.

9 Lender, "The Enlisted Line: The Continental Soldiers of New Jersey," (Ph.D. dissertation, Rutgers University, 1975), 127–34. See also Lender, "The Social Structure of the New Jersey Brigade: The Continental Line as an American Standing Army," in Peter Karsten, ed., *The Military in America: From the Colonial Era to the Present* (New York, 1980), 29–34.

10 Kohn, "American Generals of the Revolution," in Higginbotham, ed., *Reconsiderations of the Revolutionary War,* 119–20. Kohn compared his data with findings in James Kirby Martin, *Men in Rebellion: Higher Governmental Leaders and the Coming of the American Revolution* (New Brunswick, N.J., 1973), *passim.*

11 White, "Standing Armies in Time of War," 279.

12 Knollenberg, *Washington and the Revolution, A Reappraisal: Gates, Conway, and the Continental Congress* (New York, 1940), *passim.*

13 White, "Standing Armies in Time of War," 272.

14 Taaffe, *The Philadelphia Campaign,* 174.

15 Mackesy, *The War for America,* 183.

16 Wallace, *Appeal to Arms: A Military History of the American Revolution* (New York, 1951), 190.

17 Mark Edward Lender, "The Politics of Battle: Washington, Lee, and the Monmouth Campaign," *New Jersey Heritage,* 2 (2003), 10–21.

18 Shy, "American Strategy: Charles Lee and the Radical Alternative," in *A People Numerous and Armed,* 159.

19 Ibid., 161.

20 Weigley, *The American Way of War: A History of United States Military Strategy and Policy* (New York, 1973), 25.

21 Ibid., 18–39. These words are the same as Weigley's chapter title.

22 Mackesy, "The Redcoat Revived," in W. M. Fowler, Jr. and Wallace Coyle, eds., *The American Revolution: Changing Perspectives* (Boston, 1979), 182–83.

23 Royster, *A Revolutionary People at War,* 70–71.

24 Neimeyer, *America Goes to War,* 135. See also James Kirby Martin, "A 'Most Undisciplined, Profligate Crew': Protest and Defiance in the Continental Ranks, 1776–1783," in R. Hoffman and P. J. Albert, eds., *Arms and Independence: The Military Character of the American Revolution* (Charlottesville, Va., 1984), 119–40.

25 Shils and Janowitz, "Cohesion and Disintegration in the *Wehrmacht* in World War II," *Public Opinion Quarterly,* 12 (1948), 280–315; and Stouffer, et al., *The American Soldier: Adjustment during Army Life,* Studies in Social Psychology in World War II, 4 vols. (Princeton, N. J., 1949), 1: 106–30.

26 Tate, "Desertion from the American Revolutionary Army," (M. A. thesis, University of North Carolina, 1948), *passim.*

27 Lender, "The Enlisted Line," 203–34. See also Robert Middlekauff, "Why Men Fought in the American Revolution," *Huntington Library Quarterly* (1980), 144–48. On patterns of desertion and courts-martial, see James C. Neagles, *Summer Soldiers: A Survey and Index of Revolutionary War Courts-Martial* (Salt Lake City, Utah, 1986), *passim.*

28 Lender, "The Enlisted Line," 217.

George Washington, by James Peale, after Charles Willson Peale, c. 1787–1790. Independence National Historical Park. *Delegates named George Washington, a dignified and reserved Virginia planter of great landed wealth, commander in chief. Although he had fought in the French and Indian War, the 43-year-old Virginian had never commanded large numbers of troops. Yet Washington believed firmly in the worthiness of the American cause and was willing to dedicate himself completely to winning the war. Unknown to them in 1775, they had selected a person whose strength of character and depth of commitment to the goal of establishing a republican order would have a profoundly positive influence on the success of the cause.*

Above: Nathanael Greene, by Charles Willson Peale, from life, 1783. Independence National Historical Park. *The lame Quaker from Rhode Island, who had studied manuals on the art of war, became most indispensable to the Continental army. His brilliant campaigning in the South, beginning in late 1780, helped win the War for Independence*

Opposite top: The first adjutant general of the Continental army was Horatio Gates, a retired British officer and adopted Virginian. In 1777 he was in command of American forces at Saratoga before suffering a humiliating defeat at Camden, South Carolina, in August 1780. Painting by James Peale, c. 1782. Courtesy National Portrait Gallery, Smithsonian Institution, gift of Mr. Lawrence A. Fleischman and Gallery purchase.

Opposite bottom: Benedict Arnold. Courtesy North Wind Pictures Archives. *Arnold, as deeply committed a republican as could be found in the patriot population of 1775, had become convinced by 1779 that such sentiment had been both a temporary illusion and a sham. After suffering a lack of recognition and promotion from the army, Arnold betrayed his cause and joined the loyalists, becoming one of the greatest villains in United States history.*

B Arnold

Jean Baptiste Donatien De Vimeur, Comte de Rochambeau, by Charles Willson Peale, from life, 1782. Independence National Historical Park. *George Washington received assistance from a French army of 5,000 under the talented, sensible Comte de Rochambeau, which had landed at Newport in July 1780. Both Rochambeau and Washington were eager to mount a major offensive during the 1781 campaign season.*

Opposite: Charles, Lord Cornwallis, British General. Courtesy North Wind Pictures Archives. *A large detachment under Cornwallis nearly caught the rebel force under General Nathanael Greene at Fort Lee, New Jersey, in 1776. Later in the war, Cornwallis aggressively commanded British forces in the South before surrendering his trapped army at Yorktown, Virginia, in October 1781.*

Cornwallis

The mythical Molly Pitcher firing her dead husband's cannon at the Battle of Monmouth. Courtesy North Wind Pictures Archives. *Washington accepted the presence of women in the army. Camp followers were to be found traveling with almost all eighteenth-century armies. These women usually came along with husbands or lovers, or because they could not find other ways to survive economically. They were not just followers or prostitutes. Women as well as men were "on rations"; in return for half-rations, armies assigned these women a variety of duties, including cooking, caring for the sick and wounded, washing and mending clothes, scavenging the field for clothes and equipment, and burying the dead after battle.*

Above: Thayendanegea or Chief Joseph Brant. Courtesy North Wind Pictures Archives.
The Mohawk chief Thayendanegea was a Native American leader of great sagacity who organized and led his fellow Iroquois warriors and also loyalist rangers in attacking white settlements and trying to defeat rebel forces in the hotly contested frontier region of New York.

Overleaf: Action between the Serapis *and* Bonhomme Richard, *1779. What claim to dash and élan the Continental navy earned has focused on boisterous, free-wheeling John Paul Jones, a man whom sailors considered a rigid disciplinarian but extraordinary seaman. In 1779, Jones transformed an old merchant craft into a 40-gun warship, the* Bonhomme Richard. *On September 23, while sailing in the North Sea, the American commander engaged and captured the Royal navy's better-armed (50 guns) frigate* Serapis—*a major capstone to American naval action during the Revolution.* Courtesy North Wind Pictures Archives.

CHAPTER FIVE

Moral Defeat and Military Turnabout, 1779–1781

Dispersed Warfare

While the pace of active campaigning slackened considerably in the North after 1778, acts of warfare did not let up elsewhere. As already noted, the British launched a southern offensive before the end of 1778 and retook Georgia. This effort expanded greatly in 1780 with Sir Henry Clinton's invasion of South Carolina. Similarly, combined British/Indian pressures on the frontier resulted in a series of patriot reactions—most dramatically with George Rogers Clark's invasion of the Illinois country in 1778 and then with General John Sullivan's punitive expedition against the Six Nations of New York in 1779. The war at sea, especially with respect to patriot involvement, took on more global significance, largely as a result of formal French involvement. These three developments would combine in almost synergistic fashion to propel the War for Independence forward to its culminating events while also escalating the level of pressure in Britain for an end to hostilities and the construction of a final peace settlement.

Warfare along frontier lines represented an endless series of bloody local clashes, most often characterized by raids in which acts of human butchery prevailed. Both sides actively contended for Indian support because the most powerful tribes, as Don Higginbotham has observed, "were in a position to influence the balance of power in the hinterland."[1] By and large, Native American nations, when they did not seek to remain neutral, linked arms with the British, who did not represent so direct a threat to tribal territory. Crown officials had an established record, dating back to the early 1760s, of trying to check the encroachment of white settlers onto native lands, and they still had an effective Indian agent network firmly in place.

Directly influencing powerful tribes in the Great Lakes region, for example, were Crown officers at the trading post and fortress of Detroit. There Henry Hamilton, a lieutenant governor under the Quebec government, held forth as the Indians' friend. Contemporaries referred to him as the Hair Buyer. Warriors seeking scalp bounties struck with fury and vengeance. Although historians disagree about how much Hamilton encouraged this butchery, Detroit did an active business in human scalps. Hamilton claimed that he admonished his native allies not to slaughter innocent women and children, but his alleged pleas dissuaded few warriors. They clearly understood, given the history of white aggression, that they were fighting for their survival as independent nations. Certainly, too, the warriors were reacting to the white record of systematic brutality toward Indian peoples.

By 1778, the Virginians were ready to deal with Hamilton, the Hair Buyer. They had no prospect of troop support from the Continental army, which with its constrained strength could do little to protect settlements on the periphery of the war. Governor Patrick Henry called upon physically imposing George Rogers Clark, who was pressing for the assignment. A red-haired 25-year-old of rugged countenance and brash determination, Clark believed that exposed frontier regions like Kentucky could be protected if Virginia irregulars gained control of the Illinois-Indiana country. Thus began his legendary western adventures. With no more than 175 recruits, Clark headed for French settlements at Kaskaskia, Cahokia, and Vincennes. There his small band of rangers convinced the settlers to accept Virginia's authority (news of the French alliance was a powerful aid) and threatened into submission local Indians, who also seemed to believe Clark's stories that the British were just waiting for an opportunity to tax them.

Clark's daring venture stirred Hamilton from his lair in Detroit. The Hair Buyer moved south with 235 followers, including 70 Indians and 130 Frenchmen, in October 1778. He attacked Vincennes, easily overwhelming a small detachment of Virginians there, and reasserted royal authority. He settled in for the winter season, waiting for the spring thaw before moving against Clark's main force at Kaskaskia. At the same time, as historian Gregory Evans Dowd has shown in *A Spirited Resistance,* Hamilton kept working to construct a pan-Indian alliance with the goal of launching during 1779 "a coordinated strike against the Anglo-American intruders" in Kentucky and western Virginia.[2]

When Clark learned about Hamilton's presence, he quickly assembled his force of 172 followers and marched for Vincennes in the first week of February 1779. Torrential winter rains flooded the 180-mile route, which included four swollen river crossings. Food became scarce, and at one critical point his column had nothing to eat for two days. When it was not raining, sharp blasts of cold wind nearly froze the band in its muddy tracks. Overcoming every adversity (in a fashion reminiscent of Benedict Arnold's march to Quebec), Clark's irregular troops approached Vincennes on February 23. Warning local French inhabitants to stay out of the way, Clark besieged the small fortress controlled by Hamilton. When the Lieutenant Governor refused to surrender, Clark brought forward some recently captured Indians. When taken, they had white scalps tied to their belts. In full view of the fortress, Clark's men held down four of the Indians, "tomahawked them" to death, as one soldier wrote, and "threw them into the river." Deciding his position was helpless, Hamilton surrendered.

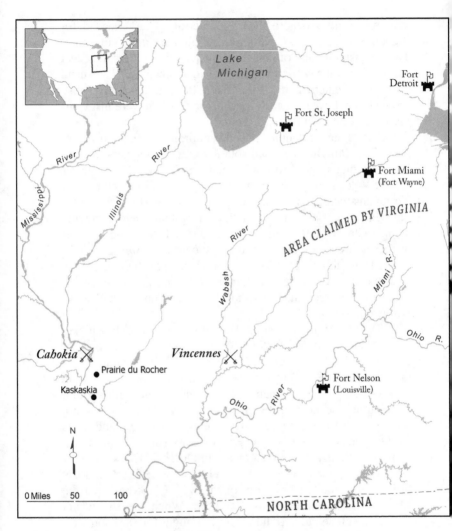

CLARK'S WESTERN CAMPAIGNS, 1778–1779

Clark sent the Hair Buyer to Virginia where he languished in prison for several months before being exchanged. Furthermore, the red-haired adventurer whom the Indians called Long Knife, persisted in his western campaigning, claiming all lands before him in the name of Virginia. His small irregular force, however, lacked the capacity to secure full control of a region of such territorial magnitude. Clark's Rangers did help to hold down the number of damaging Indian raids after 1778, and their exploits did serve to underpin patriot claims to the "Old Northwest" region when peace negotiations began in 1782. To argue for more on behalf of Clark and his small force would be stretching the point, particularly since the British (with their native allies) regained *de facto* control of the territory north of the Ohio River after the war and held it into the 1790s.

Of more immediate impact was John Sullivan's Continental expedition in 1779 against the Six Nations Confederacy of Iroquois in New York. Although some Iroquois favored neutrality and others, such as the Oneidas, supported the rebel cause, most, including the Mohawks and Senecas, allied with the British. Fort Niagara on Lake Ontario was the staging area for their devastating raids, sometimes led by Major John Butler, his son Walter, and their following of loyalists. Butler's Rangers represented former civilians who had resided west of Albany and had been caught up in the furious partisan clashes that enveloped the New York frontier after 1775. Also joining the Rangers were many Iroquois, who quite often operated under the Mohawk chief, Thayendanegea. He was better known among whites as Joseph Brant, a person of great sagacity and humanity who had received formal schooling in Connecticut before the war.

During 1778, the followers of the Butlers and Brant devastated the Pennsylvania and New York frontiers. In early July they fell on white settlers in the Wyoming Valley, located in north-central Pennsylvania. Foolishly, the local militia, numbering 360 (against more than 450 Indians and 110 loyalists), ventured beyond the protection of the local stockade. In what proved to be a particularly gory example of frontier warfare, the Rangers and Indians all but exterminated them. Reputedly, one

Indian woman ordered twelve captured militiamen to be arranged in a circle; while she chanted and danced, she ruthlessly tomahawked each of them. Other whites died by roasting on a spit or by fire at the stake.

Other blood-stained incidents, although not so dramatic in numbers, continued well into the autumn of 1778. In early November, the season of atrocities culminated with the Cherry Valley massacre in New York's Mohawk Valley region. When resisters in that community refused to surrender, Walter Butler allowed the indiscriminate slaughter of 32 men, women, and children—over the vigorous protests of Brant, who considered such random violence both senseless and sure to provoke an uncompromising patriot response.

As 1779 dawned, the distresses of so many backcountry inhabitants led Congress to instruct General Washington to muster a punitive expeditionary force. The goal was to secure the Pennsylvania–New York frontier from further Indian/loyalist depredations. John Sullivan, the man of ill-luck at Brandywine Creek and the Rhode Island campaign of 1778, accepted the assignment. Nearly 3,000 Continental soldiers began gathering at Easton, Pennsylvania, during May. Then they marched into the backcountry, hacking out a road as they moved toward the Wyoming Valley. In July they turned north, pointing them straight toward the heart of Iroquois country. At Newtown (Elmira), New York, Indians under Joseph Brant, with backup support from Butler's Rangers, chose to make a concentrated stand. Sullivan prepared carefully for the battle that came on August 29. Softening up the Newtown defenders with cannon fire and "a pleasing piece of [regimental] music" that the Indians could not "be prevailed upon to listen to," Sullivan's troops, noted one participant, mowed right through their opponents, who kept "firing and retreating to another tree, loading and firing again, still keeping up the war-whoop." Neither side suffered significant casualties, but the Indian/loyalist force accepted retreat instead of extinction.

The victory at Newtown opened up Iroquois settlements to Sullivan's expeditionary force. Over the next month, the Continentals burned and destroyed villages and crops wherever they could find them. They ransacked and leveled at least 41 Indian towns. A New Jersey lieutenant, William Barton, wanted some remembrance from so much destruction. Discovering some dead Indians, his men "skinned two of them from their hips down for boot legs, one pair for the major, the other for myself." As for the Indians, one group fell upon a scouting party under Lieutenant Thomas Boyd. They butchered them, completely mutilating Boyd and one of his riflemen. When the main army found them, their remains had been "stripped naked and their heads cut off, and the flesh of Lieutenant Boyd's head was entirely taken off and his eyes punched out." The commentator, sickened by the scene, indicated that the two slain Continentals were "immediately buried with the honor of war."

As these examples suggest, frontier warfare was often harshly brutal but hardly the product of what some commentators used to describe as the "ignoble savagism" of the Indians. Historian Bernard Sheehan has pointed out that frontier whites were just as savage as the Indians. Although "indiscriminate murder, scalping, torture, the taking of prisoners for adoption . . . struck white men as the very antithesis of civilized behavior," they engaged in the same practices. Sheehan concludes that "the irony" of war beyond the established settlements "lay in the apparent determination of the white man to draw the sharpest distinction between civilization and savagery and at the same time to conquer the Indian by becoming more like him."[3]

Although brutality was a shared characteristic of both sides, its overall impact did not immediately affect Native American resistance to the patriot cause. Sullivan's raid, for instance, forced hundreds of Iroquois warriors and their families to become wholly dependent on the British during the winter of 1779–80. Food and clothing supplies at Fort Niagara were inadequate, and great numbers of Iroquois starved to death before spring. However, as historian Joseph R. Fischer has pointed out in his study of the Sullivan expedition (*A Well-Executed Failure*), some 900 warriors under Brant and Butler "rekindled the war" in the Mohawk Valley in 1780, "destroying 1,000 homes,

1,000 barns, and 600,000 bushels of grain."[4] In this sense, Sullivan's campaign, while diminishing Iroquois tribal numbers, was less important in the long run to the removal of the Six Nations from New York than was the failure of Britain's peace negotiators at the end of the war to insist upon the maintenance of established territories for their native allies. Active support of the royal standard became an excuse for American patriots, once the war was over, to clear many regions of their Native American proprietors.

Patriot Naval Exploits

The campaigns of George Rogers Clark and John Sullivan gave cause for cheer among the patriots, even though the war in the eastern theater did not seem to be getting off dead center. At the same time, the exploits of the fledgling American navy represented a source of some rejoicing. With trepidation, the Continental Congress ventured into naval affairs during the fall of 1775. John Adams was among the few enthusiasts who had grand visions for a respectable American fleet, especially in challenging British war vessels sent out to blockade the coastline and harass commercial carriers and port towns. Other delegates, however, feared the costs associated with a massive naval building program.

On October 30, 1775, Congress partially side stepped the issue by establishing its navy committee (later called the marine committee). Within severe financial constraints, the delegates authorized the committee to find and outfit armed vessels for defending the provinces. By January 1776, Congress had purchased eight ships and ordered the construction of 13 new frigates. (Frigates were smaller but normally faster and more maneuverable than ships of the line. The latter could carry as many as 120 guns and crews of up to 1,000; the former rarely held more than 50 pieces of ordnance and 300 sailors.) Worried about bankrupting the rebel cause, Congress gave support to what may fairly be described as a modest naval program throughout the war.

The rapid advent of various state navies, as well as privateering vessels, also militated against the need for a sizable Continental navy. All told, combined state navies never had more than 40 craft at their disposal. By comparison, over 2,000 American privateers entered the fray before 1783. Anyone with a ship who had secured a letter of marque (a license to raid enemy craft) from one of the states or Congress could join the ranks of these privately owned vessels to prey upon enemy commerce. Any prize coming from a captured and condemned vessel would be turned over to owner, captain, and crew, according to proportions of investment and crew rank on the craft. Many privateers made fortunes for their owners during the war, as long as they were not caught or destroyed by British war vessels trying to blockade the American coastline.

Privateering was nothing more than a form of legalized piracy in time of war, and its long and well-developed tradition ably served the American cause. Estimates vary as to how many enemy vessels, quite often carrying vital supplies to the British army, were taken. One figure credits American privateers with 600 prizes, with another 200 going to the American navy. On the other hand, David Syrett, in his detailed study of British transport activities, *Shipping and the American War, 1775–83*, points out that overseas trading operations in 1775 involved 6,000 British vessels (including American-owned bottoms). Of these, 3,386 fell into enemy hands, with 495 being recaptured and 507 ransomed back to their original owners. Permanent seizures, which also would have involved French, Spanish, and Dutch maritime exploits, amounted to 2,384 vessels.[5] If this number is even close to accurate, total privateering and naval operations had a far more profound impact on Britain's long-distance supply problems than has usually been conceded, even if the British transport service held up well for most of the war.

Whatever the outer limits of vessels seized and condemned, privateering "throttled development of a navy" in Revolutionary America, as Howard H. Peckham has stated.[6] Also inhibiting the process were the many mariners who preferred privateering duty. One key reason was that all the prize money went to owners and crew, whereas Continental naval vessels had to turn over at least half of all proceeds from condemned vessels to Congress. Another was that discipline was often less rigorous on privateering ships, even though American naval regulations (like the army's Articles of War) were not as harsh as those of European navies, befitting a virtuous citizenry-in-arms. Floggings, the standard form of discipline, could include as many as 1,000 lashes for British mariners; the American code permitted a maximum of 12 stripes, unless the crime was so severe that formal court-martial proceedings exacted a higher penalty—and then only with the approval of the naval commander in chief.

The gentlemen-sailors who commanded the American navy, beginning with phlegmatic Commodore Esek Hopkins of Rhode Island, did little to distinguish themselves or the cause of muscular naval forces, relative to more aggressive privateers. What claim to dash and élan the Continental navy earned has focused on boisterous, free-wheeling John Paul Jones, a man whom sailors considered a rigid disciplinarian but extraordinary seaman. Born John Paul in Scotland, the future "father of the American navy" went to sea at an early age and eventually took the surname Jones to cover his identity after killing a mutinous sailor. He soon joined the Continental navy and, early in the war, took many cargo prizes along the Canadian coastline. Then, at the beginning of 1778, Jones appeared in France with the 18-gun sloop of war *Ranger*. His timing was excellent. The completion of the Franco-American alliance guaranteed patriot naval and privateering captains outfitting privileges in French ports. Even before then, the American commissioners had urged Congress to send patriot war vessels across the Atlantic to harass British commercial carriers in the North Sea and Baltic areas—and even to raid enemy ports. Now guaranteed refitting privileges, Jones was about to gain infamy for his seagoing ventures around Britain.

In April 1778, Jones sailed north into the Irish Sea toward Scotland and raided the English port town of Whitehaven, while attacking British merchant vessels along the way. In the immediate shadow of the French alliance, an intrepid patriot mariner had carried the war into the vitals of the parent nation. "For the first time in more than one hundred years," as historian William M. Fowler, Jr., has remarked (*Rebels under Sail*), "a British port had actually come under close attack by an enemy."[7] Jones's raiding expedition helped unnerve a civilian population heretofore isolated from the war and spurred a wave of antiwar protest in Britain. It also underscored the important harassing role that the American navy, however limited in strength, could play. With the French alliance, the allies could strike the extended British empire at almost any point, inflicting nasty wounds from the Caribbean islands to India. After 1778, the global maneuverability of allied naval and privateering fleets made the newly defined British military task of protecting the vitals of a far-flung empire that much more of a perplexing challenge.

Jones's raid was a symbolic warning of the plight facing the British war machine. In 1779, the commander boldly issued a second manifesto. After his Irish Sea activities, Jones returned to France, dallied with a number of French women, and sought a better vessel with which to carry on further seafaring ventures. The French government finally offered him an old merchant hulk. Jones transformed this craft into a 40-gun warship, calling it the *Bonhomme Richard* in honor of Benjamin Franklin's almanac character "Poor Richard." On September 23, 1779, while sailing in the North Sea, the American commander engaged the Royal navy's better-armed (50 guns) frigate *Serapis* off Flamborough Head. What followed was one of the most memorable naval confrontations of the war. The outgunned *Richard* nearly sank under withering fire but somehow stayed afloat as Jones and his mariners finally forced the *Serapis* to capitulate (the *Richard* sank two days later). The *Serapis* had been taken within sight of England, some 3,000 miles from North America, which certainly fed fears among English subjects, especially in light of the rumored French invasion, that the war could easily spill over into their homeland.

The *Bonhomme Richard* against the *Serapis* was a major capstone to American naval action during the Revolution and represented, as historian James C. Bradford has written, "one of the few glimmers of hope" for the patriot cause "in an otherwise dark year for the young United States."[8] Certainly, too, isolated, small-scale ship battles on the high seas, especially after the French alliance, exacerbated the problems faced by Great Britain in its attempt to supply its armies and reconquer the North American continent. The unremitting harassment provided by Continental, state, and especially privateering vessels made the Royal navy's blockade of the American coastline even more paper thin. The Continental fleet was never strong enough to become a truly menacing force, since Congress lacked the resources to underwrite a comprehensive naval program. That is just one more reason why the French alliance was so important in buttressing the rebel cause. Along with critical troop reinforcements on land, the French provided significantly expanded naval capacity, both of which played an indispensable part in bringing the war to a successful conclusion for the American patriots.

Financial Morass on the Home Front

In 1778 and 1779, committed rebels took pride in the exploits of John Paul Jones, but they also were aware that the war effort seemed to be adrift. The lack of a resolution was one of many reasons why popular enthusiasm and regular army morale reached rock bottom during 1779 and 1780. Internal disagreements were also taking their toll and threatened to drain the last vital signs of life out of the cause. Youthful Alexander Hamilton, serving Washington as an aide-de-camp, summarized many of the debilitating problems when he spoke out in 1779 about "the rapid decay of our currency, . . . the want of harmony in our councils, the declining zeal of the people, [and] the distresses of the officers of the army." These were "symptoms of a most alarming nature," a worried Hamilton stated. If he had added the martial success the British were then enjoying in the South, his list of critical problems would have been virtually complete.

With each passing day in 1779 and 1780, hardened veterans in the Continental line became more discouraged. They were not thinking about the global challenges that British strategists and forces now faced. Rather, their comments focused on mounting alienation toward civilian patriots, especially those taking advantage of the cause. Private Joseph Plumb Martin may have best captured the sentiments of ordinary soldiers when he reflected on 1780: "We . . . kept upon the parade in groups, venting our spleen at our country and government, then at our officers, and then at ourselves for our imbecility in staying there and starving in detail for an ungrateful people who did not care what became of us, so they could enjoy themselves while we were keeping a cruel enemy from them." Lieutenant Colonel Ebenezer Huntington was even more caustic. "I despise my countrymen," he wrote angrily in 1780. "I wish I could say I was not born in America. . . . The insults and neglects which the army have met with from the country beggars all description." Huntington denounced his "cowardly countrymen," who were holding "their purse-strings as though they would damn the world rather than part with a dollar for their army." Their selfishness was threatening to destroy the cause of liberty—at a time when public support should have been much stronger in the wake of the French alliance.

The indignation of such dedicated soldiers as Huntington and Martin reflected directly on the growing worthlessness of Continental dollars, the primary medium of exchange with which Congress attempted to pay for the war. Beginning in 1775, the delegates, lacking any revenue source but facing the actual financial costs of defending liberty, had started to issue paper currency, but without any form of financial backing. With popular enthusiasm and moral commitment running high, the fiat Continental dollars initially held their face value. By 1777, rampant inflation had begun. An important reason, besides slackened public confidence in the war effort, was that Congress, desperately trying to cover pressing expenses, printed its currency at far too rapid a rate, literally glutting the marketplace with paper money. The states, which should have been taxing the Continentals out of circulation to help stabilize their market value, preferred to support the value of their own currencies when taxing their inhabitants.

From an initial issue of $2 million in the summer of 1775, Congress by early 1779 had put in circulation a total of $191 million. To ask military forces and their suppliers to accept the currency when it was relatively scarce and holding its value was not a problem. On the other hand, to expect republican restraint when the annual salary of a junior-grade officer would net little more than a pair of shoes was a serious issue. The befuddled state of Continental finances, given the central government's inability to tax the populace, made it extraordinarily difficult to float a stable currency, improve the supply situation, or lure in new Continental recruits with decent bonuses for enlisting. Historian H. James Henderson, in his *Party Politics in the Continental Congress,* has summarized the situation well: "Congress, in the face of these problems, was not inactive; it was simply increasingly ineffective."[9]

The hyperinflating currency helped to fracture morale where it mattered most—in the Continental army. Officers of the New Jersey line, for example, began petitioning their state legislature in 1778 asking for solutions to problems ranging from depreciated pay to insufficient stocks of food, clothing, and equipment. In response, the state claimed these were Congressional concerns. In April 1779, the officers put more pressure on their legislature by demanding immediate relief. (They understood that Congress, dependent on the states, could not do much of anything.) Their complaint pointed out that pay "is now only *minimal,* not real," that "four months' pay of a private will not procure his wretched wife and children a single bushel of wheat. . . . Unless a speedy and ample remedy be provided," they warned the legislature, "the total dissolution of your troops is inevitable." They demanded pay in specie—"Spanish milled dollars"—to meet their basic needs. When that occurred, their "complaints shall instantly cease."

This petition contained strong words, but nothing happened except for much legislative windbaggery. Then in early May, the 1st New Jersey regiment received orders to march to Easton, Pennsylvania, and bivouac with Sullivan's expeditionary force. The officers responded with a threat. In yet another petition to the legislature, they proclaimed they would resign their commissions *en masse* rather than break camp, unless civil authorities addressed their pay and supply problems. These threats "mortified and chagrined" Washington "beyond expression." The Jersey officers, he stated, had *"reasoned wrong about the means of obtaining a good end."* They had "hazarded a step which has an air of dictating terms to their country, by taking advantage of the necessity of the moment."

That was exactly the purpose of the officers' protest. Making so bold a threat seemed to be the only way to get someone to address their grievances. The Jersey lawmakers perceived the implications. Republican purists among them preferred to see "the Brigade Disbanded [rather] than Submit to the appearance of being bullied" by the military. The majority, however, believing an independent republican nation could not be achieved without regulars remaining in the field, rapidly negotiated an acceptable compromise. To maintain the subordination of military to civil authority, the officers were to withdraw their petition. Then the state would move to provide relief, "to all appearance" by its own volition. The legislature promised to obtain clothing and immediately pay each officer £200 and each enlistee $40 in the form of a bonus. Somewhat satisfied, the brigade left winter camp and marched for Pennsylvania.

Washington aptly summarized the short-term significance of this confrontation. For "notwithstanding the expedient adopted for a saving [of] appearance," the commander observed, "this cannot fail to operate as a bad precedent." His prediction was accurate. With the deteriorating financial situation, individual acts of protest had begun to take on a group dynamic. The long-term, hard-core Continentals, separately in the officer corps and in the ranks, had become more cohesive. Out of their desperate circumstances, groups of officers and soldiers became more vociferously threatening toward civilian authorities in government. If officers and soldiers had learned to cooperate in their group protests, they could very well have ripped the republic apart from the inside over the fundamental issues of civilian peculation and indifference about their basic needs. That they did not unite was a reflection of the socioeconomic gulf that both separated them and kept feeding their well-developed contempt for one another.

When common soldiers employed the tactic of group defiance, civilians called it mutiny. When the officer corps did the same, patriot leaders used such epithets as military "extortion" or "blackmail." The officers were resentful in 1778 when Congressional delegates treated their "request" for pensions as a form of extortion being exacted by threats of individual resignations. Derogatory words from Congress may have helped spur the officers to raise the issue again during 1779. This time they demanded that postwar pensions be awarded for their lifetimes rather than just seven years. In response, the delegates told them to take their claims to their respective states. When Pennsylvania, Maryland, and Virginia responded positively, the corps went back to the central government, demanding full equality in pensions for officers from states not so generous. Congress, in desperate financial straits, hemmed, hawed, and promised nothing. In July 1780, the officers drew up their most threatening petition to date. Exposed as they had been "to the rapacity of almost every class of the community," they "should be obliged by necessity to quit the service," if Congress did not guarantee them half-pay pensions for life, beginning at the war's end. Should "ill consequences" befall "their country" because of their mass resignations, "they [would] leave to the world to determine who ought to be responsible" for the collapse of the Revolution.

Here was a threat of monumental proportions. The officers no longer intended to be whipsawed between a penniless Congress and tightfisted state governments. "The officers believed," Charles Royster has written, "that they alone had maintained the *rage militaire* of 1775." They thought "that their virtue could save their country in spite of its people," and half-pay pensions would recognize their sacrifice.[10] Certainly, however, more than personal honor and public recognition motivated them. As a group, they were in serious financial trouble, having lost much personal income because of long-time service in the war, a condition made worse for them by the highly inflated state of Continental dollars. Although Congress had attempted to refinance its currency in March 1780, that scheme was not faring well. The question was whether Congress could respond effectively, given its dearth of financial resources. Likewise, some delegates would have to set aside ideological qualms and accept reality for what it was, rather than venting their concerns with such slur words as "blackmail."

Congress was virtually helpless. By 1780, it was functioning as little more than a front line representative of the states. Most delegates wanted to act responsibly but lacked the constitutional authority to do so. The obvious weakness was the lack of taxation power and consequent inability, with no fixed revenue base, to meet the most pressing needs of the republic. In 1779, for instance, the total amount of fiat Continental money in circulation had reached $200 million. At this point the delegates stopped the printing press. In March 1780, they approved the reevaluation of their paper currency at the ratio of 40 Continental dollars to one specie dollar. The states were to tax the old Continentals out of circulation. In turn, they were to release the new currency, which was not to exceed a face value total of $10 million. The relative scarcity of the new Continentals was to serve as the hedge against hyperinflation.

This refinancing plan, so sensible in theory, faltered in reality. The states neither pushed to tax the old Continental dollars out of circulation nor moved to get the new money into the marketplace. Congress had to continue operating with its all but worthless currency, depending on foreign and domestic loans to continue financing the war effort. The delegates could also encourage price fixing agreements to hold down on rapid inflation, but they lacked the authority to do anything except recommend the adoption of such plans. The states, for their part, preferred to protect their own interests, leaving the central government all but helpless to remedy the aspiring republic's growing financial morass, which in turn meant inadequate financial and material support for Washington's Continentals.

Trapped between an increasingly restive army and uncooperative state officials, Congress more and more took on the appearance of a long-winded debating society than an agency decisively supporting the republican cause. Washington complained bitterly in late 1779 that "a wagon load of money will scarcely purchase a wagon of provision," and he reflected just a few months later that "unless Congress speaks in a more decisive tone" or is "vested with powers by the several states competent to the great purposes of war, . . . our cause is lost." The states, however, remained averse to handing greater authority to the central government, when so many republican ideologues kept reminding everyone that the Revolution had occurred, in the first place, because power in the British empire had been too far removed from the people and had been abused by corrupted imperial officials. Keeping decision-making authority close to the people, specifically in the state legislatures, was necessary for the protection of liberty, these patriot pundits repeatedly claimed. Such reasoning, however, eluded Washington's officers during the war's darkest days. Thus the question lingered: Would they resign *en masse* and leave republican purists and other noncombatants to their own devices in trying to defeat the imperial foe?

The War in the Southern States

Historians have generally agreed that the year 1780 represented the nadir of the war effort. The currency finance debacle and a resentful army were only two aspects of larger problems. Another major source of demoralization was the new British offensive in the South, which appeared to be virtually uncontainable during the summer and early fall of 1780. Actually, British interest in retaking the South may be traced back to the fall of 1775. Royal governors in that region had vigorously insisted that the North ministry do everything possible to support a supposedly large and committed loyalist population. The home government sent out an expedition of regulars to link up with North Carolina loyalists. The King's forces arrived off of Cape Fear in early May 1776, far too late to be of assistance. Earlier, at the Battle of Moore's Creek Bridge on February 27, local rebel partisans had devastated those North Carolina loyalists attempting to rally around the royal standard.

Historian Clyde R. Ferguson has argued that such early rebel success in the South reflected well on "the preexisting colonial militia structure." Other scholars, according to Ferguson, have overstated the case in viewing the pre-Revolutionary militia system in the South as "degenerate" and "as little more than a social institution whose chief function was the control of slaves." Militia activity after 1775, described by Ferguson as "irregular warfare or training for partisan war," focused on loyalists and such powerful Indian nations as the Cherokee, resulted in *de facto* rebel control of the southern region. The presence of militiamen willing to serve as partisan fighters and harass local civilians not committed to the patriot cause, furthermore, would make it very difficult for British conventional forces to conquer the region when their major onslaught finally began in 1780.[11]

Sustained hit-and-run partisan tactics still lay in the future when Henry Clinton, the British general in charge of the Cape Fear expedition in 1776, sought to remove his forces and take them north. Others persuaded him not to waste the opportunity but to seize Charles Town (later Charleston), South Carolina, then the most significant port city in the South. The Americans, however, had begun to prepare for such an assault. Suspecting a major British thrust, Congress and Washington had ordered Charles Lee to go to Charleston. There the less-than-diplomatic Lee tried to badger the inhabitants into constructing strong defenses. When Clinton's combined land-naval offensive descended on Charleston in late June 1776, the local patriots, who had not always minded Lee's instructions, put up a brilliant defense and drove off the British. Clinton's forces then sailed northward to link up with William Howe on Staten Island. This retreat ended major British military actions in the South until late 1778.

Once the war took on global dimensions and the massed concentration of forces at one strategic point was no longer possible for Britain, the home government reactivated plans for drawing on reputed loyalist numbers as one key to reconquering the southern region. The counterrevolutionary strategy seemed to work well at the outset, yet Clinton was slow to follow up on the initial success in Georgia. Rather, he hung close to New York during 1779, lamenting his declining troop strength, worrying about supplies, and fretting that Washington might try to drive his force from New York. Sir Henry became quite testy with his civilian superiors in England, who kept urging him to push ahead with the southern strategy. "If you wish to do anything," he bluntly advised them, "leave me to myself, and let me adapt my efforts to the hourly change of circumstances." Besides clinging to New York, Clinton withdrew the British garrison from Rhode Island to concentrate further his remaining numbers, all preparatory to the planned offensive push that came against South Carolina in 1780.

Meanwhile, American partisans and Continentals in the army's Southern Department engaged in a concerted attempt to drive the British from Georgia. In the late summer of 1779, favorable circumstances brought together the Franco-American allies outside of Savannah. Admiral d'Estaing commanded the French land-naval contingent, which had been off campaigning in the West Indies. Benjamin Lincoln, one of Washington's most trusted generals, had charge of some 1,400 patriot troops, mostly Continentals. Once again the prospect of successful joint operations was at hand, if the allies could figure out how to work together in smashing the outnumbered enemy. In late September, the forces of d'Estaing and Lincoln put Savannah under siege. Then, with the French commander beginning to worry about the adverse effect of turbulent fall weather on his fleet and with the British defenders refusing to capitulate, the fateful decision to storm the fortifications came. The assault occurred on October 9. A slaughter followed, largely the product of an American flanking party losing its way in the swampy terrain and by the superiority of the British position. The allies sustained 837 casualties before the day was done, compared to 155 for the British. Shortly thereafter, d'Estaing sailed for France; Lincoln had no choice but to retreat to Charleston, leaving the British firmly perched in Georgia.

Satisfied by December 1779 that an allied offensive against his New York base was not in the immediate offing, Clinton sailed south with an expedition force of 7,600 troops. Violent weather blew the fleet in all directions, but it reassembled and prepared carefully for siege operations. With the enemy in the vicinity, Benjamin Lincoln worked feverishly with 3,000 Continentals and 2,500 militia to prepare to defend the city. However, the Americans were now in a relatively weak position, since the defensive works that had helped stave off the British in 1776 had fallen into disrepair. Lincoln thought seriously about abandoning Charleston and saving his army. Local leaders pressured him into staying, insisting that the fall of their port city would trigger the collapse of the patriot cause in the South. The British siege began in early April. When one Clinton sortie cut off an escape route to the North, Lincoln faced two undesirable choices: fight to a sure death or capitulate. A furious artillery bombardment convinced fickle Charlestonians that submission was the only intelligent course. Lincoln formally surrendered on May 12, 1780. For the first time in the war, the British had captured an American army, virtually the whole Southern Department of Continental forces.

The fall of Charleston, hard on the heels of rebel failures in Georgia, augured well for the British southern strategy. Clinton sailed back to New York in triumph, leaving behind strong-willed, hard-charging Charles, Earl of Cornwallis. Before embarking, Sir Henry had ordered his aggressive subordinate to proceed with caution and to make sure that loyalists had full control of the territory behind the main army. Clinton also warned that supply lines had to be secure, so that Cornwallis did not find his force cut off from the sea and having to forage off the countryside. The Earl, as events soon demonstrated, did not listen very carefully.

The renewal of ferocious partisan warfare in the region, as much as Cornwallis's vigorous campaigning, was responsible for getting British southern forces overextended and into serious trouble. A sign of the times came at the Waxhaws, near the North Carolina border, on May 29, 1780. The blood bath there involved 400 Virginia Continentals who were marching toward Charleston but had turned back when they learned about Lincoln's capitulation. Pompous and often ruthless British Colonel Banastre Tarleton set out in hot pursuit with his green-coated cavalrymen. Reaching the retreating Americans near the Waxhaws, they attacked. Although the Continentals begged for quarter, Tarleton's dragoons butchered them, with fewer than 100 of the Virginians escaping the tragic confrontation. A new phrase denoting brutality in war, "Tarleton's Quarter," became a part of the patriots' vocabulary.

The Waxhaws slaughter, in combination with the fall of Charleston, temporarily undercut partisan rebel domination; and Tarleton's bloody ravaging of the countryside certainly encouraged the loyalists. As Russell F. Weigley has noted, "southern Revolutionaries" were "especially cruel in their harassment and repression of Loyalists" before Clinton's 1780 offensive. With Tarleton setting a "bad example" and the tables turned, "the Loyalists . . . seized the advantage of British occupation to take reprisals in violence against both persons and property."[12] Soon, irregular bands of rebels, which had been so effective in controlling the region since 1775, sprang up again. Led by such determined commanders as Thomas Sumter, "Swamp Fox" Francis Marion, and Andrew Pickens, they cowed loyalist bands in vengeful raids. They also nibbled away at Cornwallis's army, all of which greatly complicated the Earl's attempts to pacify the region.

Even with this new wave of rebel partisan resistance, the low point of the patriot southern effort had not yet been reached. The bottom came on August 16, 1780, when Cornwallis routed a reorganized Southern Department army under Horatio Gates near Camden, South Carolina. Gates, so long the darling general of New England's civilian leaders, accepted the call of Congress to reassemble some semblance of a southern army in the wake of Lincoln's capitulation. Washington felt others were more capable of succeeding at such an extraordinarily difficult assignment, but Congress refused to listen. The "hero of Saratoga" headed to southern North Carolina, where he pulled together a skeleton force consisting of a few Continentals, mostly from Maryland, and large numbers of untrained militiamen.

With 3,000 soldiers present and apparently fit for duty, Gates incautiously marched this force into South Carolina. This army seemed destined for a humiliating defeat, which is exactly what happened. Once in South Carolina, Gates's columns moved toward Camden, now a British outpost, which they approached after dark. One American officer reported that "the troops . . . had frequently felt the bad consequences of eating bad provisions; but at this time, a hasty meal of quick baked bread and fresh beef, with a dessert of molasses, mixed with mush or dumplings, operated so cathartically as to disorder many of the men." Unknown to Gates, his temporarily debilitated force was marching straight into Cornwallis's waiting arms. Having received intelligence about Gates's movements, the Earl had hurried out from Charleston with several hundred troops. The two armies bumped into each other in the dead of night. Both pulled back and prepared for a general engagement at daylight.

Gates's inexperienced and incapacitated units never had a chance. The British force routed them, as reflected in the estimated American casualty rate of 750, while the British figure was slightly over 300 killed or wounded. In what some have described as a fit of cowardice, Gates abandoned his troops before the battle was over and rode hard for North Carolina. More significantly, a second Southern Department army had fallen prey to the British in less than one campaign season. The patriot cause in the South was in serious trouble, despite continued partisan resistance. "Few guerrilla campaigns have progressed farther than the phase of terrorist raids without the assistance of at least a semblance of an organized army" to support them, Russell F. Weigley has observed.[13] That army was, again, no longer there. Some drastic turnabout was necessary if the Revolutionary cause in the South were to gain redemption.

Treason, Pensions, and Mutinies

In the North, Washington continued to experience frustration in planning for a joint Franco-American land offensive against Clinton. His officers and soldiers were as restive, if not more so, than before. Bounties, which were now normally being paid in specie, were not attracting new recruits. If anything, civilians, no matter how low their socioeconomic standing, were unwilling to join the ranks. Washington openly wondered whether he would have enough troops left to claim he still had an army for the next campaign season. The unrelenting commander in chief virtually gave up making plans for the 1781 campaign season. Washington found it exasperating that he was not able to offer weakened British forces a major challenge when he had found ways to do so during their concentrated campaign efforts of 1776 and 1777.

With lack of faith and popular commitment in the cause starting to hit rock bottom in 1779, disturbing incidents began to take place. None caused greater consternation than the treason of Benedict Arnold. Too often, commentators have portrayed Arnold as a misfit of unbalanced and egotistical temperament who was little more than a greedy, self-interested, vindictive person. That Arnold worried about the declining state of his finances cannot be denied, yet so did many other high-ranking officers. Moreover, he felt strongly that the army had too often received shameful levels of civilian support, as did his comrades. In September 1780, just before going over to the British, Arnold "lamented that our army is permitted to starve in a land of plenty." His words were hardly unique among veteran officers. His disillusionment with the cause of liberty was profound, and his actions represented the most extreme form of individual protest that he could have mustered against what he considered hypocritical patriots who had treated the army, its officers and its soldiers, with cold-hearted indifference, if not outright hostility and dishonesty.

Arnold, as deeply committed a republican as could be found in the patriot population of 1775, had become convinced by 1779 that such sentiment had been both a temporary illusion and a sham. Now wanting to restore the imperial connection, he hoped through his actions to set the stage for a massive popular return in allegiance to Great Britain. For over a year he flirted with Clinton in secret correspondence, ultimately promising to deliver West Point, considered the key to control of the Hudson Highlands, in return for a substantial pension and a generalship in the British army. His plan collapsed, however, when dashing Major John André, adjutant general of the British army and a personal favorite of Clinton's, fell into American hands in the Highlands region when returning from a secret meeting with Arnold. Thus exposed, Arnold fled West Point on September 25, 1780, and became one of the greatest villains in United States history.

The popular reaction to Arnold's treason was overwhelmingly negative. Philadelphians were typical in their denunciations. They staged an elaborate parade, centering on a horse-drawn float. Exhibited on the platform was an "effigy of General ARNOLD sitting." The turncoat had "two faces, emblematical of his traitorous conduct," and at his back "was a figure of the Devil, dressed in black robes, shaking a purse of money at the general's left ear." Thousands turned out for the show. Running "through the denunciation of Arnold," Charles Royster has stated, was "the desperate claim that the public virtue of 1775 could survive as the basis for American independence."[15] Superficially, at least, the response to Arnold's treason seemed to bring new determination to a populace apparently guilt ridden by its unsupportive behavior. If it did, the new enthusiasm did not seem to extend very far beyond parades and other forms of denunciation. In October 1780, Washington had 17,586 troops in rank (13,966 effectives). Two months later he had just about half that number (8,742 in rank with 5,982 present and fit for duty).

A major effect of Arnold's treason, in combination with other problems, was to move Congress off dead center on the pension issue. In October 1780, after another go-round of debating whether pensions would result in a privileged, unrepublican military caste, the delegates succumbed to reality. They promised the officer corps half-pay for life, to begin at war's end— predicated on the rosy expectation that funds would become available. Despite strong New England antipension sentiment, Congress was not willing to take the chance that other officers, perhaps as disgruntled as Arnold, might retire from the field or, worse yet, follow his turncoat path. One highly visible "renegade from republicanism," as Arnold has been described by James Kirby Martin, was enough.[15] The officer corps seemed to be mollified. A lingering—and vital—question was whether the central government could establish a permanent revenue source to support the pensions.

The seeming resolution of the pension issue came at a critical time, since unsettling levels of group defiance among the rank and file had begun to take place. The most common form of group protest was the line mutiny. A few isolated incidents occurred before 1779, but beginning in that troubled year long-suffering Continentals started to "combine" in reaction to their horrendous conditions, as some officers described the phenomenon. The step from these secretive and dangerous "combinations" to large-scale line mutinies was quite short.

It is plausible to argue that rank-and-file soldiers came to appreciate the tactical importance of group pressure and defiance by observing their officers in the pursuit of pensions. Heightened feelings of group cohesion also helped bond together Washington's veteran campaigners. Whatever the specific factors, the year 1779 saw near uprisings among Rhode Island and Connecticut regiments, both of which were barely contained. In 1780, another mutiny involving Connecticut soldiers ended only after a dependable Pennsylvania regiment surrounded them and restored order. Group protest by the soldiery led one worried army colonel to proclaim in September 1780: "We are in a bad way, and I think a little fighting [with Clinton] would be of great service to our army at present, and put an end to feuds and broils among themselves."

The winter of 1779–80, spent at Jockey Hollow near Morristown, New Jersey, did little to ease troop dissatisfaction. The weather was as severe that year as at any time during the century, certainly worse than at Valley Forge. Supplies, again, were almost nonexistent, even with storehouses of food available in the surrounding countryside. Local merchants and farmers, however, wanted nothing to do with Continental dollars or other forms of Congressional money, and organized foraging activity did little to keep stomachs full. About all the troops could celebrate at Morristown were the reduced morbidity and mortality rates. While one-third of the soldiery appeared on the sick roles at any given time during the Valley Forge winter, the peak at Morristown was never higher than 11.1 percent, based on data compiled by Charles H. Lesser.[16] Commensurately, fewer troops succumbed to death in camp. Declining morbidity reflected the dominant presence of hard-core veterans, who likely had already endured bouts of smallpox, typhus, and other standard camp maladies and had survived and were now immune.

Reduced morbidity and mortality rates during the harshest winter of the war did not uplift soldier morale. The supply situation remained precarious, and pay arrearages became even more pronounced as one winter season gave way to another. Very much related to pay issues, the veterans began grumbling about benefits short-term enlistees had obtained for remaining in service after their terms were up. Such individuals now received bounties in hard money as well as promises of land that exceeded acreage amounts promised to longer-term enlistees. For persons who had already endured so much hardship, such apparent favoritism, while necessary to minimize Washington's declining numbers, proved to be too much. Surgeon James Thacher understated troop feelings in December 1780 when he drew attention to "repeated disappointments of our hopes and expectations" and pointed out that "the confidence of the army in public justice and public promises is greatly diminished, and we are reduced almost to despair."

For many soldiers, the situation had passed beyond despair. On January 1, 1781, the Pennsylvania line, suffering through yet another harsh winter in the vicinity of Morristown, revolted. Some 1,500 hardened comrades ostensibly wanted nothing more to do with the army. On a prearranged signal, the Pennsylvanians paraded under arms, seized artillery pieces, and marched south toward Princeton, their ultimate target being Philadelphia. They had endured their fill of broken promises, and they claimed that the period of their enlistments was up. They maintained that they had signed on for three years, not for the duration. So if they were to stay in the ranks, they wanted the same benefits that short-term enlistees and new long-term recruits were receiving.

Formal military discipline collapsed as the mutineers, commencing what Charles Patrick Neimeyer has described as "the largest and most unusual internal upheaval in the history of American arms," brushed aside officers trying to stop them.[17] The insurgents killed one officer and mortally wounded two others. Their popular commander, Anthony Wayne, trailed along after them, attempting to appeal to their sense of patriotism. The soldiers, speaking through a committee of sergeants, assured Wayne and others of their loyalty—and proved it by delivering up two spies whom Sir Henry Clinton had sent out to monitor the situation. Moreover, the soldiers, despite their anger, behaved themselves along their route and did not threaten the civilian populace.

Although most of the mutineers were duration enlistees, that point was moot at the time. When they reached Trenton, representatives from Congress and the Pennsylvania government began meeting with them. Caught in an obvious bind, the negotiators agreed to discharge any soldier claiming to have completed a three-year enlistment. Also, they offered back pay and new clothing as well as immunity from prosecution for having summarily deserted the field. Once discharged, many of the mutineers reenlisted for the new bounty payment. The net loss to the line in terms of numbers ended up being fairly small. By late January 1781, the Pennsylvanians once more were a functioning line in the Continental army.

The resolution of their most pressing grievances did not come about solely because of the justness of their complaints. Nor was a satisfactory settlement constructed because "the revolt . . . occurred in a country where many of the men were upstanding citizen-soldiers conscious of their rights and liberties," as Don Higginbotham has suggested.[18] Few, if any, of the mutineers were upstanding in any economic sense. However, they thought the long list of broken promises had violated their fundamental rights. They were also loyal to the cause and certainly as upstanding as any person in their commitment to the goal of achieving independence. They knew that Washington was in desperate need of their numbers, and they employed the threat of a mass resignation as leverage for some modicum of financial justice. Unlike the officers, they were not in a position to lobby before Congress. Hence they used the most threatening form of protest available to them—and only after less extreme measures had failed to redress legitimate grievances. Committed to the cause, the enlistees had no desire to overthrow Congress or the state governments, since they had staked their hopes for a better life on winning a war dedicated to securing freer republican institutions in America. All told, the extreme act of mutiny demonstrated, paradoxically, that they were among the most loyal and dedicated republican patriots in the new nation, even if they had come dangerously close to repudiating a dream that so far seemed like a perpetual nightmare to them.

More worrisome at the time than the issue of appropriate justice for these veterans was whether the Pennsylvania mutiny, and its aborted predecessors, would trigger additional revolts in the Continental line. Also camped near Morristown during the winter of 1780–81 were soldiers of the New Jersey line. Officers were aware that the Jersey regulars sympathized with the Pennsylvanians and were in constant communication with them. One reported that "some men of the 1st regiment have been trying to foment an insurrection yet have been altogether unsuccessful in the 3rd." Other officers naively discounted the possibility. On January 20, the New Jersey line, witnessing the success of the Pennsylvanians, rose in mutiny. Even though each of the regulars had recently received $5 in specie as a token toward long overdue pay, they were upset about better bounties and shorter terms of enlistment offered new comrades.

The New Jersey line first broke loose at Pompton, near Morristown, its leaders shouting: "Let us go to Congress who have money and rum enough but won't give it to us." Within a few days, these troops, having gained liberal concessions, were back under control, except for isolated insults directed at the most overbearing of their officers. Washington, however, had decided that enough was enough. "Unless this dangerous spirit can be suppressed by force," he wrote Congress, "there is an end to all subordination in the Army, and indeed to the Army itself." To back up his words, the commander ordered General Robert Howe and about 500 New England troops near West Point to march to Pompton and to exact an "unconditional submission." Once in control, they were to "instantly execute a few of the most active and most incendiary leaders."

Howe's contingent reached Pompton on January 27, three days after the New Jersey line had settled its grievances. Surrounding the camp just before dawn, Howe caught the Jersey soldiers off guard and ordered them to fall in without arms. The general singled out three ringleaders and ordered their summary execution, to be shot to death by nine of their comrades. A Jersey officer intervened in one case, but two mutineers were put to death. Stated Dr. Thacher in describing the scene, "the wretched victims, overwhelmed by the terrors of death, had neither time nor . . . power to implore the forgiveness of their God, and such was their agonizing condition, that no heart could refrain from emotions of sympathy and compassion."

Washington's course with respect to the New Jersey line was brutal, but the republican cause, from his perspective, depended for survival on a well-regulated army. He had to maintain control at whatever price, even at the expense of humanity itself. Perhaps because the war picture started to brighten in 1781, only a few smaller uprisings occurred after the mutiny of the New Jersey line. Or possibly Washington's harsh actions, directed against persons as loyal to the cause as any, had a chilling effect on long-term, war-weary patriot regulars.

Sudden Turnabout: The Road to Yorktown

Just when the rebel effort in the South appeared to have all but collapsed, the Americans rebounded. Three key reasons help explain why. First, Cornwallis, flushed with victory at Camden, decided to push into North Carolina. That plan turned out to be poorly calculated, as local partisans rallied. Second, they then delivered a telling blow at the Battle of King's Mountain. Third, Congress finally deferred to Washington's opinion regarding who should command the Southern Department. Washington selected Nathanael Greene, who would soon be running Cornwallis's army in circles. Greene arrived in Charlotte, North Carolina, on December 2, 1780, and immediately relieved Gates of command. Cornwallis's needless aggressiveness, unexpected patriot partisan resistance, and Greene's unorthodoxy as a campaigner thus would combine to unravel the British southern strategy.

As Cornwallis pushed northward after the Camden debacle, his left wing under Major Patrick Ferguson found itself being enveloped by rebel partisans. The British goal was to move toward the first line of the Appalachian Mountains. Enraged "over-the-mountain men," coming together in almost leaderless fashion, began to stalk Ferguson's column, which consisted largely of hated loyalists. Beginning to sense real danger, Ferguson ordered a retreat, then spied a mountain jutting up from the Piedmont in northern South Carolina. With 1,100 followers, he prepared to defend that promontory. Ferguson, no doubt apocryphally, announced: "He was on King's Mountain and . . . he was king of that mountain and God Almighty could not drive him from it." He could not have been more wrong. On October 7, 1780, the frontier irregulars surrounded Ferguson's force and started moving up from all sides. Brutally cutting the defenders to shreds, the rebels revenged themselves for the maiming and killing of loved ones victimized by the region's partisan war. Ferguson perished in the midst of the battle from several wounds. Before the over-the-mountain men were done, 157 loyalists were dead, another 163 wounded, and 698 were prisoners. By comparison, the 1,000 frontier rebels had suffered about 80 casualties.

Not only did the Battle of King's Mountain sever Cornwallis's left wing, it also served to crush the enthusiasm of many southern loyalists then supporting the British counter-revolutionary campaign. Colonel William Campbell, one of the leaders of the King's Mountain victors, permitted summary trials of the most obnoxious Ferguson loyalists. Charges ranged from entering homes and stealing property to raping and mercilessly killing members of patriot families. Nine captured loyalists were hanged; others received gallows reprieves. Again, it seemed, the loyalists were learning that British regiments would not (or could not) guarantee them protection. Fewer thus were willing to rush out and join the King's forces in the critical days ahead.

The effects of King's Mountain did not ease Nathanael Greene's burdens. The overall "appearance" of those few troops available to him "was wretched beyond description," he complained. Notwithstanding, Greene soon devised a bold strategy for dealing with Cornwallis's numerically superior forces. He did the unthinkable, dividing his troops into three separate columns to make "the most of my inferior force," all of which "compels my adversary to divide his and holds him in doubt as to his own line of conduct." Greene gave 600 regulars and militia to rifleman Daniel Morgan, who was to push south and west toward the British stronghold at Ninety-Six in South Carolina. To the southeast he sent "Light Horse" Harry Lee and his cavalry legion of 280 dragoons to work in concert with Francis Marion's partisan rebel band. With his remaining troops, the numbers of which grew to over 1,000 with hard-sell recruiting and a modest outpouring of militia support, Greene would focus on Cornwallis's main force. The effect of Greene's "unorthodoxy" in "violating the principle of concentration," Russell F. Weigley has written, was to "make the British army still more vulnerable to partisan harassment and to encounters with his own force, which was not strong enough for a major battle."[19]

Pugnacious Cornwallis, back in South Carolina after the British debacle at King's Mountain, accepted Greene's challenge. His immediate objective was to destroy the divided patriot forces by pushing toward Greene and isolating and wiping out Morgan while in transit. To that end, he dispatched Banastre Tarleton with 1,100 soldiers to drive Morgan's force into the trap. Morgan seemed to cooperate, retreating ahead of Tarleton's onrushing force. The skilled wagon master and rifleman, however, knew that he must avoid being squeezed to bits between two British columns. In mid-January 1781, Morgan reached Hannah's Cowpens, close to the Broad River. There he decided to square off against Tarleton. His numbers now swelled to 1,000 by increments of militia, Morgan set a masterful trap. With the Broad River at his back, he placed his skittish militiamen in the front lines, ordering them to fire at least two rounds before breaking and running, as experience had taught him they would do in the face of onrushing British arms. In a second set of lines not visible to the enemy, Morgan grouped his battle-hardened Continentals, whom he presumed would not falter in the face of concentrated British fire.

Not trusting his militia, Morgan wanted the Broad River behind them. "When men are forced to fight," he explained, "they will sell their lives dearly. . . . Had I crossed the river, one half of the militia would immediately have abandoned me." On the morning of January 17, after a forced five-hour march, Tarleton's troops rushed headlong into Morgan's trap. The militia line broke, but only after inflicting casualties with some damaging fire. Smelling blood, the British surged forward in disorganized haste. Tarleton and his soldiers assumed that Morgan had aligned his force in a "traditional three-line, European-style, defense in depth formation." In reality, as historian Lawrence E. Babits has observed in *A Devil of a Whipping,* Morgan's "genius lay in reversing the strength of his linear formations and creating progressively stronger defensive lines."[20] When the British, sensing victory, charged into the additional American lines, the Continentals, backed up by militia units that had reformed after retreating, ripped them to shreds with deadly fire and a bayonet charge; Morgan also threw in a flanking cavalry assault. Tarleton managed to get away, but he lost all but 140 of his troops (339 in casualties and 600 in prisoners). Morgan suffered only

12 killed and 60 wounded. The Battle of Cowpens was the second staggering rebel counterpunch in the South against the ever combative Cornwallis.

Not resting after his triumph, Morgan pushed his force north to avoid the Earl's slowly advancing main column. After joining Greene, the rifleman turned over his portion of the army and took a leave of absence, complaining of severe bouts of rheumatism. Shortly, the chase was on between Greene and Cornwallis, the Americans retreating and the British desperately trying to catch him. To speed his march, Cornwallis abandoned all heavy baggage, including his army's supply of rum. Still, he could not run down the Americans, who retired all of the way into southern Virginia before again turning south. Both armies suffered miserably in the cold, raw weather, but Greene was wearing down his adversary. When he received reinforcements early in March 1781, he decided to make a stand near Guilford Courthouse in central North Carolina. Even if he lost the engagement, Greene reasoned, his force could inflict yet further pain on Cornwallis's harried, exhausted troops.

Russell F. Weigley has characterized Cornwallis as an officer who "possessed a quality hitherto rarely displayed by British generals in this war, a thirst for battle."[21] With Greene reinforced, the Earl now had less than half the strength of Greene and his patriots (2,000 to 4,300). However, Cornwallis readily accepted the challenge. Greene chose a plan of battle similar to that put together by Morgan at Hannah's Cowpens. Early on the afternoon of March 15, Cornwallis attacked. A vicious confrontation followed with neither side gaining a decisive advantage. Finally, Greene, sensing that he had inflicted enough damage, withdrew his weary soldiers from the field. Even though the Earl could claim a technical victory, his army had taken the worst of it—506 casualties compared to 264 on the American side. The patriot soldiers had cause for cheering, especially when they learned that the much hated Tarleton lost three fingers after being shot in the hand. On the other side, Greene was irate that 1,000 North Carolina militia abandoned him during his retreat, which only further fixed him in his doubts about the steadfastness of militia.

Cornwallis, having had enough and seriously damaged with a 25 percent casualty rate, likewise retreated, all the way to the port town of Wilmington, North Carolina, 175 miles to the southeast. There he rested and regrouped his exhausted army and obtained supplies. As for Greene, he had not defeated his adversary, but he had worn him down while making it impossible for the Earl to support partisan loyalists in South Carolina. Greene had good reason to be satisfied. He and Morgan (along with the over-the-mountain irregulars) had accomplished a phenomenal turnabout in events—and with next to nothing in resources. They had taken advantage of Cornwallis's inherent aggressiveness and had turned that quality against him. In doing so, they revived the suffocating patriot cause in the South and helped clear the pathway to Yorktown. Their accomplishments in 1780 and into 1781 represented a truly luminous point in the more general atmosphere of patriot doubt and gloom. The elements were now falling into place for a critical military victory that would lead to peace negotiations and national independence.

Notes

1 Higginbotham, *The War of American Independence,* 320.

2 Dowd, *A Spirited Resistance: The North American Indian Struggle for Unity, 1745–1815* (Baltimore, 1992), 57–58.

3 Sheehan, "Ignoble Savagism and the American Revolution," in L. R. Gerlach, et al., eds., *Legacies of the American Revolution* (Salt Lake City, Utah, 1978), 157, 172.

4 Fischer, *A Well-Executed Failure: The Sullivan Campaign against the Iroquois, July-September 1779* (Columbia, S.C., 1997), 191–94.

5 Syrett, *Shipping and the American War, 1775–83: A Study of British Transport Organization* (London, 1970), 77.

6 Peckham, *The War for Independence,* 118.

7 Fowler, *Rebels under Sail: The American Navy during the Revolution* (New York, 1976), 138–39.

8 Bradford, "The Battle of Flamborough Head," in Sweetman, ed., *Great American Naval Battles,* 44.

9 Henderson, *Party Politics in the Continental Congress* (New York, 1974), 254.

10 Royster, *A Revolutionary People at War,* 315–16.

11 Ferguson, "Functions of the Partisan-Militia in the South during the American Revolution: An Interpretation," in W. R. Higgins, ed., *The Revolutionary War in the South: Power, Conflict, and Leadership* (Durham, N.C., 1979), 239-42. For an overview of the

southern phase of the war focusing on Clinton, see Ira D. Gruber, "Britain's Southern Strategy," Ibid., 205–38.

12 Weigley, *The American Way of War,* 26.

13 Ibid., 27.

14 Royster, "'The Nature of Treason,'" *William and Mary Quarterly* (1979), 191.

15 Martin, "Benedict Arnold's Treason as Political Protest," *Parameters: Journal of the US Army War College,* 11 (1981), 63–74.

16 Lesser, ed., *The Sinews of Independence,* xxx–xxxvi.

17 Neimeyer, *America Goes to War,* 15–51.

18 Higginbotham, *The War of American Independence,* 404.

19 Weigley, *The American Way of War,* 29–30.

20 Babits, *A Devil of a Whipping: The Battle of Cowpens* (Chapel Hill, N.C., 1998), 152.

21 Weigley, *The American Way of War,* 31.

CHAPTER SIX

Of War, National Legitimacy, and the Republican Order, 1781–1789

The Yorktown Campaign

"The Revolution," wrote an aging John Adams in 1818, "was effected before the war commenced. The Revolution was in the minds and hearts of the people. . . . This radical change in the principles, opinions, sentiments, and affections of the people, was the real Revolution." In attempting to give coherency to the era that enveloped so much of his life work, Adams implied that an American identity as separate from Great Britain had manifested itself before the war. This sense of distinctness as a people, in turn, gave unity to the war effort and readily lent itself to the nation-making process that followed, once the patriots had recognized their change of heart and committed themselves irrevocably to the cause of liberty. Since legitimacy as a separate people, or so Adams claimed, characterized the American mind well before 1776, the fundamental task in war was to prove the strength of common will and purpose.

Although Adams's observations have a certain romantic appeal, notably among historians who hold that consensus of purpose rather than conflict over goals and aspirations was uppermost in shaping the Revolution, the "minds and hearts" statement strains historical reality. Specifically, it limits proper appreciation of the war as a source and instrument of national legitimacy and identity. Despite the *rage militaire* of 1775, provincial citizens lacked the psychological preparation to display the depth of commitment that they would need to maintain even a facade of unity in the face of concentrated British arms. The volatility of popular enthusiasm as the war progressed indicates that a sense of national identity had not yet taken hold, that feelings of separateness undergirding national legitimacy were far from realization in 1775 and 1776. What the war effort did, above all else, was to generate a sense of unity and legitimacy of purpose, which was essential to the nation-making process that took place through and beyond the war years. Altered affections did not so much cause as they were a result of the clash of arms.

Nathanael Greene, while playing fox and hare with Cornwallis's army, appreciated the sensitive task of establishing legitimacy. He insisted that his army, regardless of how poorly treated or supplied, not plunder the property of civilians or abuse them in other ways. Cornwallis was not in a position to be so judicious. He let his regulars and loyalist minions do as they pleased. The British left "the whole country struck with terror," stated one irate North Carolinian. Loyalists with Cornwallis considered it fair "business . . . under the protection of the army to enrich themselves on the plunder they took from . . . distressed inhabitants" unable to defend themselves. As the two armies moved through the countryside, Greene thus made friends for the cause of American identity; ironically, so did Cornwallis. Like Washington, Greene comprehended that restraint toward civilians, regardless of the enormity of army grievances, was essential to having the war effort serve as a wellspring of national legitimacy and resultant nationhood.

Cornwallis blundered in this and many other ways. He did not pacify the ground behind his army, and he did not effectively use the loyalists as agents of counterrevolutionary activity. Rather, "misdirected aggressiveness," as Russell F. Weigley has stated, "carried Cornwallis . . . to his and the British army's final disaster of the war."[1] Had the Earl been a smarter strategist, he would have worked to reestablish the allegiance of thousands of citizens who had not yet made an irrevocable commitment to the republican order so craved by more deeply committed rebels.

In some situations the fate of conflicts rests on the foibles of individual human personalities. Cornwallis was a person who might have undermined the languishing patriot cause but who failed. Misplaced personal ambition and the desire for military glory were his weaknesses. The Earl could be needlessly fractious when he perceived the world as treating him unjustly. He entered one such moody period at the time of the siege of Charleston. Clinton had just learned that Lord North's ministry had rejected his longstanding request to be relieved of the North American command. Cornwallis, positioned to be Clinton's successor, thirsted for the job and the potential fame and recognition that would come with it. When he found out about the ministry's decision, the Earl "withdrew into a shell of self-pity" and "blamed Clinton for his troubles," historian Hugh F. Rankin has written.[2] Not only was Cornwallis testy with his superior, but he chose to ignore Clinton's advice about systematic pacification and maintenance of supply lines. Cornwallis also took out his frustrations by chasing after rebel armies until Greene's force got the best of him. Smashing Greene would have brought him glory and possibly renewed interest among leaders in England about replacing Clinton. Even though outdueled, the Earl refused to yield. He was going to quench his thirst for accolades, and Virginia appeared to be a most attractive oasis.

Back in December 1780, Sir Henry Clinton sent a raiding detachment of 1,500 by sea into the Old Dominion. Commanded by Benedict Arnold, the soldiers were to aid Cornwallis by drawing rebel troops away from the Southern Department army. Another goal was to establish a site for a naval base to support future British operations in the Chesapeake Bay area.

Continental forces under Steuben and Lafayette quickly gathered to challenge Arnold's marauders, who marched as far inland as Richmond and burned and sacked that thriving town.

Responding to the presence of American regulars, Clinton reinforced Arnold with 2,000 soldiers and named General William Phillips to overall command. This military buildup, meant to support Cornwallis, did much more; as if by magnetic pull, it drew him to Virginia. In April 1781, while recuperating with his battered soldiery at Wilmington, Cornwallis wrote Phillips that he would soon link forces with him and take charge of operations there. Virginia, the Earl had decided, represented a more suitable theater for the offensive kind of warfare he preferred. In marching north, he all but abandoned South Carolina, leaving behind only a small force to contend with Greene and local partisan rebels.

Cornwallis's ambition propelled him straight into the maze from which he could not escape at Yorktown. His defiance of Clinton and virtual repudiation of the southern strategy would bring the land war, at last, to a resolution. Clinton, in turn, lacked the strength of character to discipline Cornwallis. Rather, he fussed about the focus of the upcoming summer campaign, waffling among various possibilities (much as Howe had done in the spring of 1777). At one moment he thought of retaking Rhode Island; then Philadelphia struck his fancy. Next he worried about defending his New York stronghold against Washington. Clinton then took to dickering with Cornwallis about troop strength. He wrote and asked the Earl for 2,000 soldiers (the Earl now had a force of 7,500 at his disposal). Cornwallis replied that he could spare no one. If he could not keep them all, he would return to Charleston, an offer Clinton should have accepted.

In late July, Clinton ordered Cornwallis to fortify Old Point Comfort at the mouth of the James River as an anchoring point for the British navy. After consulting his engineers, the Earl concluded that Yorktown, on the southern shore of the York River near Chesapeake Bay, would make a stronger defensive site. By August 1, he had fortifications going up. All this time,

Cornwallis seethed with anger because his army was to become a garrison force with virtually no opportunity for offensive operations. He vented himself by speaking out about Clinton's ineptness in his letters to civilian leaders in England. Neither he nor Clinton, both so busily engaged in picking at each other, had fathomed the danger of posting the bulk of the British southern army in so vulnerable a location.

While the two generals squabbled, George Washington once again dusted off his plans for an assault on New York City. His trump card was a French army of 5,000 under the talented, sensible Comte de Rochambeau, which had landed at Newport in July 1780. Both Rochambeau and Washington were eager to mount a major offensive during the 1781 campaign season. In particular, the American commander appreciated the debilitating effects of the mutinous turmoil in his army, and he wondered how long his forces could hold together without definitive action. Martial survival, more than ever, depended on operations. Washington and Rochambeau met during May in Wethersfield, Connecticut, to set campaign goals. The American commander pushed for full-scale action against New York. Rochambeau countered with news that a large French fleet might be available to support their armies; he favored moving against the British force in Virginia, with the fleet, should it actually sail north from the Indies, blocking off any escape route through Chesapeake Bay.

The Wethersfield meeting signaled the prospect of close allied cooperation, whatever the enemy target. Washington, moreover, needed the French troops to put some muscle in his plans, since his own numbers were now so meager. Always persistent, he selected July 2 as the day to begin the New York assault. However, British foraging parties discovered the allied movements, which allowed Clinton to buoy his defenses and throw off the timetable. Then, in early August, Sir Henry received Hessian reinforcements totaling 2,600, which brought his strength up to 15,000, somewhat greater than that of the allies. Washington began to despair, but bad news quickly turned positive. On August 14, the American commander learned that the rumored

French fleet under the Comte de Grasse, consisting of 30 ships and 3,000 soldiers, was definitely on its way to Chesapeake Bay. Long since aware that Cornwallis had marched his force to Virginia, Washington embraced the opportunity. Within five days, the first contingents of French and American troops moved out for the long trek south.

During the summer of 1780, Washington had offered a telling observation. "In any operation and all circumstances, a decisive Naval superiority," he wrote, "is to be considered as a fundamental principle, and the basis upon which every hope of success must ultimately depend." If he could get the allied land forces in front of Cornwallis at Yorktown and the French fleet could seal off Chesapeake Bay, the Earl's army would be trapped. The French mariners soon performed their part. Admiral de Grasse reached the Bay in late August. On September 5, in a stunning engagement called the Battle of the Virginia Capes, the French fleet drove off a somewhat weaker British squadron that had sailed from New York to reach Cornwallis. With French warships in command of the Bay, the pincers that would squeeze Cornwallis into unconditional surrender were almost in place.

Leaving behind a small diversionary force to confuse Clinton and to maintain the impression that the primary allied target was still New York, Washington and Rochambeau moved their armies south with all possible haste. By the end of September, some 7,800 Frenchmen, 5,700 Continentals, and 3,200 militiamen had Yorktown surrounded on land and water. Cornwallis, grappling with his likely fate, wrote Clinton on September 23: "If you cannot relieve me very soon you must expect to hear the worst." Still hoping the Royal navy might break through, the Earl stayed within his well-fortified lines and prepared to hold out against the allied siege. Meanwhile, an exasperated Clinton pushed the navy to get on with another expedition. The relief force ultimately did arrive but with too little and too late. It reached the Bay on October 26, seven days after Cornwallis's surrender had taken place.

Washington and Rochambeau agreed to pursue formal siege operations. On the evening of October 6, the allies began digging their first parallel trench, some 600 yards out from the left side of the British defensive works. Heavy cannonading began three days later. On October 11, the allies started to construct a second parallel trench, this time 300 yards from the enemy trenches and on a direct line with Cornwallis's advanced redoubts Nine and Ten. Under cover of night on October 14, separate parties overran the two redoubts, making it possible to move in with heavy artillery and proceed with the earth-shaking cannonading.

Cornwallis's forces, besides being worn down by incessant artillery fire, now faced two other serious problems. Food supplies had become scarce, and smallpox broke out in the ranks. Early on October 16, the British commander acknowledged his desperate position by sending out a small column against the second parallel trench. Besides spiking a few cannon, which were back in operation within a few hours, the sortie accomplished nothing. That night the Earl attempted to escape with his troops to Gloucester Point across the York River. A howling storm drove them back. On the morning of October 17, his army facing possible extermination, his cannons all but silent, and his parapets crumbling under unrelenting allied artillery fire, Cornwallis sent forth a lone drummer with a brief message: "Propose a cessation of hostilities . . . to settle terms for surrender."

That the most aggressive warrior among the British generals fell into such a trap is paradoxical. Still, Cornwallis was as much at fault as anyone else. He had made a mockery of the southern strategy, and he had defied the instructions of his commanding officer in the North American theater. Clinton, too, was more than culpable. He had ordered Cornwallis's force into a defensive post. Worse yet, he had failed to perceive how vulnerable that army would be on the land side if the French fleet cut off the Earl's escape route through Chesapeake Bay.

Two days of surrender negotiations followed. Washington conceded his adversary almost nothing. He did not promise to protect loyalist partisans with Cornwallis but stated that they would be subject to the dictates of civil authorities. He insisted that British regimental colors be cased in surrender ceremonies,

an insult that General Benjamin Lincoln had endured after ca-
pitulating at Charleston. Further, the British musicians were not
to honor their captors by playing French or American melodies.
The surrender was to be unconditional in every way.

Having submitted on every point, the British army marched
out onto a large field on the bright autumn afternoon of October
19. The "indisposed" Cornwallis did not appear. His second in
command turned over his superior's sword to Benjamin Lincoln, Washington's second, but only after having tried to hand it
to Rochambeau. The Frenchman politely demurred and pointed
toward Washington, indicating through his ennobling gesture
that the victory belonged to the Americans.

As the defeated British columns began to parade that autumn afternoon, their musicians struck up a familiar melody,
"The World Turned Upside Down." No tune could have been
more fitting. The mighty and proud had fallen. A small band of
hardened American regulars, dreaming of a better life, had, with
invaluable French assistance, endured the many dark days of despair following those of sunshine enthusiasm—and now beheld
the prospect of complete triumph. Success at Yorktown would
bring the cause of establishing a republican order in North
America one more vital step closer to legitimacy in the minds of
the indifferent and uncommitted. On the other side that day, the
British had nothing to cheer. They had long since fumbled away
the initiative in America—and also seemed to be losing it elsewhere across the globe. Whether the people of Britain would allow the war to continue, once they learned about Yorktown, had
become the main question.

The scene on the afternoon of October 19 was emotional,
certainly because of everything it signified. The British war effort
had suffered another devastating blow—the loss of an army numbering 7,200 or more. Washington, communicating with Congress, praised "the unremitting Ardor which actuated every Officer and Soldier in the combined Army" that "principally led to
this Important Event." Elsewhere on the field, a distraught British
corporal spoke of his musket as he threw it on a pile of surrendered weapons: "May you never get so good a master again!"

Formulating a Peace Settlement

Contrary to popular lore, the Yorktown triumph was not solely responsible for the first rush in British peace overtures. The situation was more complex. A look at the war map helps explain why the parent nation "had lost its nerve," as Piers Mackesy has written. "It was the timing of the blow which mattered" in making Yorktown so significant.[3] During 1781 and into 1782, His Majesty's forces would experience setbacks in India and the West Indies. In February 1781, a sizable Spanish force under Bernardo de Gálvez began what would become the siege and capture of British-held Pensacola in West Florida. Also, combined Franco-Spanish forces were preparing for a major assault against highly prized Gibraltar, which they had harassed since 1779. The French navy, so important in the Yorktown victory, seemed capable of striking everywhere. Proving the point, French and Spanish vessels had reappeared in the English Channel and were seizing British supply ships bound for America. Threats seemed to face the British empire everywhere, all of which portended the loss of much more than 13 American provinces. In addition, the cost of war had become staggering after seven years of campaigning, especially with so little to show for so much effort. In the context of setbacks across the globe and a towering financial burden, Yorktown stood as a backbreaking loss.

On the other side of the ledger, the British still had 30,000 soldiers deployed in America, controlling vital points from Halifax to St. Augustine. British troop strength far outdistanced that of Washington, which did not add up to more than 20,000 (counting Rochambeau's numbers) in all posts. Likewise, the North ministry was aware of martial protests sapping the patriot war effort from the inside, dissension that did not magically go away with the elation of Yorktown. For instance, Washington sent the bulk of his army northward to the Hudson Highlands in late 1781. There the veterans settled in and allowed their grievances to fester—to the point of near open revolt by March 1783. As another instance, during 1782 a group of disgruntled Continentals in South Carolina plotted to seize Nathanael Greene and some lesser-ranking officers. Their notion was to turn them over to the enemy for ransom payments. Once uncovered, the scheme fizzled; one sergeant was summarily executed, and the other plotters fled to the British.

Even with such turmoil in the patriot ranks, Lord North's ministry could no longer realistically pursue a policy of enduring at all costs when the actual weight of reverses in battle kept undermining expectations of an upturn in events. The task now became that of minimizing imperial losses before the European allies snapped the backbone of the far flung empire.

Yorktown signaled that such a point of unbearable stress was at hand. Official word of Cornwallis's entrapment reached London on Sunday, November 25, 1781. Germain, the intractable American secretary, carried the report to Lord North, who received the news "as he would have taken a ball in the breast." Again and again, the astonished cabinet head exclaimed: "Oh God, it is all over!" North was sure that Parliament, increasingly restive about the financial burdens of war and stresses of worldwide military pressure, would not accept this stunning loss with equanimity. Even though King George III wanted to continue, North's instincts were correct. Britain was a war-weary nation that had grown tired of pronouncements that the glory of the empire depended upon maintaining all the American appendages. Sentiment for continuing the war effort reached its lowest point in March 1782, when Parliament reconvened from its winter recess. On March 4, the House of Commons decreed that any citizen wanting to pursue the war was to be considered an enemy of the realm.

North and Germain, as well as George III, had to accept that verdict. Knowing that he was fully out of step, Germain had already resigned, but not before he recalled Henry Clinton, whom he never liked. General Sir Guy Carleton, governor of Quebec Province, took over as the North American commander through the evacuation process. The much maligned Lord North surrendered his post on March 20, concluding his 12-year tenure with these words as he left the Commons: "Goodnight, gentlemen.

You see what it is to be in the secret!" Perhaps to save face, George III mumbled a bit about abdicating. Then he turned to the task of finding a new chief minister, one devoted to the construction of peace. Lord Rockingham, who held pro-American sentiments and now favored the granting of American independence, accepted the office. The moment for serious negotiations thus had arrived with the warmer spring weather of 1782.

Meanwhile, the challenge facing the designated American peace commissioners in Europe had become more complex by 1782, largely because of French and Spanish diplomatic maneuvering. The Spanish originally had entered the war on the narrowest grounds—and only as France's ally. Their foreign minister, the ever calculating Count Floridablanca, encouraged Spain to do so in 1779 with the permission of his sovereign, the Bourbon King Charles III (distantly related to the French monarch), in return for two basic guarantees: first, that France would persist in the war until Spain regained Gibraltar and, second, that any new American nation would be so strictly circumscribed with respect to territory that it could never become a threat to Spain's imperial holdings in the Americas. In particular, the Spanish court feared the emergence of a flourishing republican nation that could serve as a model for disaffected Spanish subjects elsewhere in the New World. Absolutists that they were, King Charles and Floridablanca were reluctant to support the formation of a political entity that might, at some future point, become a serious threat to Spain's long-term interests.

Vergennes, no fool, did not question Spanish logic. The French foreign minister comprehended that the creation of a vital American republic could imperil monarchical and imperial systems everywhere. The essential wartime goal, Vergennes believed, was the dismemberment of the hated British foe. Sacrificing American interests, he reasoned, would not inhibit this main objective—and might even support it, especially if France and Spain could force the Americans into a state of dependency, primarily commercial, upon these two Bourbon powers. By fusing short- and long-term objectives, France and Spain began to imagine that they were going to be major victors in the artful game of diplomatic intrigue. Great Britain and the 13 states would be the losers. The monarchical-imperial status quo would be preserved, yet with a decided shift in the overall balance of power toward the Bourbon powers.

Although the French generously supported the American war effort with troops and matériel (which Spain did not do), Vergennes worked diligently, especially after 1778, to assure that nothing more emerged from the war than a weak political entity squeezed into constraining territorial boundaries. He also envisioned the formation of an informal commercial empire with French merchants taking up where British commercial interests had left off. That French loans and direct military assistance were so critical to winning the war when that vital support was being put forth for the creation of a nonnation in North America is one of the great paradoxes of the times. Only the logic of national self-interest can help explain such contradictions.

Over the years, the three designated peace commissioners most in contact with the European courts—John Adams, Benjamin Franklin, and John Jay—had become wary of the intentions of Vergennes and Floridablanca. They had their guard up by 1781, if not before. Vergennes, having put pressure on a Congress fearful of the loss of allied support, a Congress that contained middle states' merchants eager to develop strong commercial ties with Spain and France, got the American central government to agree that, beyond the matter of independence, the peace commissioners were to claim nothing without France's prior approval. By early 1782, it appeared that Vergennes could virtually dictate the content of peace terms for the Americans that would be wholly favorable to the Bourbon powers.

Vergennes believed he was in control of the negotiations. The peace commissioners, however, chose to ignore their Congressional instructions. Outwardly pleasant, if not obsequious, toward Vergennes, they constructed treaty details with the British but did not keep the French minister up to date. Initial talks got under way between Franklin and Richard Oswald, an aging

Scottish slave trader who was Britain's first emissary to the American commissioners, during the spring of 1782. Franklin, vitally concerned about legitimate national interests, promised Vergennes that the Americans would seek France's approval for all proposed terms. Vergennes, perhaps trusting too much in the Philadelphian's republican-looking countenance, encouraged the discussion of basic points for his review. By the time he saw the proposed settlement, he had his own reasons for not trying to scuttle what the Americans had wrought.

Instability in George III's new government after Lord North's resignation helped the American effort. The ministry agreed that the former colonists had to be drawn away from the Bourbon allies. The question was how to facilitate that goal. Lord Rockingham preferred to recognize American independence and let the rebels go their own way, so long as the peace treaty did not solidify ties between the former colonists and France and Spain. Lord Shelburne, who had succeeded Germain as the colonial secretary, subscribed to independence in name only. He insisted that proper accords would effectively keep American commerce spinning as usual in the old imperial orbit. The difference in approach became a moot point in July 1782 when Rockingham suddenly died. His passing cleared the way for Shelburne, who preferred a more rigid negotiating posture. The new minister would allow certain concessions to assure that the Bourbon powers could not so weaken the American republic that the former colonists might be used in some undesirable way against British interests. Wanting to assure their dominance over American trade and give the republic enough strength to stand up to France and Spain, the British agreed to a generous territorial settlement that otherwise might not have materialized.

In the preliminary articles of peace, signed at Paris by Richard Oswald and the American commissioners on November 30, 1782, Great Britain did much more than recognize independence—and set the American patriots free. The articles established the Mississippi River as the western boundary and, in a secret provision, settled 31° of north latitude as the southern boundary. The agreement recognized American fishing rights, although as a "liberty," off the coasts of Nova Scotia and New-foundland; it also stipulated that rebel government confiscations of loyalist property had to stop; and it obligated Congress to urge the states to return seized loyalist holdings. The British promised that their army would not carry away slaves upon evacuation, but they refused to concede the vast territorial entity of Canada. On that point, Shelburne was adamant. The Americans did not need this region, he reasoned, to have enough strength to counter any Bourbon pretensions about dominating the new republic.

For years John Adams had worried that bringing an enduring republic into being would not be destroyed in war but in peace negotiations. "America," he wrote, "has been a football between contending nations from the beginning, and it is easy to foresee, that France and England both will endeavor to involve us in their future wars. It is our interest and duty," Adams concluded, "to be completely independent, and to have nothing to do with either of them, but in commerce." Generally, the preliminary peace treaty was satisfactory from that perspective. Certainly, the accords represented about as much as the one-time colonists could have expected to obtain—a sufficiently broad base on which to construct a worthy national edifice. It may be counted as double irony that Great Britain, the enemy in battle, had helped lay that foundation (admittedly in its own self-interest) when the patriots' wartime allies preferred as spindly a platform as possible for the new American nation.

Franklin accepted the task of explaining to Vergennes that the American commissioners had not obeyed their instructions. The French minister received the news rather passively. For him, the timing of the Americans' preliminary settlement with England now worked to France's advantage. By the fall of 1782, the tide of international war, so decisively running against Britain at the end of 1781, had now turned against France and Spain. In April 1782, the British naval force of Admiral George Brydges Rodney had shattered the French fleet of Admiral de Grasse in a bloody Caribbean battle. In October, a Franco-Spanish expeditionary force gave up its attempt to dislodge the British from Gibraltar. As with Britain before, the cost of continuing the war with such expensive disasters was becoming a formidable burden for Louis XVI's overextended treasury.

Against this backdrop Franklin observed, in communicating the proposed Anglo-American peace accords to Vergennes, that *"the English, I just now learn, flatter themselves that they have already divided us."* "I hope this little misunderstanding will therefore be kept a secret," added the disingenuous Philadelphian, "and that they will find themselves totally mistaken." Franklin's carefully chosen words must have amused Vergennes. Not to be outdone, the French minister used the preliminary Anglo-American treaty as an excuse for repudiating all Spanish commitments and moving forward with the broader peace settlement.

The new American state thus survived the pitfalls of diplomatic intrigue and was about to earn legitimacy among the nations of the world. Still, no person could safely predict the future of the new republican order, especially if Washington's army felt too aggrieved by its sense of civilian betrayal to lay down its arms and disband without strife.

The Newburgh Conspiracy

The prospect of peace should have made all Americans jubilant. The imminence of a settlement, however, made the Continental army increasingly restive. Washington's soldiers, some 10,000 men and an estimated 1,000 women, had settled into the army's final cantonment at New Windsor, New York, a hilly area slightly north of West Point near the town of Newburgh on the west bank of the Hudson River. The Continentals remained on wartime alert, yet the daily routine in camp was hardly demanding enough to keep these veterans from thinking about personal opportunities after the war—and obligations still outstanding. The troops worried among themselves about pay arrearages and whether other enlistment promises would ever be honored. The officers began to fear that the army would be disbanded before Congress found the means to fund pensions. The army became more anxious, if not more surly, with each passing week, so much so that Washington, who had hoped to spend the upcoming winter of 1782–83 at Mount Vernon, canceled his plans.

Historians disagree about the extent of the drama that was about to unfold. The broad issue was financial justice for an army that viewed itself as treated miserably by an ungrateful civilian populace. According to Richard H. Kohn, disunity characterized the officer corps in regard to how to ensure its interests. Washington was in the middle and was the voice of moderation. One faction, usually loyal to the commander but now troubled that a peace settlement would allow Congress to renege on the pension issue, decided to put strong pressure on the central government. Important leaders in this group were Generals Henry Knox and Alexander McDougall. Another faction, centering on Horatio Gates, second in command at Newburgh, appears to have thought in the most dangerous of all terms—those of a potential military *coup d'état,* if necessary, against the central government.

Kohn has described Gates as "an overbearing and sensitive general whose bad blood with Washington was long-standing." He was an officer whose "pretensions had suffered for years."[4] Gates, the so-called "hero of Saratoga," had been all but sacked from the army for his regrettable performance at Camden. After that debacle, he returned home but repeatedly pestered Congress for a hearing to exonerate his name. To placate him, the delegates restored Gates to rank as Washington's second in command at Newburgh. The commander welcomed him in gentlemanly fashion, but he still mistrusted Gates because he thought of him as a key player in the Conway Cabal, a person who, like Charles Lee, had imagined himself worthy of heading the Continental army.

The Knox-McDougall group seized the initiative and provoked a flurry of controversy toward the end of 1782 when they sent a strongly worded petition to Congress. The officers bluntly declared: "We have borne all that men can bear—our property is expended—our private resources are at an end." They explained that their friends were "wearied out and disgusted with their endless applications for credit." They demanded that half-pay pensions be commuted to five years of full pay; if Congress did not act and guarantee them such severance payments, they pointedly warned, "any further experiments on their patience may have fatal effects."

In 1780, at the nadir of the war effort, the officers had threatened Congress with mass resignations. Now, many of them were hinting rather directly that they might use the force of arms to exact at least a minimum of financial recompense from civilian officials. Perhaps, too, they were implying that someone, such as George Washington, might be superimposed over the central government as a dictator, as some had suggested during the most difficult days of the war. The military subverting civil authority would be one means to force the population to recognize the service of the army and to treat it with justice, even if such a precipitous action violated one of the most sacred of republican principles about the distribution of power in society. Images of Cromwell—even Caesar—were now dancing in many patriot heads.

To thicken the plot, a group of delegates, known as the nationalists, saw the petition as a tool to coerce the states into providing a permanent revenue source for Congress. This bloc centered on Robert Morris of Philadelphia, certainly among the wealthiest persons in America. That Morris was a financial genius cannot be denied. That he and other nationalists viewed the central government under the Articles of Confederation as hopelessly weak and in need of a real infusion of power was also true. The inability of Congress to deal with basic wartime issues appalled Morris and the emerging nationalist group. Their vision of the republic encompassed the need for a central government capable of providing military strength, economic stability, and political endurance. Unlike republican purists, they did not fear concentrated power. At the end of 1782, they had already tried to increase the authority of Congress—and had failed. The officers' threatening petition gave them new hope.

Important Morris associates in Congressional dealings were Alexander Hamilton, James Madison, and Gouverneur Morris (no relation to Robert). Robert Morris was serving as Superintendent of Finance, one of four administrative posts, along with war, marine, and foreign affairs, established by Congress in 1781 to bring greater coherency to the nation-making process. Before Morris assumed his duties, the delegates had approved the Impost Plan of 1781, a proposed constitutional amendment that would give the central government a permanent source of revenue from duties of 5 percent *ad valorem* on all imported goods. The Impost would assure Congress the ability to fund many of its war debts, including such obligations to the army as the officers' pensions or their commutation into lump sum severance payments. Like any amendment to the Articles, the Impost Plan, considered linchpin legislation in the nascent nationalist drive to strengthen the central government, required the approval of all thirteen sovereign states. In November 1782, Rhode Island dealt the plan a lethal blow when its legislature voted against ratification.

In this context, the Morris group grabbed onto the officers' remonstrance. To help reinvigorate their plans, as Hamilton wrote, "the necessity and discontents of the army presented themselves as a powerful engine." The idea was to use the latent threat of military force as a means of pushing the states into adopting a permanent revenue source for Congress. After all, securing such a base was critical to the army's interests, if it realistically wanted to see the payment of back salaries, commuted pensions, or other forms of financial indebtedness.

To make this threatened use of martial force fully effective, the nationalists in Congress needed Washington's involvement, perhaps even his willingness to lead the army into the field as a temporary expedient to frighten state leaders into submission. The nationalists were well aware of Washington's temperament and attitudes. Although the commander openly advocated a more powerful central government, he appreciated the dangers of the military intervening in civil affairs. Washington feared the destructive potential of his standing army of embittered veterans. Throughout the war, he had scrupulously subordinated his own feelings about key issues to civil authority. He knew that decision making resulting from martial threats and possible force was antithetical to rule by civil law and human reason. He understood that the Revolution's goal of establishing freedom-oriented republican institutions could not be realized if civilian officials were eclipsed, even once, or even seriously intimidated by united, uniformed military forces.

Washington wanted the grievances of his army properly redressed, but he refused to countenance the nationalist plotters. He could feel the imminent danger of the Revolution, begun with a spirit of citizen virtue and moral commitment, succumbing to the tyranny of military dictatorship. Such an ending would have rendered to dust all the human travail and suffering of the past eight years. The commander in chief was not about to let his army or himself be used as an instrument of coercion, the way some standing armies had been manipulated by power-hungry leaders in the past.

The Morris nationalists in Congress, despite the odds against involving Washington, were direct in their communications. As Hamilton discreetly explained to the commander in chief, "the great *desideratum* . . . is the establishment of general funds, which alone can do justice to the Creditors of the United States. . . . In this the influence of the army, properly directed, may cooperate." Hamilton sent these calculated suggestions to Washington in mid-February 1783. At that time, informal word about the preliminary peace settlement had just reached Congressional leaders in Philadelphia. If peace came and the Continental army disbanded without incident, the potential leverage of massed military pressure would be forever lost. Washington appreciated these circumstances and prepared himself for the seemingly inevitable confrontation, which he depicted as the officers throwing "themselves into the gulph of Civil horror."

What Washington suspected was that the Morris nationalists, for lack of alternatives, had struck some sort of a deal with Horatio Gates. Historians have debated whether the initiative came from Gates and officers loyal to him, their goal being to supplant Washington at the head of the army and then have the "hero of Saratoga" lead it into the field. Some deny that Gates took any such initiative or had any intentions of trying to undermine Washington.[5]

The heavy involvement of Gates's subordinates in the final stage of the crisis does not support this categorical exoneration. Gates was clearly up to something, most likely working in conjunction with, and being used by, the Morris nationalists. Richard H. Kohn has argued that the Morris nationalists apparently had turned their plotting into "a treacherous double game, fraught with uncertainty." They intended to have Gates "spark the explosion" of the army, thus serving to break state resistance to fixed revenues for Congress. However, Hamilton warned Washington of the impending uprising, hoping that he could contain the mutiny, once it had begun, and save the new nation from the likes of Gates.[6] The danger, of course, was that the upheaval could get so out of hand that Washington, despite his charisma, would be powerless to contain the turmoil. Under such circumstances, with Gates in apparent command, a politically oppressive autocracy could have become the end-product of the Newburgh machinations.

Whatever the extent of Gates's involvement, the crisis came to a head in March 1783. Word from Philadelphia reached Gates's quarters that the time for action was at hand. By Monday, March 10, John Armstrong, one of Gates's aides, had written the first Newburgh Address, a document full of inflammatory statements. Christopher Richmond, another Gates aide-de-camp, circulated copies to officers throughout the camp. In blunt terms, the Address spoke bitterly of civilian ingratitude for what the army had accomplished; it mocked "the meek language of entreating memorials"; and it advised every officer to "suspect the man who would advise to more moderation and longer forbearance," a clear negative allusion to Washington. Since Congress and the states had not provided for financial justice, the Address declared, decisive action was at last necessary: "If peace, that nothing shall separate them [Congress] from your arms but death: if war, that . . . you will retire to some unsettled country, smile in your turn, and 'mock when their fear cometh on.'" Finally, the Address urged every officer to attend a special meeting the next day to discuss grievances in full and to prepare for further action.

Washington, outraged but not surprised by the Address, given earlier warnings, prepared himself for the showdown. He had already appealed to the Knox-McDougall group for support. Their dislike of Gates helped bring them around. More secure with this base, on Tuesday morning, March 11, the commander issued general orders that labeled the Address and its proposed meeting as "disorderly" and "irregular." Washington advised the officers to meet, but on his authority at noon on Saturday, March 15—the Ides. He would not attend this gathering, or so he stated, so that everyone could speak freely. The implication was that Gates, as the second ranking officer, would be in charge. No doubt fooled by Washington's tactic, which led them to think the commander was unaware of their objective, the Gates group acceded to Washington's general order through the issuance of a second Newburgh Address. This document, also written by Armstrong, accepted the new meeting date and cautioned the officers that a short delay must not be allowed to "lessen the *independence* of your sentiments."

March 15, 1783, was a day of great tension. As the officers's meeting came to order with Gates in the chair, Washington strode into the room and walked forward toward his adversary. He asked for permission to speak and then turned to confront his angry subordinates. Searching for the right words, he urged patience, and he characterized the first Newburgh Address as a document appealing to "passions" rather than "reason and good sense." How could the army, Washington asked forcefully, turn against the country "in the extremist hour of her distress." Had the officers suffered so much for so long only to sow "the seeds of discord and separation" in civil society? "My God! What can this writer have in view," Washington queried rhetorically, "by recommending such measures? Can he be a friend to the army? Can he be a friend to the country? Rather is he not an insidious foe?"

Sensing that he was still not convincing his comrades, Washington stated that he wanted to read a letter. He reached into his pocket and pulled out a pair of eyeglasses. The gathering took immediate notice; none had seen their leader wear glasses before. Catching their surprise, Washington calmly explained: "Gentlemen, you must pardon me. I have grown gray in your service and now find myself growing blind." His words and their larger meaning caught the assemblage off guard. The commander had verbalized for all of them their sense of personal sacrifice, of thwarted dignity, and of sullied honor.

The officers suddenly grasped Washington's message. The army had already established the point that such concepts as self-sacrifice and citizen virtue, upon which the republic was to rest, had gained true meaning in America. Regardless of the fickleness of so many "sunshine" patriots, the high example set by the long-term officers and the regulars had brought the dream of a republican polity to the verge of reality. Even if the nation never remembered who had made the real sacrifices nor gave them deserved recognition or financial recompense, that did not seem to matter so much now. Washington wanted everyone who had truly sacrificed to take comfort in what they had accomplished—and the legacy they had left. To destroy everything on the verge of success would have been the most cruel of ironies. The assembled officers thus reflected on the ideal of deeply committed virtue; and some, including the most cynical veterans, openly wept. Washington had reconciled his officers to the cause of liberty, despite their sense of betrayal by the Congress, the states, and the American populace they had served so well.

The Newburgh Conspiracy quickly passed into oblivion, handed down by writers to our own time as a minor tempest, until studied more intensively in recent times. To downplay its significance, however, is to support the myth of unbounded harmony and unity in the cause, to keep maintaining the impression that American patriots knitted together seamlessly made the republican experiment the harvest of their arduous martial labor. Reality did not follow so idyllic a path. The Newburgh confrontation, representing the culmination of various group protests within the Continental army, took place because Washington's officers felt such profound alienation toward patriot civilians on whose behalf they had supposedly been giving their all, even to the point of life itself.

The officers could not predict whether the rank and file would have followed them into the field, since the two groups had never identified their interests closely enough to protest effectively in common. No doubt the fear of standing alone brought some of the officers into line, but recalling their sense of duty cannot be overly stressed. As a culminating event to unstable relations between army and society, the crisis also showed that the officers were capable of subordinating self-interest to the public welfare, the essential test of virtuous citizenship. Because of their restraint, a military coup, with some American Caesar rising out of the chaos, did not eventuate. Washington had controlled his new modeled army, a potentially fearsome creature unwanted in 1775 and 1776 but made necessary because of laggard popular support for the cause. Most significantly, the army had remained on the side of liberty and republicanism while tempted, even dared by civilians who withheld support and encouragement from 1777 on, to become a praetorian force. When most sorely enticed, Washington's army reaffirmed the principle of subordinating military power to civil authority. Paradoxically, this same hardcore group of regulars, so shortchanged by so many patriots (and feared by ideologues as the antithesis of the republican ideal of the militia) set the highest example of selfless behavior in Revolutionary America.

Transition to a Postwar World

Newburgh was one ending in the transition to peace. There would be others as the new nation extricated itself from war and sought legitimacy as an independent republic. News of preliminary peace started to spread across the landscape, and Congress proclaimed a cessation of hostilities on April 11, 1783. Final peace terms, involving separate treaties among the belligerents, would be formally ratified in Paris during September. Meanwhile, Great Britain began to evacuate its military forces. Congress, despite the sentiments of such nationalists as Robert Morris and Alexander Hamilton, was anxious to demobilize the Continental army before some new threat to civil authority developed. In the aftermath of Newburgh, Congress did commute officers' pensions into lump-sum payments equivalent to five years of full salary. The central body also framed a new impost plan with a 25-year limitation clause, but the states never ratified this plan, the effect of which was to keep the central government both penniless and powerless. Without revenue, Congress could not honor its lump-sum severance payments. By June 1783, the "furlough" of Washington's regulars was well under way. Congress did not want to disband the Continentals officially until British regiments had left New York, Charleston, Savannah, and other east-coast points of troop concentration.

Most of Washington's regulars returned to civilian life in relative peace. Each furloughed soldier received three months' pay in "final settlement certificates," a pittance of what Congress owed them. The certificates represented a form of fiat money to mollify the soldiers, so that they would not leave the army "enraged, complaining of injustice—and committing enormities on the innocent Inhabitants in every direction," explained Washington. Not all went off quietly. An angry group of Pennsylvania veterans marched on Philadelphia in June, and some troops from the southern theater bolstered them. They surrounded the State House, where Congress and the Pennsylvania assembly met, and demanded immediate financial satisfaction. The intimidated delegates, warned ahead of time of the danger, begged the Pennsylvania government for militia protection. State officials offered neither solace nor assistance. While the soldiery shouted insults, the Congressional delegates filed out of the State House and left the scene. So irate were these civilian leaders, some of them nationalists, that they relocated themselves first to Princeton, New Jersey, then soon thereafter to Annapolis, Maryland. They could do little else. They had no financial resources and no real power; and with the coming of peace, they had to bow before republican purists who believed that a central government with any tangible authority was a likely engine for political tyranny.

The confrontation at the State House in Philadelphia was the last major protest from any group of Continental soldiers. As for Washington, he still hoped that his veteran troops would receive proper compensation. In early June 1783, he sent a circular letter to the various states and called for a strengthened Congress and a just financial settlement. With respect to the central government, the issue was whether the new nation was to be "respectable and prosperous, or contemptible and miserable." The former condition depended on providing Congress with "a Supreme Power to regulate and govern the general concerns of the Confederated republic, without which the Union cannot be of long duration." Washington exhorted the states to give the central government the capacity to discharge the wartime national debt (including obligations owed the army). He added, poignantly, that he had personally pledged himself to officers and troops alike, "that their Country would finally do them complete and ample Justice."

In the end, the down and outers who proved to be Washington's steadiest soldiers never received much compensation for loyal services rendered the infant nation. Private Joseph Plumb Martin, in later life, described these circumstances with exceptional candor: "The country was rigorous in exacting *my* compliance to my engagements to a punctilio, but equally careless in performing her contracts with me; and why so? One reason was because she had all the power in her own hands, and I had none."

Besides settlement certificates, the furloughed soldiers retained their muskets, ammunition if they decided to take it, and the clothes on their backs. Furlough papers, which proved honorable discharges, could be used at a later date to claim land warrant certificates for promised bounty lands. The land warrants soon became another form of fiat currency, to be traded off quickly for the necessities of life. The result was that few soldiers who dreamed of a freehold stake in the new republic realized their goal. Land speculators soon started snapping up the warrants for sums far below their face value and eventually made easy profits in selling off claims to the "soldiers' lands" in the Ohio country. Meanwhile, most of Washington's veterans reentered civilian life at the same poverty level that they had left behind—and remained there for the rest of their lifetimes. Ultimately, only former slaves, redemptioners, and felons benefited in some immediate way from Continental service. The bulk of them gained their personal freedom.

Joseph Plumb Martin described the initial readjustment process in this unvarnished fashion: "When the country had drained the last drop of service it could screw out of the poor soldiers, they were turned adrift like old worn-out horses, and nothing said about land to pasture them upon." Martin, who became a humble dirt farmer in Maine, never regretted his personal sacrifices and contributions. He felt immense satisfaction in having measured up to the self-sacrificing ideal of citizen virtue, and his classic memoirs convey unquestionable pride in his years of Continental service, despite the pitiful severance settlement he received in 1783.[7]

Martin also expressed great affection for President James Monroe and others, who in 1818 cleared the way for veterans' pensions in the form of financial relief for destitute Continental veterans. (Modest disability pensions had been available before war's end for those unfortunates who had suffered nearly total destruction of life and limb.) Then in 1832 Congress granted all Revolutionary veterans, including militiamen, pensions without restrictions. Historian William H. Glasson (*Federal Military Pensions in the United States*) has estimated that the average living pensioner was 74-years-old in 1831.[8] Perhaps as many as 60,000 to 65,000 veterans were still alive some 49 years after the final peace settlement and, no doubt, those poor enough to get pensions were grateful for the financial compensation.

Historian John Resch has argued that pensions became possible because the War of 1812 with Great Britain had a liberating effect on popular conceptions of Revolutionary era Continental soldiers. "No longer was the Revolution imagined as a conflict waged by a virtuous and patriotic citizenry and its band of amateur soldiers," Resch has stated. The "soldiers, rather than the populace as a whole, became the symbol of the spirit of '76." As such, "regulars emerged in the memory of the war from the recessed ranks of the distrusted to the front lines of esteemed patriots."[9]

Joseph Plumb Martin would have disagreed. What distressed the aging veterans most of all, he wrote during the 1820s, was the psychological reaction of friends and neighbors to this long delayed recompense. Martin's neighbors apparently took to arguing that the pensions were unfair because the Continental army had been "needless." They continued to assert "that the militia were competent for all that the crisis required," and that "it would have been much better for the country to have done it than for us [the Continentals] to have been eating so much provisions and wearing out so much clothing, when our services were worse than useless." Martin considered "it cruel to be thus vilified," but he had the personal fortitude to slough off such "hardhearted" sentiment and to accept it for what it was—cracker-barrel commentary. In the end, he took solace in what he and his Continental brethren had accomplished in forging a chain of "Independence and liberty" out of so little in the way of basic war matériel and popular patriot support.

The crushing burdens of poverty and public ingratitude also fell on veterans' wives and families. A few of the hundreds of women who became a part of rebel forces received pensions, but the vast majority did not. Many instead shared the hard lot of widows and orphans left by the war. Recognizing at least partial responsibility for their plight, the states had provided some small assistance to these unfortunates. Even this aid, however, came grudgingly.

The ordeal of Electa Campfield, for example, the widow of a Continental, typified what happened to most women when they applied for relief. She first wrote to the county court, stating that her husband's death had left her "with one Child and without any kind of support," and that she had suffered "innumerable difficulties during the whole of the war." To receive benefits, she next had to locate her husband's former officers and obtain sworn statements establishing his service record in his New Jersey regiment. The minister of her local congregation also had to supply a deposition testifying to the legality of her marriage, and the local Overseer of the Poor then swore to her legal residency. All this information went to the court, which approved her application and sent it to the state legislature. Widow Campfield then waited seven months for the assembly to approve her request and to authorize payments from the state treasury.

Other orphans and widows apparently never heard that help was available, and some who had applied became thoroughly disheartened with the arduous application procedures. Worn down by the process, they neglected to follow up on submitted claims, which occasionally meant that approved benefits were never collected. The situation abetted many personal tragedies but was also indicative of society's misgivings about awarding pensions of any kind.

Antipension sentiment also bit deeply because it disparaged the fortitude and sacrifices of those men and women who had stood up with Washington for the long-term fight. Howard H. Peckham's compilation of American casualties (*The Toll of Independence*) conservatively estimates a total death figure of 25,674 among Revolutionary soldiers and sailors (7,174 in battle, an estimated 10,000 who succumbed to disease in camp, and an estimated 8,500 prisoners who died while in enemy hands). Another 8,241 were wounded in battle and survived, while 1,426 were missing in action—some of whom may have died with others deserting or returning unnoticed after battle to the ranks.[10] If the basic estimate of 175,000 total participants, including regulars and militia actually in the field, is more or less accurate (Peckham uses the higher base of 200,000), one out of every five soldiers did not come away from the war personally unscathed. Furthermore, since the bulk of the fighting fell to the Continentals, they likely experienced a casualty rate as high as 30 to 40 percent from all causes, dramatically higher than the figure of 13 percent in losses suffered by Union troops during the much bloodier Civil War.

In his analysis, Peckham points out that the War for Independence, among all wars involving American armies, ranks only behind the Civil War in numbers of casualties relative to total population.[11] Since not that many patriots chose to stay in the Continental ranks for extended periods, the debt owed to

Washington's hardened, long-term veterans did not deserve to be minimized, especially since a substantial portion of them became wartime casualties or were long since dead and gone by 1818. Society's memories, however, have a way of deceiving reality and becoming self-serving, as Martin's neighbors so strikingly demonstrated.

By early 1784, the Continental army had ceased to exist for all practical purposes. Only some 600 troops were still in the ranks with the responsibility of guarding military stores at West Point and Springfield, Massachusetts, and for assisting with the restoration of civilian government in New York City. For many nationalists, the new republic needed some form of ongoing military establishment, however circumscribed in numbers. However, they saw little hope for their goal of strengthening the central government. Disgusted by the inchoate state of public affairs, many had given up and gone home. Typical were Robert Morris, who had left the superintendency of finance, and Alexander Hamilton and James Madison, who had resigned their seats in Congress even before their terms were up. With localists back in control of Congress, the likelihood was remote that a creditable type of national military establishment would be maintained.

The leading nationalists firmly believed in a strong military constabulary, even during peacetime. However, the coming of peace meant that their "hopes for a large, centrally controlled standing army evaporated," as Walter Millis has described the situation.[12] All that was left were those 600 troops, not much of a security force to stand up against new external threats or domestic turbulence of any kind.

Washington, now in retirement at Mount Vernon, yet a strongly committed nationalist (as were many of his former officers), wanted Congress to keep up a respectable force. Even before furloughing the army had begun, he prepared his "Sentiments on a Peace Establishment," derived from the advice of key officers and from wartime experience. The commander knew that a large peacetime force flew in the face of antistanding-army ideology. Thus he recommended a small regular army of 2,631 to protect the new nation's borders and to deal with possible Indian uprisings and domestic turmoil. To back up this core of regulars, Washington called for well-trained militia units to include all white, male citizens between the ages of 18 and 50. To avoid wartime problems, all militia would drill according to uniform guidelines and regulations. Furthermore, some male citizens between the ages of 18 and 25 would be singled out for more rigorous duty in elite units. Although the total force would consist mostly of volunteers, a reflection of the martial obligations embedded in citizenship, it would also be better trained than were colonial militia and would have regulars at the core with vital support from a limited number of elite militia units. Also, the whole constabulary would be subject to Congressional as opposed to unpredictable and divided state authority.

The "Sentiments" did not go as far as Washington would have liked. Because he was always "aware of fiscal and political limitations," as Dave R. Palmer has written in *Provide for the Common Defense,* the retired commander "wielded a practical pen." His plan "represented what he thought to be within reach, not all that the new nation actually needed."[13] Washington would have preferred a more numerous core of standing regulars, but he had experienced the national failure to mobilize such a cadre even during the urgency of war. Furthermore, he accepted ideological constraints. Washington pointed out to Hamilton, in conveying the plan to Congress, that "a large standing Army in time of Peace has ever been considered dangerous to the liberties of a Country." Thus "a few Troops" were all that any should ask for, but they were "indispensably necessary." "Fortunately for us," he concluded, "our relative situation requires but few."

There was also another side to Washington's thinking. The idea behind compulsory training for all male citizens related to the obligations of citizenship in the context of wartime troop shortages and the inconsistent performance of militia. The commander wrote in the plan: "It may be laid down as a primary position, and the basis of our system, that every Citizen who enjoys the protection of a free Government, owes not only a proportion of his property, but even his personal services to the defense of it." Here was an unequivocal restatement regarding the fundamental duties of each citizen in a republican polity.

Washington was doing much more than merely endorsing the concept of the citizen-soldier and universal military obligation, as essentially argued by the first modern student of the "Sentiments," John McAuley Palmer in *Washington, Lincoln, Wilson*.[14] He was trying to support the legitimacy of the newly enshrined republican order by establishing a mechanism that would result in mandatory virtuous behavior. At the same time, he was upholding his convictions about the necessity of having a core standing force as the primary unit of defense. Also, as Russell F. Weigley has stressed in *Towards an American Army,* Washington hoped to broaden the hard core base with "a militia in which some men, at least, would be much like regulars." Those in the elite units would become "a special force of carefully trained men, capable of immediate resistance to European regulars, within the general militia."[15]

Despite the efforts of Hamilton and other nationalists, Washington's "Sentiments," as well as similar plans presented by Baron von Steuben and others, would not be realized for several years. Congress, reduced to virtual insignificance, declared on June 2, 1784, that the remaining establishment should be discharged, except for 80 troops to guard military stores. Piously, the delegates concluded that "standing armies in time of peace are inconsistent with the principles of republican government." This action epitomizes how weak and helpless the central government had become within a year of the end of hostilities.

Myth and Tradition: A Political/Military Settlement

The new nation, somewhat reassured of its republican fervor and virtuous fiber with independence now a reality, easily retreated into traditional antistanding-army thinking. When Washington officially resigned from the service on December 23, 1783, everyone present was on the verge of tears. No Caesar or Cromwell he, the man who could have become a dictator offered his "sincere Congratulations to Congress" in "presenting myself before them to surrender into their hands the trust committed to me." Once again, images of Cincinnatus abounded, for it seemed to those present that Washington desired nothing more than the thanks of a grateful citizenry and the chance to return to his plow.

Republican ideologues did not forget that some persons had urged Washington during the darkest days of the contest to seize power as Caesar and Cromwell once had. When Henry Knox and Baron von Steuben led the officer corps in establishing the Society of Cincinnati in 1783, many shrill voices rose in clamorous denunciation of an apparent desire for a military aristocracy, if not something worse. The officers themselves sought an exclusive fraternal group to which only persons of their grade who had been in rank for a minimum of three years or were in uniform at the end of hostilities could belong. Furthermore, they proposed that membership be hereditary with only first sons of succeeding generations being eligible for affiliation. Besides exclusiveness, they had an agenda that included lobbying for commutation and setting up a charity fund to assist former comrades who failed in making the economic transition back to civilian life. The officers, through the Cincinnati, wanted to offer each other the recognition that civilian patriots had so long withheld from them. Critics, by comparison, complained that the Society was not only inherently unrepublican but also had tyrannical designs. Gossip spread widely—for instance, that the real purpose of the charity fund was to have monies available for the officers' planned takeover of the government.

Part of the reaction to the Cincinnati, too, reflected the officers' largely pronationalist preferences in politics, a logical outgrowth of wartime frustrations. That they had insisted on pensions, now wanted more power at the center, and desired a respectable peacetime military establishment made them very suspect to attacks by insecure republican localists (later called Antifederalists). Furthermore, the retired officers seemed to be taking too much credit for the Revolution's triumphal course. They were not being fair in neglecting the contributions of noncombatants, who with peace at hand were demanding a larger share of recognition.

Some contemporary commentators began to explain away why the citizenry had not been more eager to defend liberty. Soon they would declare that the people were actually worthy participants all along, hard evidence to the contrary notwithstanding. An early instance of this kind of imaginative historical reconstruction may be found in Mercy Otis Warren's treatment of the war years in her *History of the Rise, Progress and Termination of the American Revolution,* initially published in 1805.[16] Warren's study typifies how a contemporary's concern with public virtue served to modify historical reality and underpin a misleading tradition. Writing most of her study shortly after the war, Warren admitted that participation fell off after 1776. The real problem, she asserted, had to do with self-serving leaders ambitious for personal profit and high political and military offices. What saved the cause from these nascent nationalists was the middle-class citizen-soldier, who behaved with a keen sense of decorum and duty throughout the war. Citizen-soldiers were always pure in word and deed and did, after all, compose the bulk of the army in the field. As one example of Warren's proof, she claimed that the "mutinous disposition" of the soldiers who marched on Congress in June 1783 "did not appear to have infected the whole army: many of the soldiers were the substantial yeomanry of the country."[17]

In this transformation of reality, the army's down and outers were now troublemakers, as neatly juxtaposed to ever virtuous citizens-in-arms. According to republican ideology, they should have been the great stabilizing influence, so apparently they were. In turn, those who threatened the cause after 1783 were militarists of the nationalist stripe, individuals who favored the formation of the Society of the Cincinnati, and the lower orders, who could always be duped by designing persons grasping after power for its own sake.

Warren's characterizations were both highly partisan and inaccurate, but that did not matter in the postwar world. To republican purists, such power-hungry persons as Robert Morris, Henry Knox, and Alexander Hamilton, not the virtuous citizenry, were the ones who had to be watched. Very little ground stood between the partisan reminiscences of Warren and other republican ideologues and the grandly ornate flourishes of George Bancroft, all of which provided a firm base for the myth of widespread citizen virtue and unremitting commitment in support of the cause of liberty.

In our own time, however, the hold of mythology over the War for Independence has been lessening. John Ellis, for instance, in his provocative study of *Armies in Revolution,* has compared levels of popular participation in the American war with those of the English, French, Russian, and Chinese revolutions. He found in the English and Chinese civil wars a harmonious "integration of the civilian and the military" on a mass scale, in the sense that "the act of being a soldier is made inseparable from the desire to be a more fulfilled citizen."[18] In the case of the American war, Ellis observed that "parochial notions of family and district" with no "particular sense of being American," as separate from being an British subject, held down on high levels of popular involvement and support. He goes on to conclude that "though the enemy had been identified," the colonists still lacked a "cohesive sense of solidarity" because they "had little conception of a collectivity beyond that of town or county." With a weak central government, "there was no way in which the more enthusiastic patriots could begin to remedy the deficiencies in national feeling." Consequently, the most committed rebels "found themselves caught in a vicious circle: regional diversities and divisions fed upon themselves to create an atmosphere of political apathy and helplessness."[19]

To state the proposition somewhat differently, the enemy had been clearly identified by 1776. However, the sense of being an American (a separate political being) was not yet prevalent enough to ensure unity in the cause, once the *rage militaire* had passed. The challenge was to move beyond parochial, localist identities, to attach the affections of the people to a paramount sense of national legitimacy. That task meant altering the feelings of the Philadelphian who asserted early on in the contest: "Let who would be king, he well knew that he should be a subject." Over time, the actual experience of making war helped to effect that change, until, with the arrival of a victorious peace settlement persons started claiming that national duty rather than parochial self-interest had governed their actions during the war.

Success in war, above all else, completed a vital step in the political conversion process. A more widely held sense of national legitimacy was a critical product of the travail of those few who stood the test of Continental service. In "The Military Conflict Considered as a Revolutionary War," John Shy has observed that the conflict with Britain served as "a political education" by convincing "thousands of more or less unwilling people to associate themselves openly and actively with the cause."[20] This process of forced involvement may be brought to mind by recalling military operations in the South after 1778. The spread of warfare into so many locales helped to break down parochialism in favor of feelings of national identity and legitimacy.

These newfound sentiments were blossoming across the landscape by war's end. They were essential to the next step in the process of establishing a fully legitimate national political order. After 1783, the crucial question was what form the republican polity should take. Purists persisted in their faith in public virtue as an organizational concept. The nationalists, by comparison, could not imagine, after the experience of the war, that citizen virtue could ever serve as a stable and enduring base for political stability. Something had to be done, they kept telling each other. Their chance finally came during 1787 in the wake of Daniel Shays's Rebellion in Massachusetts. The national Constitution they designed and pushed through to ratification provided for a structure of government that, from their perspective, would guarantee a national political order that could resolve pressing problems effectively and could endure through time, but with no dependence on public virtue.

Walter Millis has argued that the Constitution of 1787 "was as much a military as a political and economic charter."[21] Having failed to institute an effective peacetime military constabu-

lary in 1783, the nationalists now made sure that a worthy establishment would be possible in the future. Congress now had the
stated power to "provide for the common defense" through
taxes, import duties, and excises, as well as the authority to declare war, make peace, provide for and maintain a navy, issue
letters of marque, and "raise and support Armies." The president, as the highest civil official, was also to serve as commander in chief. There was to be militia, too, which while subject to state authority, could "be employed in the Service of the
United States." Equally important, state units were to be trained
according to standard procedures of "discipline prescribed by
Congress."

The nationalists, in their role as founding fathers, drew
heavily upon plans advocating a standing regular force to be
supplemented by well-trained militia. As a group, these leaders
were not afraid of military power, with all that it implied, so
long as it remained subordinate to civil authority. Had they been
blatant militarists, they would not have adopted English precedent and limited military appropriations to a maximum of two
years before renewal. There can be no doubt, as Richard H.
Kohn has stated, that the nationalists consciously worked to
give "the new government sharp military teeth," or that they
"wanted a government able both to protect the nation from foreign countries and to protect a minority from popular despotism, from the majority, and from the licentiousness of the
people."[22] In the process, though, they did not abandon republican tenets. Rather, they designed them so that standing forces
would be present in peace as well as war to fill the void in public virtue.

There is fundamental irony here. The likelihood of virtue
and abiding commitment being sustained in the absence of
broad-scale consensus about national legitimacy was quite slim.
That proved to be the case in 1776. Once that consensus had begun to be achieved, however, the possibility that the populace
might be more willing to sacrifice their particular interests
for the good of the larger national community became much

greater—both in peace and in war. Events after the war, however, did not convince the nationalists that the transition to an independent republican nation had altered what they viewed as the self-serving character of the people. As a result, they carried through on sweeping constitutional change in 1787.

The experience of war with its parallel quest for national legitimacy served as an essential reference point in the definition and formation of enduring republican institutions in the United States. Those who prevailed in 1787 put the emphasis on order and structure rather than on the abstract concept of public virtue, which from their perspective might forever be wanting. They also did so because they viewed military strength as essential to stability and durability as a nation. Opposition whig writings may have served as the framework in their deliberations, but experience cannot be minimized. Thus while carefully providing for the subordination of military to civil authority, the nationalists also sought to emulate European models favoring the need for regular military institutions. The Constitution, so much a product of its times, confirmed that blending of traditions.

Once the new government began to function in 1789, fulfilling the goal of military effectiveness proved to be difficult. Although the nationalists strove for a respectable establishment, their political adversaries challenged them almost every step of the way. The opposition party (they soon took to calling themselves Jeffersonian Republicans) branded their political adversaries as militarists eager to ensnare the people in despotic traps. At least rhetorically, the Jeffersonians retained their faith in militia and the virtuous citizen-soldier well into the nineteenth century. Only time produced a working balance between the regular force and militia traditions.

In actual historical circumstance, the regular force tradition could take solace and pride in the War for Independence. Its accomplishments rested on the determination of the small band of committed long-term soldiers who stood with Washington after so many citizen-soldiers went home in 1775 and 1776. The volunteer force tradition, based on ideological pronouncements about public virtue, in turn, came to dominate in oral and written legend and myth about the War for Independence. In the end, however, Washington's Continental establishment was, of necessity, a standing army, fighting for a populace rather than representing the social composition of that population in war. Even though the army grew to resent and despise patriot civilians, it remained faithful in its quest. That force, because of its own virtuous fiber, set the stage for the lasting republican order of the United States. Back in 1783, Henry Knox stated the proposition aptly when he explained there was "a favorite toast in the army," that of "'a hoop to the barrel,' or 'Cement to the Union.'" That may be the way Private Joseph Plumb Martin and his comrades would prefer to be remembered, not as the myth has made them, but as the real human beings they were—individuals who secured, militarily, the origins of a stable and enduring American republic.

Notes

1 Weigley, *The American Way of War,* 37.

2 Rankin, "Charles Lord Cornwallis: Study in Frustration," in G. A. Billias, *George Washington's Opponents: British Generals and Admirals in the American Revolution* (New York, 1969), 202.

3 Mackesy, *The War for America,* 435–36.

4 Kohn, *Eagle and Sword,* 17–28.

5 Kohn specifically condemns Gates. See Ibid., 25, and also Kohn, "The Inside History of the Newburgh Conspiracy: America and the Coup d'État," *William and Mary Quarterly,* 3d Series, 27 (1970), 187–220. For a defense of Gates, see Paul David Nelson, "Horatio Gates at Newburgh, 1783: A Misunderstood Role," *William and Mary Quarterly,* 3d Series, 29 (1972), 143–58, which also includes a response by Kohn. See also Nelson, *General Horatio Gates: A Biography* (Baton Rouge, La., 1976), 266–97.

6 Kohn, *Eagle and Sword,* 26–27.

7 See James Kirby Martin, ed., *Ordinary Courage: The Revolutionary War Adventures of Joseph Plumb Martin,* 2d ed. (St. James, New York, 1999), 162–65.

8 Glasson, *Federal Military Pensions in the United States* (New York, 1918), 95–96.

9 Resch, *Suffering Soldiers,* 197–98. Resch does not reference Joseph Plumb Martin or his memoir.

10 Peckham, ed., *The Toll of Independence: Engagements and Battle Casualties of the American Revolution* (Chicago, 1974), 130.

11 Ibid., 131–34.

12 Millis, *Arms and Men,* 37.

13 Palmer, *Provide for the Common Defense: America, Its Army, and the Birth of a Nation* (Novato, Calif., 1994), 28–29.

14 Palmer, *Washington, Lincoln, Wilson: Three War Statesmen* (Garden City, N.Y., 1930), 10–27, 55–71.

15 Weigley, *Towards an American Army: Military Thought from Washington to Marshall* (New York, 1962), 12.

16 Warren, *History of the Rise, Progress and Termination of the American Revolution,* 3 vols. (Boston, 1805), 3: 268–82. See also commentaries in Lawrence D. Cress, "Republican Liberty and National Security: American Military Policy as an Ideological Problem," *William and Mary Quarterly,* 3d Series, 38 (1981), 73–96; and Lester H. Cohen, "Explaining the Revolution: Ideology and Ethics in Mercy Otis Warren's Historical Theory," Ibid., 3d Series, 37 (1980), 200–18.

17 Warren, *History . . . of the American Revolution,* 3: 277.

18 Ellis, *Armies in Revolution* (New York, 1974), 238–39.

19 Ibid., 46–47.

20 Shy, "The Military Conflict Considered as a Revolutionary War," in *A People Numerous and Armed,* 222.

21 Millis, *Arms and Men,* 41.

22 Kohn, *Eagle and Sword,* 80. See also Millis, *Arms and Men,* 40–46.

A NOTE ON REVOLUTIONARY WAR HISTORY AND HISTORIOGRAPHY

Until recent decades, military history about the War for American Independence has had a decided "guns and battles" orientation. Many such volumes, dating well back into the nineteenth century, had strong antiquarian interests. Governing questions concerned what personality, battle, or battlefield tactic contributed most to momentary triumphs or defeats during the war. Almost always in the background was the patriotic mythology of a determined provincial freeholding populace marching forward arm-in-arm in the struggle to overcome perceived British tyranny.

By modern standards, such history was narrow in conception and generally uninformative about larger issues affecting the course of the Revolution. As with any genre of literature, there were exceptions. Readers may still benefit from such works as, for example, Lyman C. Draper, *King's Mountain and Its Heroes* (Cincinnati, Ohio, 1881); Richard Frothingham, *History of the Siege of Boston, and the Battles of Lexington, Concord and Bunker Hill,* 4th ed. (Boston, 1873); Henry P.

Johnston, *Campaign of 1776 around New York and Brooklyn* (Brooklyn, N.Y., 1876); and William S. Stryker, *The Battles of Trenton and Princeton* (Boston, 1898).

Other important exceptions include the compilations of those persons who sought out and preserved documents from the Revolutionary period. Peter Force was such an individual. His massive collection, *American Archives,* 4th and 5th Series, 9 vols. (Washington, D.C., 1837–1853), contains a storehouse of information on the early phases of the war through 1776. As a second example, Benson J. Lossing's *Pictorial Field-Book of the Revolution,* 2 vols. (New York, 1851–1852), remains a foundational guide to Revolutionary Era sites. From yet another angle, Emory Upton's *Military Policy of the United States since 1775* (Washington, D.C., 1904), written several years before its publication, decried the lack of concern about maintaining regular armies and assuring military preparedness in the post–Civil War era. At least some of the blame, claimed Upton, lay with Revolutionary patriots who failed to establish a viable tradition for standing military institutions.

Upton's distaste for militia and focus on values, policies, and institutions served to undergird the production of various studies that reached beyond battle-related discussions. Claude H. Van Tyne emphasized the ineffectiveness of militia as opposed to Washington's regulars in *The War of Independence: American Phase* (Boston, 1929). By comparison, Don Higginbotham has emphasized the many contributions made by short-termers, in "The American Militia: A Traditional Institution with Revolutionary Responsibilities," Don Higginbotham, ed., *Reconsiderations of the Revolutionary War: Selected Essays* (Westport, Conn., 1978), 83–103, as does Mark V. Kwasny in *Washington's Partisan War, 1775–1783* (Kent, Ohio, 1996).

How leaders in the early republic attempted to balance the two traditions is of paramount concern in the early chapters of John McAuley Palmer, *Washington, Lincoln, Wilson: Three War Statesmen* (Garden City, N.Y., 1930); and Russell F. Weigley, *Towards an American Army: Military Thought from Washington to Marshall* (New York, 1962). Marcus Cunliffe, *Soldiers and*

Civilians: The Martial Spirit in America, 1775–1865, 2d ed. (New York, 1973), analyzes the evolution of the "professional," "antiprofessional," and "antimilitarist" traditions in the American experience through the Civil War. The most complete study of conflicting attitudes, as expressed in postwar policies affecting military institutions for the new nation, is Richard H. Kohn's *Eagle and Sword: The Federalists and the Creation of the Military Establishment in America, 1783–1802* (New York, 1975). Also noteworthy are Lawrence Delbert Cress, *Citizens in Arms: The Army and Militia in American Society to the War of 1812* (Chapel Hill, N.C., 1982); Dave R. Palmer, *Provide for the Common Defense: America, Its Army, and the Birth of the Nation* (Novato, Calif., 1994); Reginald C. Stuart, *War and American Thought: From the Revolution to the Monroe Doctrine* (Kent, Ohio, 1982); and John Todd White, "Standing Armies in Time of War: Republican Theory and Military Practice during the American Revolution" (Ph.D. dissertation, George Washington University, 1978).

Such scholarship has shown that studies of war and its related experiences can transcend the details of particular engagements and inform the broader sweep of human history. Still, the emphasis on "guns and battles," as if the Revolutionary War had virtually no connection to the new republic's pursuit of identity, legitimacy, and stability, characterized a number of volumes produced after World War II. Representative publications include John R. Alden, *The American Revolution, 1775–1783* (New York, 1954); Robert W. Coakley and Stetson Conn, *The War of the American Revolution: Narrative, Chronology, and Bibliography* (Washington, D.C., 1975); R. Ernest Dupuy, et al., *The American Revolution: A Global War* (New York, 1977); John C. Miller, *Triumph of Freedom, 1775–1783* (Boston, 1948); Howard H. Peckham, *The War for Independence: A Military History* (Chicago, 1958); Willard M. Wallace, *Appeal to Arms: A Military History of the American Revolution* (New York, 1951); and Christopher Ward, *The War of the Revolution,* 2 vols., J. R. Alden, ed. (New York, 1952). As companion pieces, two useful primary source collections are G. F. Scheer and H. F. Rankin, eds., *Rebels and Redcoats* (Cleveland, Ohio, 1957); and R. B. Morris and H. S. Commager, eds., *The Spirit of 'Seventy-Six: The Story of the American Revolution as Told by Participants,* 2 vols. (Indianapolis, Ind., 1958).

A number of studies relating to particular regions, communities, and campaigns have appeared in recent years, many of them influenced by questions about relationships between military institutions and societies. Representative of these volumes are David Hackett Fischer, *Paul Revere's Ride* (New York, 1994); Robert A. Gross, *The Minutemen and Their World* (New York, 1976); Adrian C. Leiby, *The Revolutionary War in the Hackensack Valley: The Jersey Dutch and the Neutral Ground, 1775–1783* (New Brunswick, N.J., 1962); David Hackett Fischer, *Washington's Crossing* (New York, 2004); Stephen R. Taaffe, *The Philadelphia Campaign, 1777–1778* (Lawrence, Kans., 2003); John S. Pancake, *1777: The Year of the Hangman* (University, Ala., 1977); Wayne Bodle, *The Valley Forge Winter: Civilians and Soldiers in War* (University Park, Pa., 2002); Joseph R. Fischer, *A Well-Executed Failure: The Sullivan Campaign against The Iroquois, July–September 1779* (Columbia, S.C., 1997); and Russell F. Weigley, *The Partisan War: The South Carolina Campaign of 1780–1782* (Columbia, S.C., 1970). Lawrence E. Babits, *A Devil of a Whipping: The Battle of Cowpens* (Chapel Hill, N.C., 1998), investigates what soldiers experienced in combat during this pivotal engagement in building on John Keegan's pioneering *The Face of Battle* (New York, 1976), which reconstructs the battles of Agincourt (1415), Waterloo (1815), and the Somme (1916).

The Leiby and Weigley volumes are indicative of the many possibilities inherent in regional history, as are two suggestive essays by Clyde R. Ferguson. These include "Carolina and Georgia Patriot and Loyalist Militia in Action, 1778–1783," in J. J. Crow and L. E. Tise, eds., *The Southern Experience in the American Revolution* (Chapel Hill, N.C., 1978), 174–99; and "Functions of the Partisan-Militia in the South during the American Revolution: An Interpretation," in W. R. Higgins, ed., *The Revolutionary War in the South: Power, Conflict, and Lead-*

ership (Durham, N.C., 1979), 239–58. Among other noteworthy regional studies of the war in the South are John Buchanan, *The Road to Guilford Courthouse: The American Revolution in the Carolinas* (New York, 1997); Wayne E. Lee, *Crowds and Soldiers in Revolutionary North Carolina: The Culture of Violence in Riot and War* (Gainesville, Fla., 2001); John W. Gordon, *South Carolina and the American Revolution: A Battlefield History* (Columbia, S.C., 2003); and Walter B. Edgar, *Partisans and Redcoats: The Southern Conflict that Turned the Tide of the American Revolution* (New York, 2001).

Certainly a major thrust of recent military history has been to get beyond battlefield tactics and campaign logistics. The new history has sought to grapple not only with war and its conduct but also with its consequences and impact on governments, societies, and peoples. A number of studies have helped uncover the rich prospects of the new history. In the first chapter of *Arms and Men: A Study in Military History* (New York, 1956), Walter Millis discussed the impact of the Revolutionary War on social and political developments in the new nation. In "The Military Conflict Considered as a Revolutionary War," *A People Numerous and Armed: Reflections on the Military Struggle for American Independence* (New York, 1976), 193–224, John Shy looked at the war as an educational experience, particularly in regard to political identity and loyalties. John Ellis's *Armies in Revolution* (New York, 1974), compared rebel armies in the English, American, French, Russian, and Chinese revolutions. He analyzed the role that these armies played in breaking down local attachments and in creating a sense of national purpose and legitimacy among peoples caught up in revolutionary situations. Richard Buel, Jr., in *Dear Liberty: Connecticut's Mobilization for the Revolutionary War* (Middletown, Conn., 1980), produced a study that looked at how the war effort in one state seemed to wear down the populace and cause a somewhat unbalanced if not unstable economic and political climate in the postwar years. Buel expanded his arguments in *In Irons: Britain's Naval Supremacy and the American Revolutionary Economy* (New Haven, Conn., 1998). Don Higginbotham's classic *The War of American Independence: Military Attitudes, Policies, and Practice, 1763–1789* (New York, 1971), showed the many linkages between fighting the war and the course and direction of the Revolution.

Investigating the relationships between military institutions and societies has also resulted in extensive research about the socioeconomic composition of armed forces as a reflection of ideologies and societal values. Some historians continue to support the patriotic myth that Revolutionary soldiers were property-holding freeholders and tradesmen, as earlier represented in such works as Charles K. Bolton's *The Private Soldier under Washington* (New York, 1902), and more recently presented in John Resch, *Suffering Soldiers: Revolutionary War Veterans, Moral Sentiment, and Political Culture in the Early Republic* (Amherst, Mass., 1999). Numerous studies, however, have weakened the hold of this long-standing belief. Among these are Charles Patrick Neimeyer, *American Goes to War: A Social History of the Continental Army* (New York, 1996); Steven Rosswurm, *Arms, Country, and Class: The Philadelphia Militia and the "Lower Sort" during the American Revolution* (New Brunswick, N.J., 1987); Gregory T. Knouff, *The Soldiers' Revolution: Pennsylvanians in Arms and the Forging of Early American Identity* (University Park, Pa., 2004); Mark Edward Lender, "The Social Structure of the New Jersey Brigade: The Continental Line as an American Standing Army," in Peter Karsten, ed., *The Military in America: From the Colonial Era to the Present* (New York, 1980), 27–44; Lender, "The Enlisted Line: The Continental Soldiers of New Jersey" (Ph.D. dissertation, Rutgers University, 1975); Edward C. Papenfuse and Gregory A. Stiverson, "General Smallwood's Recruits: The Peacetime Career of the Revolutionary War Private," *William and Mary Quarterly,* 3d Series, 30 (1973), 117–32; John R. Sellers, "The Common Soldier in the American Revolution," in S. J. Underdal, ed., *Military History of the American Revolution: Proceedings of the Sixth Military History Symposium,* USAF Academy (Washington, D.C., 1976), 151–61; and Sellers, "The Origins and Careers of the New England Soldier: Noncommissioned

Officers and Privates in the Massachusetts Continental Line" (paper delivered at the American Historical Association Convention, 1972). As a group, these investigations conclude that middle- and upper-class Americans were not willing to risk the hardships of long-term campaigning, despite repeated rhetorical flourishes about the need for enduring citizen virtue. Given mythology and reality, it is worth comparing the data presented in these studies with those compiled by Sylvia R. Frey's *The British Soldier in America: A Social History of Military Life in the Revolutionary Period* (Austin, Tex., 1981).

That the social characteristics of regular soldiers on both sides were so similar suggests that European practices heavily influenced American values regarding what kinds of persons should bear the burden of extended combat. Drawing heavily on poor and politically defenseless persons had become an ingrained part of the American experience by the later colonial wars. The implications of these findings in relation to the image of the citizen-in-arms may be traced in John Shy, "A New Look at the Colonial Militia," *A People Numerous and Armed*, 23–33; Fred Anderson, *A People's Army: Massachusetts Soldiers and Society in the Seven Years' War* (Chapel Hill, N.C., 1984); Harold E. Selesky, *War and Society in Colonial Connecticut* (New Haven, Conn., 1990); James Titus, *The Old Dominion at War: Society, Politics, and Warfare in Late Colonial Virginia* (Columbia, S.C., 1991); Gary B. Nash, *The Urban Crucible: Social Change, Political Consciousness, and the Origins of the American Revolution* (Cambridge, Mass., 1979); and John E. Ferling, *A Wilderness of Miseries: War and Warriors in Early America* (Westport, Conn., 1980).

In a similar vein, other contributing groups, among them women, are beginning to get long overdue attention. The much neglected role of women in the Revolutionary army has been studied in Holly Mayer, *Belonging to the Army: Camp Followers and Community during the American Revolution* (Columbia, S.C., 1996); Alfred F. Young, *Masquerade: The Life and Times of Deborah Sampson, Continental Soldier* (New York, 2004); Linda Grant De Pauw, "Women in Combat: The Revolutionary

War Experience," *Armed Forces and Society,* 7 (1981), 209–26; and John Todd White, "The Truth about Molly Pitcher," in J. K. Martin and K. R. Stubaus, eds., *The American Revolution: Whose Revolution?,* rev. ed. (New York, 1981), 99–105. These studies supersede Walter H. Blumenthal's straight-laced look at *Women Camp Followers of the American Revolution* (Philadelphia, 1952). In regard to African Americans in the Continental service, studies have not yet surpassed Benjamin Quarles, *The Negro in the American Revolution* (Chapel Hill, 1961), with some additional material in Sylvia R. Frey, *Water from the Rock: Black Resistance in a Revolutionary Age* (Princeton, N.J., 1991). As with women and African Americans, collective information on those persons who served as Continental officers still needs further development. Essential reading on this subject are Richard H. Kohn, "American Generals of the Revolution: Subordination and Restraint," in Higginbotham, ed., *Reconsiderations of the Revolutionary War,* 104–23; and Jonathan Gregory Rossie, *The Politics of Command in the American Revolution* (Syracuse, N.Y., 1975).

Issues about the nature and extent of military service by property-holding patriots are critical to discussions of the role of republican ideology as a basis for actual behavior on the part of the Revolutionary populace. Background information on the ideology of liberty may be found in Bernard Bailyn, *The Ideological Origins of the American Revolution* (Cambridge, Mass., 1967); and Gordon S. Wood, *The Creation of the American Republic, 1776–1787* (Chapel Hill, N.C., 1969). Concepts about the military obligations of citizens with an economic stake in society date back at least to the period of the Renaissance in Italy. J. G. A. Pocock's *The Machiavellian Moment: Florentine Political Thought and the Atlantic Republican Tradition* (Princeton, N.J., 1975), explores that issue. A thoughtful analysis of anti-standing-army ideology as it affected the coming of the Revolution appears in John Shy, *Toward Lexington: The Role of the British Army in the Coming of the American Revolution* (Princeton, N.J., 1965); and in John Phillip Reid, *In Defiance of the Law: The Standing-Army Controversy, the Two Constitu-*

tions, and the Coming of the American Revolution (Chapel Hill, N.C., 1981). For a valuable discussion of reputation and personal honor as an extension of the ideal of public virtue, see Caroline Cox, *A Proper Sense of Honor: Service and Sacrifice in Washington's Army* (Chapel Hill, N. C., 2004).

In light of the emphasis Revolutionary leaders placed on the concept of citizen virtue, one should expect to find sustained enthusiasm for the American cause. On the short-lived passage of patriot enthusiasm for arms, see Allen Bowman, *The Morale of the American Revolutionary Army* (Washington, D.C., 1943); and Charles Royster, *A Revolutionary People at War: The Continental Army and American Character, 1775–1783* (Chapel Hill, N.C., 1979). Besides indicating that the populace felt deep commitment for the cause, even while eschewing military service, Royster has claimed that those persons who made up Washington's new modeled ranks were largely motivated to arms by ideological considerations. In juxtaposing ideology and material concerns, Royster has set up a rigid dichotomy of interests. By comparison, this volume concludes that the individual dreams and expectations of Washington's rank-and-file troops paralleled the broader quest for a new republican order—as represented in the search for greater economic security and personal freedom. Likewise, the true republicans (those who measured up to ideological standards of virtuous commitment) were these same men and women. This small band of long-term soldiers, rather than the general populace, earned the laurels of military victory that were then taken from them by the general populace at war's end. This postwar displacement phenomenon, perhaps more than any other factor, helped establish the myth about widespread popular involvement in and commitment to the war effort.

For balanced presentations on the composition and motivations of Washington's soldiers, readers should consult the findings of Neimeyer, Rosswurm, Knouff, Lender, Sellers, Papenfuse, and Stiverson, cited above, as well as Robert Middlekauff, "Why Men Fought in the American Revolution," *Huntington Library Quarterly,* 43 (1980), 135–48; and John Shy,

"Hearts and Minds in the American Revolution: The Case of 'Long Bill' Scott and Peterborough, New Hampshire," *A People Numerous and Armed,* 165–79. Also of importance is Richard H. Kohn, "The Social History of the American Soldier: A Review and Prospectus for Research," *American Historical Review,* 86 (1981), 553–67, which covers the whole of the American experience. For commentary from Revolutionary War veterans themselves, see John C. Dann, ed., *The Revolution Remembered: Eyewitness Accounts of the War for Independence* (Chicago, 1980); and James Kirby Martin, ed., *Ordinary Courage: The Revolutionary War Adventures of Joseph Plumb Martin,* 2d ed. (St. James, N.Y., 1999).

Besides soldiers and societies, the new military history has other interests, including civil-military relations and maintaining civilian control of military institutions. An essential work on this subject is Richard H. Kohn, "The Inside History of the Newburgh Conspiracy: America and the Coup d'État," *William and Mary Quarterly,* 3d Series, 27 (1970), 187–220. Another area has to do with strategy as it relates to a balanced perspective on the successes and failures of each side. Suggestive inquiries include Ira D. Gruber, "Britain's Southern Strategy," in Higgins, ed., *Revolutionary War in the South,* 205–38; Dave R. Palmer, *The Way of the Fox: American Strategy in the War for America, 1775–1783* (Westport, Conn., 1975); John Shy, "British Strategy for Pacifying the Southern Colonies, 1778–1781," in Crow and Tise, eds., *Southern Experience in the American Revolution,* 155–73; Russell F. Weigley, *The American Way of War: A History of United States Military Strategy and Policy* (New York, 1973); William B. Willcox, "Too Many Cooks: British Planning before Saratoga," *Journal of British Studies,* 2 (1962), 56–90; Willcox, "British Strategy for America, 1778," *Journal of Modern History,* 19 (1947), 97–121; and Willcox, "Rhode Island in British Strategy, 1780–1781," Ibid., 17 (1945), 304–31. A third area has focused on the war from the perspective of Great Britain. Of great significance is Eric Robson's *The American Revolution in Its Political and Military Aspects, 1763–1783* (New York, 1955), which questions whether British forces could ever have won the war, and Piers Mackesy's *The War for America, 1775–1783* (Cambridge, Mass., 1964), a masterful study of the war with respect to its international components and the strengths and weaknesses of Britain's leaders. Also of consequence are Jeremy Black, *War for America: The Fight for Independence, 1775–1783* (Stroud, U.K., 1991); Stephen Conway, *The War of American Independence, 1775–1783* (London, 1995); David Syrett, *Shipping and the American War, 1775–83: A Study of British Transport Organization* (London, 1970); and R. Arthur Bowler, *Logistics and the Failure of the British Army in America, 1775–1783* (Princeton, N.J., 1975). On France's martial involvement, see Lee B. Kennett, *The French Forces in America, 1780–1783* (Westport, Conn., 1977); and Jonathan R. Dull, *The French Navy and American Independence: A Study of Arms and Diplomacy, 1774–1787* (Princeton, N.J., 1975).

Great numbers of biographies have also influenced the body of knowledge about the Revolutionary War period. Two indispensable collections featuring the war's major military figures are G. A. Billias, ed., *George Washington's Generals* (New York, 1964); and Billias, ed., *George Washington's Opponents: British Generals and Admirals in the American Revolution* (New York, 1969). In addition, a sampling of the varieties of available biographies are Marcus Cunliffe, *George Washington: Man and Monument,* rev ed. (New York, 1982); Don R. Gerlach, *Proud Patriot: Philip Schuyler and the War of Independence, 1775–1783* (Syracuse, N. Y., 1987); Louis R. Gottschalk, *Lafayette Joins the American Army* (Chicago, 1937); Ira D. Gruber, *The Howe Brothers and the American Revolution* (Chapel Hill, N.C., 1972); Don Higginbotham, *Daniel Morgan: Revolutionary Rifleman* (Chapel Hill, N.C., 1961); Bernhard Knollenberg, *Washington and the Revolution, A Reappraisal: Gates, Conway, and the Continental Congress* (New York, 1940); James Kirby Martin, *Benedict Arnold, Revolutionary Hero: An American Warrior Reconsidered* (New York, 1997); Max M. Mintz, *The Generals of Saratoga: John Burgoyne and Horatio Gates* (New Haven, Conn., 1990); Paul David Nelson,

General Horatio Gates: A Biography (Baton Rouge, La., 1976); Hugh F. Rankin, *Francis Marion: The Swamp Fox* (New York, 1973); and William B. Willcox, *Portrait of a General: Sir Henry Clinton in the War of Independence* (New York, 1964).

The studies listed in this bibliographical essay represent a fraction of the literature that is available on the War for Independence in the era of the American Revolution. For more detailed bibliographical information on diaries and reminiscences by participants, readers should consult J. Todd White and Charles H. Lesser, eds., *Fighters for Independence: A Guide to Sources of Biographical Information on Soldiers and Sailors of the American Revolution* (Chicago, 1977). On casualty estimates, Howard H. Peckham, ed., *The Toll of Independence: Engagements and Battle Casualties of the American Revolution* (Chicago, 1974), represents a helpful compilation of statistics. On the numbers of troops in the Continental service during various stages of the war, Charles H. Lesser, ed., *The Sinews of Independence: Monthly Strength Reports of the Continental Army* (Chicago, 1976), is invaluable. On the organization of Washington's forces, Robert K. Wright, Jr., *The Continental Army* (Washington, D.C., 1984), offers a comprehensive analysis. On supply and logistics, E. Wayne Carp, *To Starve the Army at Pleasure: Continental Army Administration and American Political Culture, 1775–1783* (Chapel Hill, N.C., 1984), represents a noteworthy investigation. On crime and discipline, a useful starting point is James C. Neagles, *Summer Soldiers: A Survey and Index of Revolutionary War Courts-Martial* (Salt Lake City, Utah, 1986).

All the studies listed herein, as well as others too numerous to mention, have served to broaden our comprehension of the War for Independence as it came about and as it influenced the character of American values, institutions, and traditions during the Revolutionary Era and beyond. We know that we still have much to learn, even as historians continue to raise new questions, rethink old issues, and conduct archival research, all being essential to comprehending ever more completely the formative impact of the experiences of the Revolution on its participants and on the course of United States history.

INDEX

A Respectable Army:
The Military Origins of the Republic, 1763–1789,
Second Edition
Developmental editor: Andrew J. Davidson
Copyeditor and Production editor: Lucy Herz
Proofreader: Claudia Siler
Cartographer: Jason Casanova, Pegleg Graphics
Indexer: Pat Rimmer
Printer: Versa Press